States, Markets, and

Why do some donor governments pursue international development through recipient governments, while others bypass such local authorities? Weaving together scholarship in political economy, public administration, and historical institutionalism, Simone Dietrich argues that the bureaucratic institutions of donor countries shape donor–recipient interactions differently despite similar international and recipient country conditions. Donor nations employ institutional constraints that authorize, enable, and justify particular aid delivery tactics while precluding others. Offering quantitative and qualitative analyses of donor decision-making, the book illuminates how donors with neoliberally organized public sectors bypass recipient governments, while donors with more traditional public-sector-oriented institutions cooperate and engage recipient authorities on aid delivery. The book demonstrates how internal beliefs and practices about states and markets inform how donors see and set their objectives for foreign aid and international development itself. It informs debates about aid effectiveness and donor coordination and carries implications for the study of foreign policy, more broadly.

SIMONE DIETRICH is Associate Professor of Political Science at the University of Geneva. Her work in international political economy and development has appeared in leading academic journals. She is a member of advisory networks to donor governments and the Organisation for Economic Co-operation and Development. Prior to her academic career, she was development practitioner in Bosnia and Herzegovina.

States, Markets, and Foreign Aid

SIMONE DIETRICH
University of Geneva

CAMBRIDGE
UNIVERSITY PRESS

CAMBRIDGE
UNIVERSITY PRESS

University Printing House, Cambridge CB2 8BS, United Kingdom

One Liberty Plaza, 20th Floor, New York, NY 10006, USA

477 Williamstown Road, Port Melbourne, VIC 3207, Australia

314–321, 3rd Floor, Plot 3, Splendor Forum, Jasola District Centre, New Delhi – 110025, India

103 Penang Road, #05–06/07, Visioncrest Commercial, Singapore 238467

Cambridge University Press is part of the University of Cambridge.

It furthers the University's mission by disseminating knowledge in the pursuit of education, learning, and research at the highest international levels of excellence.

www.cambridge.org
Information on this title: www.cambridge.org/9781316519202
DOI: 10.1017/9781009007290

First published 2021

A catalogue record for this publication is available from the British Library.

Library of Congress Cataloging-in-Publication Data
Names: Dietrich, Simone, author.
Title: States, markets, and foreign aid / a political economy of aid delivery tactics Simone Dietrich.
Description: Cambridge, United Kingdom ; New York, NY : Cambridge University Press, 2021. | Includes bibliographical references and index.
Identifiers: LCCN 2021025069 (print) | LCCN 2021025070 (ebook) | ISBN 9781316519202 (hardback) | ISBN 9781009001755 (paperback) | ISBN 9781009007290 (epub)
Subjects: LCSH: Economic assistance, American. | Economic assistance, European. | Non-governmental organizations. | BISAC: POLITICAL SCIENCE / International Relations / General | POLITICAL SCIENCE / International Relations / General
Classification: LCC HC60 .D495 2021 (print) | LCC HC60 (ebook) | DDC 338.91–dc23
LC record available at https://lccn.loc.gov/2021025069
LC ebook record available at https://lccn.loc.gov/2021025070

ISBN 978-1-316-51920-2 Hardback
ISBN 978-1-009-00175-5 Paperback

To Sophia Maria
and her generation that inherits this world.

Contents

List of Figures   *page* viii

List of Tables   x

Preface and Acknowledgements   xiii

1   Understanding Donor Pursuit of Foreign Aid Effectiveness   1

2   How National Structures Shape Foreign Aid Delivery:
    A Theory   39

3   Examining the Causal Mechanism across Donors:
    The United States, the United Kingdom, Sweden,
    Germany, and France   77

4   Country-Level Evidence Linking Donor Political
    Economies to Variation in Aid Delivery   123

5   Testing the Argument with Evidence from Aid Officials
    from the United States, United Kingdom, Sweden,
    Germany, France, and Japan   153

6   Examining Public Opinion as an Alternative Explanation:
    Evidence from Survey Experiments with Voters in the
    United States and Germany   188

7   Implications for Aid Effectiveness, Public Policy, and
    Future Research   222

Bibliography   238

Index   269

Figures

1.1 Proportion of bypass aid for OECD donors in select
    recipient countries, 2010   *page* 15
4.1 Proportion of aid delivered through bypass channels
    in 2010   127
4.2 Domestic government outsourcing across
    individual donors   131
4.3 Delivery patterns for binary political
    economy division   133
4.4 Marginal effects of political economy types across
    quality of recipient governance   143
4.5 Marginal effects of political economy types across
    quality of recipient governance   146
4.A1 Domestic government outsourcing across
    individual donors   150
4.A2 Marginal effects of political economy types across
    quality of recipient governance   152
5.1 Point estimates and 95% confidence intervals for 'no
    bypass/yes government engagement' aid delivery
    rank-order   169
5.2 Point estimates and 95% confidence intervals for 'no
    bypass/yes government-to-government' share of all
    bilateral aid by donor political economy across
    governance scenarios   171
5.3 Simple distribution of aid officials' responses   177
6.1 Distribution of responses across the German and
    US samples   198
6.2 Predictive margins for government-to-government
    aid across experimental conditions for German and
    US samples   203
6.3 Distribution of responses across the German and
    US samples   204

6.4 Predictive margins for government-first ranking
     across experimental conditions for German and
     US samples   207
6.5a Aid to recipient government – good governance   210
6.5b Channel rankings – good governance   210
6.6a Aid to recipient government – bad governance   211
6.6b Channel rankings – bad governance   211

Tables

3.1 Summary of select neoliberal reforms and their outcomes across donor countries since 1980   *page* 102

3.2 Summary of managerial practices in the management of foreign aid   121

4.1 Donor political economies and bypass, 2005–2015   139

4.A1 Donor political economies and bypass, 2005–2015   151

5.1 Difference-in-difference estimates of aid delivery ranking by donor political economy   172

5.2 Simple differences   174

5.A1 Number of interviews by donor country and agency   187

6.1 Summary of experimental conditions   196

6.2 Response to question about aid delivery through government   199

6.3 Response to question about aid delivery ranking   205

6.A1a Balance checks for control vs. good governance treatment   214

6.A1b Balance checks for control vs. government corruption treatment   215

6.A1c Balance checks for control vs. weak institutions treatment   216

6.A1d Balance checks for control vs. political violence treatment   217

6.A2a Regression-based analyses for government aid   218

6.A2b Regression-based analyses for ranking government first   218

6.A3a Cross-tabulations of treatments and government aid: German respondents   219

6.A3b Cross-tabulations of treatments and government
            aid: US respondents   220
6.A4a Cross-tabulations of treatments and ranking
            variable: German respondents   221
6.A4b Cross-tabulations of treatments and ranking
            variable: US respondents   221

Preface and Acknowledgements

The motivation behind this book stems from a memorable incident that took place in Sarajevo, Bosnia and Hercegovina, in 2003. At the time, I was working for the Organization for Security and Cooperation in Europe on projects related to development and peace-building. One such project entailed a collaboration with the Office of the High Representative (OHR), the international institution responsible for over-seeing the implementation of civilian aspects of the Peace Agreement ending the war in Bosnia and Hercegovina. At the urging of the High Representative, Paddy Ashdown, representatives of international financial organisations, the United States government, and local business elite launched a public–private partnership to reduce and remove laws and regulations perceived as barriers to private investment and job creation. The OHR figuratively embraced the interventionist nature of the project by naming it the 'Bulldozer Initiative' and setting the task of having '50 reforms enacted within 150 days'. For years, economic development of this kind was elusive and for good reasons: these efforts took place in a highly complex, post-conflict environment, presided over by foreign administrators, where politics remained deeply divided along ethnic lines and hope for a functioning and prosperous multi-ethnic state was a rare commodity.

The Bulldozer Initiative was designed to enable the international community and local businesses to identify important business reforms by working around often obstructive national governments, and to apply the OHR`s political clout to 'bulldoze' or get reforms passed in divided parliaments. My professional assignment was to work with a group of young entrepreneurs from different ethnic backgrounds to develop one legislative reform proposal that could fit the bill. The group delivered and the proposal was passed in parliament in the set time period alongside 49 other reforms.

When the time came to promote the success of the Bulldozer Initiative to local and international media, Paddy Ashdown, flanked by national leaders, did so in front of a full-sized yellow bulldozer. The group donned matching yellow construction helmets and held up a large sign that read, '50 economic reforms in 150 days'. As a member of the audience, I heard Ashdown emphasise the importance of 'getting things done' and 'delivering concrete and quantifiable results' and all within in a particularly difficult political context. A representative from the United States added that the initiative's success boded well for replicating it in similar contexts around the world.

In spite of the initiative's apparent success, not all in attendance that day were enthusiastic. In sideline conversations, I overheard representatives from Germany or France express concerns with the project's delivery tactics. These dissenters were uncomfortable with how the project had been initiated and driven, not by the local authorities and institutions but by the internationally appointed OHR. They stressed the importance of working with the political authorities and institutions instead of setting up parallel structures that worked around them. Although they agreed that better solutions were needed, some went so far as to mock the 'bulldozer approach'. These critics suggested 'bulldozing' simply would not work as a long-term development practice and might even be counter-productive. A better approach would be to help developing countries strengthen their own institutional capacities so that they could organise and develop their own local reforms and solutions.

As a young field worker, I found this experience confusing. How could such divergent, even opposing, approaches to development co-exist? How could they possibly be reconciled? Given how complex international state-building already was, how did donor disagreements over aid delivery complicate things further? How could resources be coordinated across donors and applied to the immense challenges of development? I began to see my encounter as reflective of what were deep, underlying tensions among different donors on how to go about promoting institutional reform or development under similar circumstances. A host of issues surrounded and were perpetuated by these divergent approaches. And if donors disagreed, not just about the Bulldozer Initiative but about delivery tactics for a range of projects under similar conditions, what was the origin of these different, even opposing, impulses and approaches?

Reflecting on this incident several years later as a foreign aid scholar, I recognised that two interlocking questions 'why do some donors bypass national authorities while others prefer government-to-government engagement under similar circumstances?' and 'why do some donors focus on achieving results, while others strive to build capacity?' had not been addressed by existing theories in political science or economics. Yet, I felt that answering them promised new insights not only into the origins of donor motivations. It seemed as if understanding why donors deliver aid differently would also advance debates about foreign aid effectiveness or international state-building that have been going on for many years. After all, bypass and engagement with the recipient government are fundamentally different forms of donor–recipient interaction that promote different objectives in development; require different time-horizons for evaluating aid success; and that shape political and economic development in the recipient country in different ways.

My key to understanding marked variation in donor delivery tactics is to focus on decision-makers in national aid bureaucracies and to pay attention to the structures that shape their interests and dictate their behaviour. As many social scientists before me, I consider material interests as the driving force that explains aid delivery decisions. My book implies that the reactions of donor officials who were present at the Bulldozer celebrations in Sarajevo in 2003 may have been rooted in organisational rules and practices. Their support or opposition was shaped by organisational guidelines, by standard operating procedures and decision-making frameworks that make bypass or government engagement tactics more likely. While on the one hand, the viewpoints of US officials were guided by an explicitly neoliberal guide book, developed to optimise aid success in the short-run, opposition by German and French officials had its origin in a more traditional set of public-sector oriented principles that privilege long-term, institutional capacity building in international aid.

My full appreciation of the constraining role of such ideological structures in aid delivery evolved slowly over the course of many research trips that were structured around conversations and interviews with representatives of different donor governments, aid agencies, as well as staff from NGOs or international organisations that implemented aid for donors in recipient countries. I found my interactions with aid practitioners across countries and organisations deeply rewarding. The more interviews I conducted, the more I learned about the marked differences in aid bureaucratic rules and practices; how these rules were underwritten by different views about the role of states and markets in governance; how these guidelines encouraged aid officials to either bypass or engage more with the recipient governments; and how taking one approach often precluded a switch to the other.

Conversations with practitioners also impressed on me the many trade-offs associated with bypass or government engagement tactics. For example, facing formidable aid challenges, some officials may adopt the tactic of circumventing existing institutions to obtain results to show progress, while others may shy away from exacerbating the same issues by setting up parallel structures to deliver services. Listening to aid practitioners made me acutely aware how navigating these trade-offs exacerbates and even creates problems in and for international state-building and development, especially in poorly governed countries that are most in need of assistance. Overcoming them will require extensive dialogue among donors, regardless of how divergent their organisational rulebooks and goals may be, as well as between the donor community and recipient countries. My sincere gratitude goes to the many practitioners who reserved time for me to discuss foreign aid delivery in their jobs, who shared their experiences and personal reflections and who participated in the survey that forms the empirical core of Chapter 5 in the book.

States, Markets and Foreign Aid took long to write and has accumulated many debts over the years, for which I now want to say thanks. The idea to write this book was born during my year as postdoctoral researcher at the Niehaus Center for Globalization and Governance at Princeton University, where I could have not asked for a better and more stimulating environment to lay the early foundations for the research. As the project evolved theoretically and empirically, I have benefitted from many conversations, advice and support from mentors, colleagues and friends. I received helpful reactions or guidance to parts of the argument or empirical strategy from John Ahlquist, Lucio Baccaro, Leo Baccini, Monika Bauhr, David Bearce, Sarah Bermeo, Tim Büthe, Sarah Bush, Michael Bernhard, Stephen Chaudoin, Christina Davis, Axel Dreher, Cooper Drury, Jörg Faust, Robert Franzese, Andreas Fuchs, Desha Girod, Don Green, Emily Hafner-Burton, Jude Hays, Susan Hyde, Ryan Jablonski, Stephen Kaplan, Peter Katzenstein, Robert Keohane, Jonathan Kriekhaus, Doug Lemke, Brad LeVeck, Pat Lown, Gabriella Montinola, Paolo Morini, Amanda Murdie, Dan Nielson, Grigore

Pop-Eleches, Bernhard Reinsberg, Jonah Schulhofer-Wohl, Jake Shapiro, Christina Scheider, David Stasavage, Martin Steinwand, Haley Swedlund, Mike Tierney, Dustin Tingley, Frederic Varone, Hugh Ward, Meredith Wilf, Matthew Winters and Joe Wright. Irfan Nooruddin was a big believer in the project from the beginning and his feedback at early critical junctures had an important impact on the argument. Raymond Hicks generously read and commented on early versions of the project and provided guidance on the technical implementation. I am grateful for all these contributions.

Different versions and parts of the book were presented at many seminars, workshops and conferences, including the World Trade Institute at the University of Bern, Paris School of Economics, London School of Economics, University of Gothenburg, University of Hamburg, University of California at Berkeley, European University Institute, University of Antwerp, University of Mannheim, Hertie School of Governance, Oxford University, German Institute of Global and Area Studies, Overseas Development Institute, German Development Institute, the University of Munich, as well as annual conferences of the International Political Economy Society (IPES), American Political Science Association (APSA) and the International Studies Association (ISA). I want to thank participants at these events for their engagement and feedback. An early version of the argument was published as an article in *International Organization* in 2016.

Before the manuscript went out for review, it was the subject of a day-long workshop at Princeton University. This opportunity to get feedback from some of the best scholars in the field was extraordinary, and I am deeply grateful to Sarah Bermeo, Desha Girod, Amaney Jamal, Jon Pevehouse, Christopher Kilby, Helen Milner and Jim Vreeland for reading the manuscript in its entirety and offering advice for sharpening the book's theoretical argument and for leveraging the empirical evidence more effectively. I am indebted to Jon Pevehouse for suggesting the title of the book. I am thankful to Patricia Trinity for organising the meeting and to the Niehaus Center for Globalization and Governance and the University of Geneva for supporting it financially.

These final words are written at the University of Geneva, several years after I first had the idea to write this book. In between, I had the privilege to work in different academic environments in different countries, all of which offered excellent conditions for research and learning from students. I also benefitted from productive research stays at the Quality of Government Institute at the University of Gothenburg and the Leibniz Institute for Economic Research at the University of Munich.

My research was supported financially from travel and research grants from the University of Missouri, the University of Essex, the University of Geneva and the International Studies Association. I thank Kristina Enger and Katharina Fleiner for their outstanding research assistance in identifying and collecting original data sources; conducting thorough research of secondary literature and archival documents; and indexing the book. My thanks go to Kate Davies from the Bill and Melinda Gates Foundation and Jennifer and David Hudson for allowing me to add my survey experiment to their Aid Attitude Tracker survey in Germany and the United States, which I used to do the empirical analyses in Chapter 6.

I would like to thank John Haslam of Cambridge University Press for supporting the book and sending the manuscript to two incredible anonymous reviewers who thoroughly engaged with it and offered excellent suggestions as to how to further strengthen it. Robert Judkins and Sindhuja Sethuraman made sure that the production of the book stuck to its schedule and Kevin Hughes helped polish the writing. All errors remain my own.

Finally, I am indebted to my family and friends. In particular, I am grateful to my parents, Margit und Ulrich Dietrich, and my brother, Florian, for their unconditional love and support. Although we have lived in different countries for more than twenty years now, their steady encouragement, reassurance and compassion provided the emotional support I needed to finish this book. I thank Paul Labun for countless discussions on the manuscript, his willingness to read and criticise drafts, and for helpful suggestions. As an experienced aid practitioner, he constantly challenged me to consider the argument's policy relevance. I dedicate this book to my daughter, Sophia, who has been a steadfast anchor throughout this project. She has graciously embraced at times challenging transitions between State College (PA), Princeton, Columbia (MO), Colchester (UK) and now Geneva. As this book has taken shape, she has grown into the most delightful, curious and sensitive daughter I could have hoped for.

1 | *Understanding Donor Pursuit of Foreign Aid Effectiveness*

1.1 Introduction

Powerful nations use wealth to intervene in the affairs of weaker nations. This practice has ancient roots. Yet, the notion of the use of foreign aid to advance development in poorer countries only appeared in the post–World War II era. Since then, industrialised countries have built up extensive foreign aid programmes that reflect, in part, a commitment to an internationalist agenda that seeks to address developmental inequalities through international efforts. One indication of the consensus in favour of such efforts is that taxpayer-funded global aid budgets have surpassed USD 100 billion in every year since 2007. In a post–Cold War context, donor governments have raised the stakes of this agenda by promising to help even in countries where there is a high risk of foreign aid vanishing because of high levels of corruption or weak state institutions.

While there has been sustained support and financing for foreign aid for over half a century, the process by which donors go about promoting prosperity in developing countries, especially in poorly governed countries, remains poorly understood. During my own field visits to donor countries, I was confronted, time and time again, by representatives of donor nations who agree on promoting prosperity but diverge on the tactics they use to deliver aid. For example, while an aid official from the United States might circumvent or 'bypass' corrupt recipient governments to ensure that aid gets delivered to the people, in the same set of circumstances, a German official opts for chanelling aid through the recipient government, citing capacity-building as the central motive. Such divergent tactics for delivering aid under similar international economic and recipient country conditions are puzzling. Questions about why and how donors decide to bypass recipient governments or, in contrast, work with them, and under what conditions this is done, remain largely unanswered by existing theories that study donor behaviour. In fact, the systematic study of aid delivery is in its infancy.[1]

This lack of understanding of why and how donors go about promoting prosperity abroad is surprising given how long and intensely scholars have debated the topic of foreign aid in recent decades. Prominent aid supporters, such as Jeffrey Sachs, advocate for more aid and cite aid initiatives such as the Global Fund to Fight AIDS, TB, and Malaria or the Global Alliance on Vaccines and Immunizations as global aid successes, which have saved lives by the millions at remarkably low cost.[2] Prominent aid critiques such as Peter Bauer,[3] William Easterly,[4] and Nobel Prize winner Angus Deaton,[5] on the other hand, claim that aid not only falls short of helping developing countries develop but that it also perpetuates countries' struggles to promote economic growth. Over the years, this debate has developed in a more or less binary fashion,[6] attracting scholars, practitioners, and celebrities to join either camp. What has largely been missing in this debate, however, is a more nuanced treatment of the varied ways through which foreign aid can influence development abroad. Directly building up recipient capacity or incentivising governments to promote macroeconomic reform is one channel where international development runs through and engages with the recipient government. Delivering vaccines through international organisations (IOs) or building drinking wells through non-governmental organisations (NGOs) or building roads through private contracting firms are other possible channels that bypass recipient structures and implement development through non-state actors. While both tactics can promote development abroad, they are built on fundamentally different models of donor–recipient interaction. I define 'bypass' as aid that does not directly engage government authorities and goes to non-state actors for implementation. These non-state or bypass actors include, for example, IOs, NGOs, or private development firms. I define engagement with the recipient government as any activity that involves the recipient government as an implementing partner.

---

[1] Political scientists and economists have increasingly turned towards studying aid delivery mechanisms, including Dietrich and Wright (2015); Dietrich and Murdie (2017); Swedlund (2017); Bermeo (2018); among others.
[2] Sachs (2005).   [3] Bauer (1976).   [4] Easterly (2007).   [5] Deaton (2015).
[6] Tsopanakis (2016).

In this book, I seek to accomplish two objectives. My first goal is to shed light on the different tactics by which donor governments intervene in recipient countries. Until recently, research on donor motivations in political science and economics has paid too little attention to the different tactics that donors employ when delivering aid abroad.[7] Instead, it has focused on donor decisions about whether or how much aid to give. This focus has masked important and unexplored variation in how donors pursue development abroad. As a French official suggests during an author interview, 'Fifty percent, if not more of total annual ODA-aid effort, meaning more than half of the hundred billion Euros, is about *delivering* the aid to the beneficiary in the recipient country. It is all about selecting the right interface, the right channels of delivery to ensure that aid is effective. And, this estimate is a conservative one.'[8]

My second goal is to provide a political economy explanation of foreign aid delivery. By shedding light on why donors deliver aid in the way that they do, and why some bypass more than others, this book contributes to long-standing questions about the origins of donor motivations. I also contribute to the debate on foreign aid effectiveness by clarifying what goals donors pursue with their development efforts.

I locate the origin of bypass or government-to-government tactics inside aid organisations. The argument of this book originates in the intuition that aid decision-makers, who are the central actors in foreign aid decision-making, need to be understood in the context of the national aid organisations for which they work. Aid organisations, like other state organisations, function on the basis of institutional guidelines, standard operating procedures, or rulebooks that prescribe how aid officials deal with risk in aid implementation at any given time. These rules and practices act as constraints on aid officials insofar as they justify particular aid delivery tactics, while precluding others. In developing the argument, I derive aid officials' preferences for bypass or engagement from formal rules of the game that become manifest in particular bureaucratic structures and administrative practices that prescribe particular aid delivery tactics.

---

[7] Examples for recent research that explain different ways of giving aid include Molenaers et al. (2015); Bush (2016); Swedlund (2017); Allen and Flynn (2018); Bermeo (2018); Adhikari (2019).

[8] Author interview with Senior French Official AFD, Paris 2009.

Institutions alone, however, are insufficient for explaining why donor officials diverge in their preferences for aid delivery tactics, or for answering the more fundamental question about the origin of bypass or engagement. They merely explain an ordered regularity in aid delivery of any given aid organisation. They tell us why rational, incentive-oriented aid officials behave the way they do given their institutional environment. Institutions, in their functions as constraints, however, do not shed light on why donor governments, or more specifically their aid officials, deliver aid differently. Neither can they tell us much about the substance of aid politics: why it is that, today, aid officials in the United States and Germany are constrained differently. The questions of 'why bypass?' or 'why engage?' require me to think, as Robert Lieberman reminds us, about the substance of aid politics.[9] It requires me to think about the ideas that motivated and gave rise to the rules that aid officials follow inside their organisations. After all, aid organisations, alongside other state institutions, are created and reformed over time, and their organisation and rules thus need to be understood in a national, historical context. By integrating insights from historical institutionalism, I claim that, at different times in different donor countries, national orientations about the appropriate role of the state in public sector governance have shaped the organisation and character of state institutions. In the United States and the United Kingdom, for example, during moments of critical juncture, when the welfare state was in crisis and opportune political circumstances presented themselves, neoliberal reformers significantly reshaped rules and administrative practices across state organisations, including national aid organisations. They locked in neoliberal ideas to generate stable patterns of aid delivery in the future. In other words, how aid organisations are structured has little to do with the specific challenge of delivering aid to countries with poor governance today. Rather, the aid organisation's structure reflects an institutional legacy that expresses how political actors many decades ago sought to deal with broader societal challenges, how they sought to reorder the relationship between the state and markets in the economy.

My theory thus endogenises institutions insofar as they lock in a particular ideological view. Neoliberal doctrine is consequential for aid delivery in the United Kingdom and the United States because these

---

[9] Lieberman (2002).

countries create rules that prescribe and incentivise aid officials to select bypass under conditions of poor recipient governance. More traditional public sector ideas are consequential for aid delivery in Germany and France because their national aid organisations were set up to promote government-to-government aid delivery. These organisational rules create different types of political games and shape donor–recipient interactions differently. Marked cross-donor variations in organisational incentives are not yet accounted for in empirical academic research on donor motivations. The decision to interlock ideas with institutions enables me to provide a political economy explanation that accounts for this marked variation in aid delivery across donor governments.

The argument developed throughout the book focuses on the micro-institution and its character. It puts the aid official front and centre in decision-making. It looks at what happens in the institution. I show that aid officials are constrained by institutional rulebooks that authorise, enable, and justify a particular aid delivery tactic, while precluding others. A direct analysis of agents in their respective national institutional environments allows me to flesh out the causal mechanism and isolate it from alternative explanations. It allows me to make more direct claims about aid officials that go beyond Williamson's classic description of agents as 'self-interest seeking with guile'.[10]

At this point, readers might wonder which of these tactics is more effective? Both bypass and engagement with recipient governments can promote development but each does so in a very different way. A key virtue of government-to-government aid is that it involves the recipient government and thus has the potential of increasing recipient country ownership over the development process. In collaboration with governments, donors can pursue potentially transformational projects that contribute to the capacity of local structures, making development more sustainable in the long run. Yet, critics may be quick to point out its limitations: working together with recipient governments can be costly insofar as engagement requires extensive dialogue and effective due diligence systems to ensure that recipient governments stay true to their word. Compared to bypass, government-to-government delivery thus requires more patience and longer time horizons for assessing its success. Finally, government-to-government aid may be more

---

[10] Williamson (1985) as cited in Hawkins and Jacoby (2006).

vulnerable to corruption or serve to prop up dictators insofar as it can be used to buy political support.[11]

A key virtue of bypass, on the other hand, is that donors can circumvent recipient structures when they pose an obstacle to aid implementation. By working around the government, donors can bring aid directly to the people who need it. Yet, critics may be quick to argue that bypass may be no panacea either insofar as it can have deleterious effects on development. Bypass may divert attention from riskier and potentially transformational projects that include recipient governments as partners but that may be difficult to measure and may require longer time horizons to become successful.[12] By delegating aid delivery to non-state actors, donors set up parallel structures whose design is largely shaped by technocrats in donor or implementing organisations and thus may not reflect developmental needs or priorities of recipient authorities.[13] Or, bypass can be complicit in the stagnation of indigenous development. It can, for example, undermine local capacity to formulate and implement their own development policies.[14]

To illustrate the difficult trade-offs associated with bypass in development, I turn to the global effort to contain the spread of HIV/AIDS. In setting up one of the largest vertical health programmes in the history of foreign aid, the Global Fund and its partners delivered treatment through their own systems and structures, saving millions of lives in the world's poorest countries. Simultaneously, however, these targeted efforts create pathologies that work to undermine the development of broader healthcare structures in recipient countries. For example, a singular focus on HIV/AIDS leads to a decline in spending in other important health services,[15] making it difficult for local structures to provide adequate treatment of other illnesses such as diabetes or chronic respiratory diseases, among many others. Or, the generously funded HIV/AIDS programmes attract doctors and nurses from other health services, thus compounding existing and often chronic shortages in other areas of health. Finally, the implementation of a programme that relies on external systems and structures does not encourage the kind of knowledge transfer that would be

[11] Kono and Montinola (2009); Ahmed (2012).   [12] E.g. Muller (2018).
[13] E.g. Easterly (2014).   [14] E.g. Chasukwa and Banik (2019).
[15] England (2007).

required to continue the programme in the absence of parallel structures. Such pathologies contribute to what Pritchett, Woolcock, and Andrews have called 'capability traps', in which states' ability to develop themselves in the long run is severely constrained and limited.[16]

Aside from their adverse effects on development, bypass tactics can affect politics in recipient countries. For example, service provision by external, non-elected actors may undermine citizen confidence in elected leaders and raise questions about their legitimacy.[17] Or, bypass aid may mute popular resistance in dictatorships by subsidising government spending, thus rendering citizens less willing to openly challenge the incumbent through protests.[18] Or, bypass may cause repressive governments to lash out against implementing actors and potentially weaken civil society in the country.[19] These are all outcomes that donors care about and that present aid officials with difficult trade-offs. My argument about institutional path dependency in foreign aid delivery suggests not only that neoliberal doctrine has lasting consequences for which tactics donors choose to promote development but also that these locked-in tactics may have transformative consequences for developmental or political trajectories of recipient countries.

In this book, I do not examine the effectiveness of bypass or engagement tactics in aid delivery. Nor do I explore the effects of bypass on recipient country politics. Nor do I wish to make normative claims about which I believe is better suited to promote prosperity. Instead, I approach the question of effectiveness indirectly. I argue that the way that aid officials look at the success of their aid projects and programmes is endogenous to the spirit of the institutional rulebook by which they operate, and which structures donor–recipient interaction: while aid officials whose work environment is organised by neoliberal principles prioritise cost-effectiveness and direct delivery to the poor, their counterparts in more statist organisational environments prioritise capacity-building and government ownership.

---

[16] Pritchett et al. (2010).

[17] For research on external goods and service provision and state institutions see Sacks (2012); Dietrich and Winters (2015); Winters et al. (2017); Dietrich et al. (2018, 2019); Baldwin and Winters (2020).

[18] DiLorenzo (2018).   [19] Dupuy et al. (2015, 2016).

In other words, aid success means different things to aid officials from different political economies.

More broadly, I suggest that the core mission or mandate of the aid organisation is not objectively defined. Rather, it reflects the ideological context in which the institution was created many decades earlier to deal with societal problems at the time. Historically, approaches to solving societal challenges promoted a particular blend of roles between states and markets in public sector governance.[20] The aid organisation's mandate is thus endogenous to the ideological orientation of the organisation at the time it was created: whether it embraces a larger role of the state or promotes a greater role for markets in public sector governance. Institutional rules and practices that lock in these views then steer aid officials towards goals that either promote state-strengthening or direct provision to the poor. Even if aid officials were committed to employing what they may consider an optimal solution to aid delivery at any given moment in time, organisational incentives would steer them towards institutionally prescribed solutions. The orientation of the institutional rulebook also dictates where aid officials come down on the difficult trade-offs associated with bypass or government-to-government tactics in development.

My argument rejects the claim that aid officials can easily optimise aid delivery following whatever tactic appears to be most promising at any given time. For innovative ideas to be consequential they need to be compatible with the underlying institutional rulebook. Ultimately, the choice for bypass is somewhat disconnected from what works best in international development insofar as neoliberal donors will gravitate towards it even in the absence of concrete empirical evidence that doing so is more effective.

My argument establishes that, in the world of foreign aid, there are not just tensions between donors and recipient governments. There are tensions among donor governments of different political economy types in how they think about aid effectiveness and, consequently, about how to pursue aid delivery abroad. These tensions reflect a broader struggle for authority in the aid discourse, where donors compete over which conception of aid effectiveness is better. By pursuing bypass or engagement tactics to varying degrees, each donor brings to bear its domestic experience, expertise, and resources to accomplish

[20] Evans (1995).

the goals it has set out in foreign aid. For public policy, my argument has a few implications: first, it suggests that lasting and robust changes in aid delivery tactics require institutional reforms that change institutional rulebooks. Neoliberal doctrine and the organisational changes that have accompanied it have altered aid priorities and delivery modalities of Anglo-Saxon and Scandinavian donors at different points in time over the last four decades. For example, a focus on measurable outcomes crowds out aid activities that are difficult to measure but that some consider central to foreign aid.[21] It makes it more difficult to maintain aid projects where results are not readily measurable or that take time to bear fruit, such as efforts to strengthen recipient capacity.

Because traditional public sector donors do not share these same priorities, my argument also implies that political economy differences may explain the lack of donor coordination in the field. For years, scholars and practitioners have bemoaned that too many cooks in the kitchen undermine aid effectiveness.[22] To decrease transaction costs of too many national aid programmes and projects that are implemented following a donor country's national structures, the Organisation for Economic Co-operation and Development's Development Assistance Committee (OECD DAC) recommends that donors coordinate their activities in the field.[23] Yet, despite all the lip service offered in support of more coordination, little progress has been made on this front and scholars continue to document fragmented aid delivery in the field.[24] My argument implies two things for this particular debate. On the one hand, institutional differences may remain fundamental obstacles for donor coordination across different political economy types unless donor political economies converge on the same type, or recipient countries converge on a good quality of governance. On the other hand, it may be that donor coordination efforts may vary in success across political economy types insofar as 'like-minded' donors who share aid objectives and delivery preferences find more common ground for coordination.

To test my argument, I employ a mixed-methods approach. I present quantitative analysis of aid delivery patterns across twenty-three OECD donor countries. I present quantitative and qualitative evidence from

[21] Wilson (1991).
[22] For research that has studied the problem of uncoordinated aid-giving for recipient governments see Ross (1990); Ashoff (2004); Balogun (2005); Rogerson (2005); Acharya et al. (2006).
[23] OECD (2003).   [24] Winters (2012); Steinwand (2015).

extensive field research with donor officials across different OECD donor countries, the United States, United Kingdom, Sweden, Germany, France, and Japan. I selected these countries because they represent key donors in the international development community and because they exhibit variation in their political economy type. As will be discussed in subsequent chapters, decision-makers were remarkably candid about the goals that matter for their national aid organisations as well as the constraints imposed on them when fulfilling their duties as aid officials. These interviews provide invaluable insights about foreign aid cross-nationally.

The predictions of my argument are supported by the tests that I conduct in the empirical sections of the book, both at the cross-country level and the level of aid decision-makers. This book is about the institutions that shape donor officials in their decisions on how to deliver foreign aid. My empirical strategy reflects this insofar as a substantial part of the evidence is collected through open- and closed-ended surveys of officials in their aid organisations. Then I show that the individual-level decisions map onto aggregate country differences in bypass.

In what remains of this introductory chapter, I first establish my dependent variable and make a case for why the study of aid delivery is important for understanding donor motivations. In a next step, I establish the empirical and theoretical puzzle motivating this book. I then provide an overview of the existing literature. Subsequently, I provide a synopsis of the theoretical framework and summarise the central empirical findings of this book. I then highlight the book's primary theoretical contributions, its implications for policy and foreign aid effectiveness. I conclude with a road map for the subsequent chapters.

1.2 A Focus on Foreign Aid Delivery

One plausible reason for why so many of the questions about donor motives raised in the previous section remain unanswered may be that, despite the tremendous knowledge generated by economists or political scientists over the years, we still know relatively little about the different channels through which foreign aid works. Although scholars have recently turned to studying variation in aid sectors, aid tying, or budget support,[25] the bulk of research has studied donor motives by focusing

---

[25] Radelet (2004); Faust et al. (2017); Bermeo (2018); Ganga and Girod (2019).

on aid levels as the dependent variable. In doing so, scholars have often resorted to the assumption that foreign aid is delivered through the government-to-government channel, although this may not have always reflected reality.

The lack of systematic, historical data on aid delivery mechanisms surely explains, in part, why scholars have focused on studying donor motives by examining aid levels and making convenient assumptions about its government-to-government delivery. The OECD Development database, the primary data source for foreign aid flows, has only been collecting systematic data on aid delivery channels since 2005. However, a focus on levels masks the range of choices that donor governments have in aid delivery.

In reality, foreign aid can be delivered by a multitude of different actors. These include the recipient government but also non-state development actors. Donors can outsource the delivery of foreign aid to non-state actors, including international and local NGOs, international organisations such as the United Nations or the Global Fund, and public–private partnerships, and private sector companies.[26] As channels of aid delivery, NGOs can be important development partners for donors. Their issue focus and local knowledge about what types of projects are needed make them attractive to donors who seek to deliver services effectively. Because not all local NGOs in developing countries are equally capable and virtuous,[27] donor governments usually channel funds through international NGOs such as Care International, Doctors Without Borders, or Catholic Relief Services, who often deliver services in cooperation with local NGOs but do so with monitoring frameworks in place. In regions of the world where international NGO partners are less present, or where projects require economies of development, donors can turn to international organisations for service delivery. International organisations such as the WHO or UNHCR can quickly mount and sustain interventions on behalf of donor governments and have increasingly turned to bilateral aid as a source of finance. This form of funding is different from multilateral aid that records core contributions to IOs,

---

[26] Dietrich (2013, 2016).   [27] Barr et al. (2005).

which they can use as they see fit.[28] In addition, donors can channel their aid through public–private partnerships and private contractors.

Such a variety of aid delivery channels suggests that donor–recipient relations are not always government-to-government, but may involve non-state actors. Over time, bypass tactics have become more popular, and global aid flows increasingly rely on bypass channels for implementation.[29] In 2015, OECD governments delegated nearly 40 per cent (approximately US$ 49 billion) of their bilateral aid to non-state development actors for implementation, effectively bypassing the recipient government.[30] These non-state delivery channels enable donors to accomplish their goals through means other than government-to-government aid.

Accounting for aid delivery channels helps us make sense of puzzling findings generated by a literature that has conventionally studied donor motives through the lens of aid commitments. For example, previous research has found that countries that are more corrupt receive larger amounts of foreign aid.[31] Because the study's authors had assumed (but not tested) that aid was given through the government-to-government channel, the result encouraged some to infer (ex post) that donor governments did not care about risks associated with aid in corrupt countries; and, per further leap of inference, donor governments did not care about development outcomes. The conventional approach to studying donor motives through the lens of aid commitments thus masks the range of choices that donors have to implement aid in the recipient country.

It also masks the importance of risk in donor decision-making. In a previous systematic study of the determinants of aid delivery, I show that this inference, based on the simplified assumption that all aid is government-to-government, has the potential to be misleading about donor motives. I show that donors, on average, systematically resort to bypass tactics to deliver aid in countries like Sudan or Sri Lanka, where need for aid is high but corruption or weak state institutions

---

[28] Eichenauer and Reinsberg (2017); Eichenauer and Hug (2018); Chasukwa and Banik (2019); Dietrich et al. (2019). Scholars who study more traditional multilateral aid include Rodrik (1995); Kilby (2006); Milner (2006); Girod (2008); Milner and Tingley (2012); Humphreys and Michaelowa (2013); Schneider and Tobin (2013); Strand and Zappile (2015); Denly (2021).
[29] Dietrich (2013); Bermeo (2018).   [30] OECD DAC (2017).
[31] Alesina and Weder (2002).

pose severe risks for aid implementation. In country contexts where governance is relatively better, on the other hand, donor governments are more likely to engage with the government, ceteris paribus. What motivates this decision by donor governments to bypass the regime in countries under poor governance are risks of aid capture by the recipient government. When recipient countries have better systems of governance, donor governments perceive lower levels of risk associated with aid capture and are thus more likely to engage with the recipient government in aid implementation.[32] This finding suggests that donors can and do account for risk by channelling the aid through bypass channels in countries that arguably are in more need than well-governed recipient countries.[33]

Accounting for aid delivery thus enables scholars to better specify models of donor decision-making. By introducing non-state development actors as ready alternatives for donors, aid delegation choices become more complex and require theorising about why and when donor governments prefer to engage with or bypass the recipient government. This presents a challenge for realists who think of bilateral aid as an instrument of statecraft, to be used to buy influence and promote foreign policy objectives.[34] If bilateral aid is channelled through non-state actors for implementation, the way in which donor governments manage to maintain influence over recipient governments is not self-evident. As I will show in the next section, disaggregating foreign aid into its various delivery channels helps us uncover new empirical and theoretical puzzles in the study of foreign aid and international relations that existing theories cannot answer.

1.3 Empirical and Theoretical Puzzles of Foreign Aid Delivery

Donor government officials from different countries often advocate dissimilar tactics when confronted with similar development challenges, such as poor governance in the aid receiving countries. I now want to see whether this heterogeneity persists at the cross-country level. Indeed, when plotting donor delivery tactics across different

---

[32] Dietrich (2013).
[33] See Winters (2010b), who shows that the risk of aid capture systematically influences World Bank lending decisions.
[34] Baldwin (1985); Morgenthau et al. (2005); Bueno de Mesquita and Smith (2009).

recipient countries, I note that donors do not converge under similar conditions. Instead, I see marked variation when comparing donor delivery tactics in poor governance environments: while some donor governments choose to bypass, others engage through the government-to-government channel.

In Figure 1.1, I plot individual donor delivery in Sudan, Sri Lanka, Tanzania, and Cape Verde in 2010.[35] These four recipient countries differ in quality of governance. Sudan is effectively a 'failed' state, which lacks a functionally competent government with whom donor governments could engage. Here, we expect donors to bypass government structures not only because the functional logic dictates bypass but also because donors do not have options to meaningfully engage with the recipient government. Sri Lanka, on the other hand, does have a functionally competent government but scores relatively low on recipient governance. Tanzania has relatively better governance quality than Sri Lanka, with similar development needs. Last but not least, Cape Verde ranks highest on the quality of governance dimension. In terms of aid delivery tactics we observe the following: in Sudan, which, with a low governance score of 0.86, ranks at the very low end of the governance scale, all donor governments, with the exception of Greece, bypass the Sudanese government with more than 50 per cent of their bilateral aid. In the case of Sri Lanka, which scores higher than Sudan but remains at the low end of the governance scale, we note that differences exist across donors in the extent to which they use bypass channels to deliver foreign aid. While a majority of donors bypass with more than 50 per cent of their aid, others donors, such as France or Germany, do so to a more limited extent. Moving to Tanzania, whose governance score ranks it ahead of Sudan and Sri Lanka, we note that a clear majority of donors deliver more than half of their aid through the government-to-government channel. In Cape Verde, which scores 2.98 on the governance scale, donors channel only a small proportion through bypass actors. This initial inspection of the raw data shows differences across donors in comparisons in a given year.

We find a similar pattern of differences across donors when we inspect what happens to donor behaviour as the quality of governance changes over time. Here, I select one country, Uganda, which experienced a high-level corruption scandal. In 2011, news broke suggesting

---

[35] Dietrich (2013).

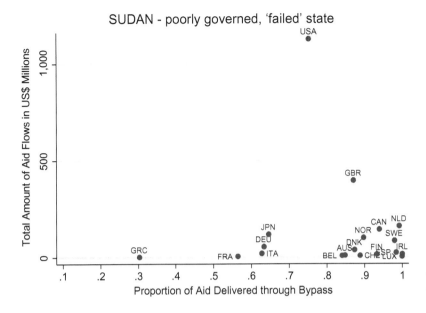

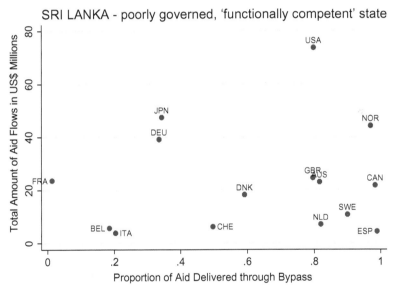

Figure 1.1 Proportion of bypass aid for OECD donors in select recipient countries, 2010. Y-axis is total aid commitments in constant US Dollars in millions. X-axis is fraction of aid delivered through non-state development actors.

Source: Dietrich (2013)

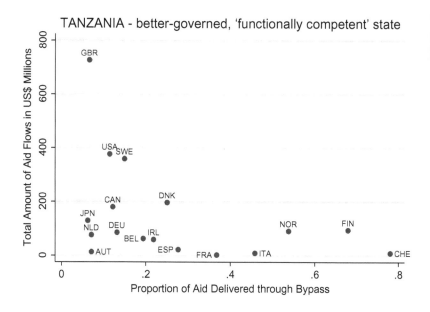

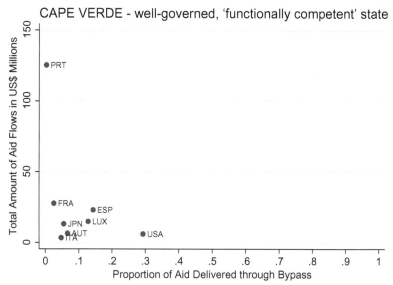

Figure 1.1 (*cont.*)

that the office of Uganda's prime minister had engaged in numerous cases of fraud and embezzlement. These involved diverting millions of foreign development assistance aimed at rehabilitating parts of northern Uganda devastated by decades of insurgency in order to enrich public officials' private accounts.[36] This high-level corruption scandal marks a decrease in governance quality, and raises risks associated with government-to-government aid delivery. Again, we note marked differences: the United Kingdom, Ireland, Sweden, and Norway announced the immediate suspension of all government-to-government aid to Uganda, while continuing aid delivery through IOs and NGOs. France and Japan, on the other hand, did not suspend significant amounts of government-to-government aid.[37] This suggests that donors react differently to changes in the quality of governance over time; and that not all follow the same problem-solving approach under similar conditions, as risks of aid capture increase from one aid budget period to the next.

Together, these two aid delivery scenarios present a similar picture: they show that some donors use bypass tactics to mitigate aid delivery risks, while others make more limited use of it. Instead, countries like Germany and France pursue tactics that engage the recipient government but incorporate more hands-on mechanisms of control and oversight. It is these contrasting approaches that raise the main empirical puzzle of this book: why do some OECD donors choose to withhold the majority of government-to-government aid in response to bad governance while others continue to provide substantial amounts through the government-to-government aid channel?

This pattern also presents a puzzle for international relations theory. Because aid capture poses significant obstacles to effective aid delivery, scholars and practitioners have suggested that donors reduce the risk of aid capture by pursuing a strategy of country selectivity where aid goes to countries with better governance.[38] And, while there is some evidence suggesting that donors were more selective in the early to mid-1990s,[39] current patterns suggest that donors continue to provide significant amounts of aid to countries where the risk of aid capture is

[36] Piccio (2012); Swedlund (2017).
[37] OECD CRS Database. Accessed 10 May 2013.
[38] Collier and Dollar (2002).
[39] Berthélemy and Tichit (2004); Levin and Dollar (2006); Bandyopadhyay and Wall (2007); Claessens et al. (2009); Annen and Knack (2019).

very high. This pattern raises another set of questions: Why would donors continue to allocate aid when programmes and projects are likely to fail, or develop pernicious consequences? If channelled through the recipient government, as shown by studies, aid as a non-tax resource has been shown to reduce the need for incumbent governments to tax their own citizens, which not only undermines long-term development goals but also reduces the political accountability of governments and thus inhibits democracy.[40] Aid may also be used to support patronage networks or a state's coercive apparatus, or thwart social resistance, which all strengthen the stability of dictatorships.[41] Some scholars have gone so far as to claim the existence of an 'aid curse' akin to the 'natural resource curse'.[42] At a minimum, however, foreign aid risks being captured by corrupt recipient governments, or wasted because of weak state institutions.[43] This suggests that giving aid directly to governments can have negative consequences for outcomes that donors care about.

One sensible answer to these questions would be that although foreign aid is justified as a response to needs in poor countries, we know that donors use aid as an instrument of statecraft. As research has long recognised, bilateral aid serves multiple purposes that include buying influence and policy concessions,[44] domestic stability,[45] counterterrorism,[46] UN votes,[47] democratisation,[48] and the promotion of trade,[49] among others. While this assertion is sensible and has found empirical support in the literature, existing heterogeneity across donor delivery patterns raises the question of why, if aid was largely an

---

[40] Bräutigam and Knack (2004).

[41] Morisson (2009); Licht (2010); Ahmed (2012).   [42] Djankov et al. (2008).

[43] Jablonski (2014); Winters (2014).

[44] Bueno de Mesquita and Smith (2009); Empirical studies have shown that policy influence via conditionality only works if recipient country interests are aligned (Mosley et al. (1991); Collier et al. (1997); Killick et al. (1998); Girod (2018)) or if the recipient country is more dependent on foreign aid, see (Girod and Tobin (2016)).

[45] Collier and Hoeffler (2002); Kono and Montinola (2009); Braithwaite and Licht (2020); Campbell and Spilker (2020); Steele, Pemstein, and Meserve (2020).

[46] Boutton and Carter (2014); Heinrich, Machain, and Oestman (2017); Savun and Tirone (2018).

[47] Wittkopf (1973); Kegley and Hook (1991); Kuziemko and Werker (2006); Dreher et al. (2008, 2018); Lim and Vreeland (2013).

[48] For example, see Round and Odedokun (2004); Morgenthau et al. (2005); Bermeo (2011); Cornell (2013); Resnick and van de Walle (2014); Bader and Faust (2014); Dietrich and Wright (2015); Pospieszna (2019); Dunton and Hasler (2021).

[49] Bearce and Tirone (2010); Bearce et al. (2013).

instrument of statecraft, the United States and the United Kingdom, both global powers in world politics, would divert significant proportions of their aid away from government-to-government aid and give it to non-state development actors for implementation. These important questions of delegation require a theory that can explain why donors pursue different aid delivery tactics under similar circumstances.

1.4 Foreign Aid in the Literature

I now turn to the literature on foreign aid. Although the systematic study of aid delivery is in its infancy, existing research on foreign aid allocation guides my thinking on what factors matter in aid decision-making. It will help me identify a political economy explanation that answers two important questions: first, I ask 'what factors are systematically associated with bypass or engagement tactics in aid delivery?'; and, second, and more importantly, I ask 'what makes some donors promote more bypass than others under similar conditions?'

Recipient Characteristics as Determinants of Foreign Aid

As a first step, I turn to a vast literature in economics and political science that has tried to understand donor motivations by looking at the effect of recipient characteristics on foreign aid spending. These studies have asked whether foreign aid is responsive to recipient need or donor interests.[50] The conventional prediction states that more aid to countries in need would be evidence of altruistic motives, while more aid to countries where donors hold non-development interests, including but not limited to the promotion of trade and investment, or support for strategically important countries and former colonies, is said to support the conclusion that donors prioritise selfish motives. The results reveal robust support for the hypothesis that donors follow their political motivations, while the evidence for needs-based, altruistic motives is more mixed. Most recently, Bermeo's research shows that in the post-Cold War era, donor political motives no longer exclude development-oriented aid allocation. Instead, many political agendas of donors are served by effectively promoting development abroad.[51]

---

[50] McKinlay and Little (1978, 1979); Mosley (1981); Maizels and Nissanke (1984); Baldwin (1985); Schraeder et al. (1998); Kilby and Dreher (2010).
[51] Bermeo (2018).

This large body of work has shed much light on the determinants of foreign aid commitments and guides my theorising about whether donors engage with or bypass the government. It guides the specification of the model that I employ in my empirical tests in subsequent chapters. It is, however, also subject to critique. Scholars in this tradition have tended to infer donor motivations from allocation behaviour; where the existence of hypothesised interests is confirmed by looking at how much aid is allocated across different countries, and where. They do not directly measure donor interests.

What is more, this literature treats donors mostly as homogenous actors who respond in similar ways to political or altruistic motivations. As subgroup analyses show, however, not all donors fit into aid allocation patterns that scholars have identified at the aggregate level. Major donors, for example, have been found to provide aid to project military or commercial interests,[52] while smaller donors are found to give more for altruistic reasons, as indicated by a positive relationship between recipient need and aid commitment.[53] Or, there remains unexplained variation in foreign aid effort across donors, with the Nordic countries, among others, showing uncommon levels of generosity.[54]

As I have shown, we observe marked differences in how donor governments deliver their foreign aid under similar conditions. The state of the world in aid-receiving countries alone cannot explain differential responses. To understand why donors deliver aid differently under similar conditions, I need to understand why bypass is more common in the United States or the United Kingdom than it is in Germany or France. I want to understand donor motivations ahead of time, before donor governments deliver their aid. I thus need to turn my attention to what is going on inside donor countries, and search for the origins of foreign aid delivery tactics. To that end, I turn to a growing literature that links foreign aid to domestic politics.

---

[52] Maizels and Nissanke (1984); Schraeder et al. (1998).
[53] Alesina and Dollar (2000); Alesina and Weder (2002).   [54] Hoadley (1980).

Donor Politics as Determinants of Foreign Aid

Political scientists and economists have tried to explain why donors differ in aid policy by focusing on domestic politics.[55] One set of explanations links foreign aid spending to public opinion and citizens' moral views. Lumsdaine's seminal study claims, for example, that generous aid budgets have their origin in domestic egalitarian values.[56] Subsequent studies in this tradition find that donor welfare institutions and foreign aid are correlated; and that political parties or legislators, depending on the public's spending preferences or social welfare values, will promote or oppose foreign aid when in government or cast legislative votes in favour or against foreign aid.[57] The focus on values and redistribution is sensible given the specific nature of foreign aid but the empirical support is mixed[58]: sometimes left-leaning parties appear more generous, while, at other times, conservative governments allocate more aid.[59] Other scholars suggest that political actors to the left promote aid for different reasons than their right-leaning counterparts.[60]

These differences may emerge because the hypothesised link between domestic solidarity and international solidarity is not self-evident. Rather, it depends on other characteristics, including, for example, an individuals' foreign policy orientation, or the institutional context in which individuals live.[61] Nor do partisan beliefs about the role of the state in the economy necessarily translate into straightforward predictions about foreign aid. Furthermore, the hypothesised link between public opinion and foreign aid decision-making may be tenuous because foreign aid is primarily formulated out of public view. Nor may aid considered a salient issue for voters at the ballot box. So, even

---

[55] Stokke (1989); Pratt et al. (1989); Lumsdaine (1993), Therien and Noel (2000); Lancaster (2006); Chong and Gradstein (2008); Frot (2009); Tingley (2010); Milner and Tingley (2011); Lundsgaarde (2012); Paxton and Knack (2012); Brech and Potrafke (2014); Prather (2014); Heinrich et al. (2016); Bayram (2017); Dietrich et al. (2019a); Bayram and Holmes (2020); Wood (2018).

[56] Lumsdaine (1993).

[57] Noël and Therién (1995); Therién and Noël (2000); Tingley (2010); Milner and Tingley (2010, 2011); Paxton and Knack (2012).

[58] Fuchs et al. (2014).

[59] Goldstein and Moss (2005); Dreher et al. (2015); Dietrich et al. (2020).

[60] Fleck and Kilby (2006, 2010); Brech and Potrafke (2014); Greene and Licht (2018); Dietrich et al. (2019a).

[61] Bauhr et al. (2013); Kertzer et al. (2014); Prather (2014); Rathbun et al. (2016).

if voters had a clear preference over how to spend aid, it is not clear that this preference would be consequential for how people cast their vote in elections.[62]

Another explanation links ideas and beliefs to aid allocation. In *Ideas, Interests, and Foreign Aid*, Van der Veen argues that cross-donor differences in foreign aid spending exist because donor governments, as they make decisions about where to spend and how much, turn to the world of ideas.[63] Key decisions are guided, so goes the argument, by national beliefs about what the objective of foreign aid should be. These national beliefs, as measured through aid frames, differ across countries and explain why donors differ in their aid policy. Van der Veen's research is a landmark contribution insofar as it establishes national ideas as key drivers of foreign aid policy but it is not without limitations. Similar to other studies that examine foreign aid policy from a macro perspective, it brackets out the fact that aid decision-making takes place at the micro-level. It takes place inside aid organisations that organise donor–recipient interactions through rules and practices. The tendency to view aid-decision-making as effectively unconstrained masks and understates the role of micro-institutions.

The idea that micro-institutions help us better understand world politics has recently spurred research. Over the past ten years, more and more studies have emerged that study the features of international organisations and link them to their behaviour.[64] In this context, some scholars have studied bureaucratic structures and formal rules of the game, such as layers of bureaucracy,[65] institutionalisation,[66] delegation,[67] and voting rules.[68] Others have studied the influence of institutional culture. As Barnett and Finnemore show in *Rules for the World*, organisational culture can be a powerful explanatory factor insofar as 'the rules, rituals, and beliefs that are embedded in the organization' can creates pathologies and undermine organisational goals.[69] In *Currency of Confidence*, for example, Nelson develops a

---

[62] Dietrich et al. (2020).   [63] Van der Veen (2011).
[64] Wendt (2001); Barnett and Finnemore (2004); Barnett and Coleman (2005); Johnson (2014).
[65] Hardt (2009); Carcelli (2019).   [66] Hofmann (2009).
[67] Hawkins et al. (2006); De Hoogh et al. (2015).
[68] Scharpf (1997b); Tsebelis and Xenophon (2002); Bayer et al. (2015); Iannantuoni et al. (2020).
[69] Weaver (2008); Yanguas and Hulme (2015).

causal link between neoliberal ideas and beliefs that underwrite the IMF and the IMF officials' lending decisions. In a world characterised by uncertainty, shared beliefs in neoliberalism between the IMF official and borrower authorities generate confidence that borrowers will act responsibly, leading to some borrowing countries being treated more favourably than others.[70] This important empirical study enriches our knowledge of how ideas can shape behaviour at the micro-level, yet it might underplay the importance of formal rules that may account for why IMF officials play favourites with neoliberally oriented governments. As I will argue in subsequent chapters, ideas become consequential and explain stable patterns of behaviour when they point in the same direction as formal rules and practices that structure donor–recipient interactions.

The conjecture that institutions constrain behaviour of aid officials has been around at least since Martens, Mummert, Murrell, and Seabright's *Institutional Economics of Foreign Aid*.[71] As in other areas of institutional economics, aid agencies are at heart bureaucratic organisations that are built on distinct rules of the game that generate incentives for aid agents to behave in particular ways that can lead to problems and affect agency performance. Recent empirical studies have provided important insights about the constraining effect of institutions on foreign aid policy and the effectiveness of foreign aid.[72] Hailey Swedlund argues, for example, that the frequent failure of aid agreements results from the inability of both donor and recipient governments to credibly commit to the terms of contract.[73] In another study, Dan Honig points to variation in institutional autonomy across aid agencies as an important determinant of whether aid projects are implemented successfully across different recipient country contexts.[74] This and other research at the micro-level has significantly advanced our understanding of foreign aid decision-making and aid effectiveness.[75] But, they are also subject to critique insofar as organisational practices within aid organisations have been assumed to be largely similar across donor agencies, thus making plenty of assumptions

---

[70] Nelson (2017). [71] Martens et al. (2002).

[72] Sjöstedt (2013); Vestergaard and Wade (2013); Lebovic (2014); Bush (2015); Yanguas and Hulme (2015).

[73] Swedlund (2017). [74] Honig (2018).

[75] Arel-Bundock et al. (2015); Bush (2015); Buntaine et al. (2017).

about what makes agents tick, including their preferences, knowledge, understanding, and expectations.

Finally, scholars have investigated the nexus between interest groups and foreign aid.[76] Milner and Tingley argue that the tugs and pulls of interest groups effectively constrain decision-making. In their book, Milner and Tingley document, for example, that interest groups that are interested in development contracts frequently lobby USAID or legislators for more and larger contracts and are called on for testimonials in Congress.[77] In a similar vein, Roberts' research documents the politics and influence of what she calls the US 'industrial development complex'.[78] This focus on distributive politics advances our understanding of the role that non-state actors, especially private sector interests, can play in shaping US aid decision-making. It is not clear, however, to what extent interest group politics can explain aid decision-making beyond the United States or perhaps neoliberal donors whose political economies offer plenty of entry points where vested interests can exert influence and ensure that outsourcing persists.

1.5 The Explanation in Brief

The political economy explanation of foreign aid delivery that I advance begins with identifying the key actors and their institutional environments. The key actors are senior officials in aid organisations who make decisions about how to promote international development; and, more specifically, how to deliver aid in developing countries. My argument is built on several interlocking claims.

As a first step, I claim that the world of aid officials across donor governments is characterised by risk and rational expectations. In this world, aid officials who make decisions about foreign aid delivery are concerned with minimising risks in aid implementation. They all express a desire to minimise risk in aid delivery and promote development abroad. To them, one important source of risk is a corrupt and weak recipient state. As analytical and empirical work on records of aid implementation shows, aid transfers between donor and recipient governments are at great risk of aid capture through agency

---

[76] Roberts (2014); Milner and Tingley (2015); McLean (2019).
[77] Milner and Tingley (2015).   [78] Roberts (2014).

problems.[79] I define aid capture broadly as resulting from the mismanagement of aid in the recipient country, either by intentional diversion through corrupt authorities or the waste of aid due to weak institutions and/or lack of absorptive capacity.[80] When making decisions about aid delivery, aid officials seek out information about risks associated with aid implementation and turn to measures that proxy the quality of governance in aid-receiving countries.

As a second step, I argue that aid officials do not make these decisions in a vacuum: as they consider solutions to address the risk of aid capture abroad, their choice set is shaped by the institutional environment in which they operate. As decision-makers, aid officials are governed by institutional rules and practices that seek to help organisations accomplish their goals. By following rules and responding to institutional incentives, aid officials can optimise professional gains, such as career promotions or bigger budgets.[81] As we know from decades' worth of scholarly research on institutions, rules of the game and organisational practices guide the behaviour of people working in organisations and influence policy.[82] It is these rules and practices that influence how aid officials are going to respond to risks of aid capture abroad. Institutions authorise, enable, and justify particular delivery tactics, while precluding others. They ensure that aid officials of the same organisation respond to aid delivery in similar ways.

At the same time, I introduce important cross-donor variations in institutional environments that help explain why aid officials, and ultimately donor governments, differ so markedly in their aid delivery tactics.[83] I argue that the rules and practices that structure donor–recipient interactions within aid agencies are of markedly different

---

[79] Svensson (2000); Brautigam and Knack (2004); Reinikka and Svensson (2004); Gibson et al. (2005); Djankov et al. (2008).

[80] This definition differs from the following authors' who define aid capture solely as acts of corruption: Jablonski (2014); Winters (2014).

[81] There will always be some agents who are not driven by institutional incentives, but we can expect the majority of decision-makers to follow the institutional playbook.

[82] Weber (1978); North (1990); Powell DiMaggio (1991); Hall and Taylor (1996); Campbell (1998); Mattli and Bühte (2013).

[83] Within any given aid organisation, I assume bureaucratic structures and practices to be the same and expect the majority of aid officials to behave in ways that are consistent with incentives and contribute to the organisation's goals and objectives (a minority may not act according to set incentives).

character and have to be understood in a historical context. They are institutional legacies that reflect predominant beliefs and practices of the times during which the aid organisations were created. As Przeworski reminds us, institutions built at any given moment in time produce stable patterns of behaviour because they mould and integrate behaviour of people who work within them. They make predominant beliefs and values stick.[84]

In this book, I make a broad distinction between national aid organisations that are neoliberal in character and aid organisations that are organised around more traditional public sector ideas. To avoid the blurring of the concept of neoliberalism, which has been used in many ways, I want to specify briefly how I use the concept and what it means in the context of state institutions. As an ideology, neoliberalism promotes a particular institutional form on which aid organisations are built. I conceive of neoliberalism as using the state and its power to bring about and institutionalise a particular bureaucratic order where state agents, or aid officials in my case, conceive of themselves as managers who coordinate service provision through the principle of competition and the associated price system.[85] A neoliberal state order breaks with the traditional public sector model insofar as it replaces authoritative coordination and control with one of dispersed competition. It emphasises individual over collective action. As Dardot and Laval claim, among others, neoliberalism is a government rationality that structures and organises the actions and interactions of the state and society in accordance with the principle of competition.[86] I thus conceive of neoliberalism as a mode of government that internalises a market-based rationality and creates rules and practices that reflect the culture of private firms and that, once imposed, govern the behaviour of state agents. These rules and practices require aid officials to monitor the output of any agent who delivers goods and services for the state, and to evaluate them on the basis of relatively short-term horizons for effectively delivering the results that were pre-specified in the contract. A neoliberal state order further incentivises officials to

---

[84] Przeworski (1975).
[85] E.g. Hibou (2015) For a more general discussion of the neoliberal state and political order see Foucault (2004).
[86] See Dardot and Laval (2009) for an excellent overview of the political and economic circumstances of neoliberalism.

outsource goods and service provision to non-state actors because it believes them to be superior to the state.

The desire to bring business efficiency to government by corporatisation, performance indicators, more focus on effective management, and outsourcing goes hand in hand with, or is often preceded by, sustained efforts of state dismantlement that go further than reducing bureaucratic capacity. Importantly, lower levels of capacity render the state more dependent on and susceptible to the interests of non-state implementers. This suggests that a neoliberal state order not only incentivises aid officials to deliver aid through non-state actors via rules and practices. A neoliberal state order reinforces policy directions by empowering vested interests. Today, private contractors like Chemonics or DAI, wield more influence in Washington than three or four decades ago.[87] In order to acquire more and larger grants, they donate to political campaigns. They rotate personnel into and out of aid agencies and provide expertise and help write legislation. By promoting their pecuniary interests, interest groups reinforce the effect of neoliberal institutional rules and practices on aid delivery. They pull aid officials towards more bypass. In this book, I conceive of interest group empowerment as a political dynamic that has its historical origin in neoliberal doctrine and that reinforces aid officials' preferences towards more bypass. The tugs and pulls of interest groups through representative institutions and politicians and their collective influence on bureaucratic decision-making ensure that neoliberal ideology becomes vested and political. This mechanism reinforces and works to sustain bypass tactics. It makes it even less likely that aid agencies return to a more statist orientation.

To assess whether aid organisations are neoliberal in character, I look at two dimensions that are associated with organisation: an aid organisation's bureaucratic structure and practices. In the United States, the United Kingdom, and Sweden, for example, neoliberal reforms have, at different points in time, dramatically reorganised the structures of their public sectors. Although, initially, reforms took place in Anglo-Saxon countries, economic and financial crises shook Scandinavian economies in the 1980s. In Sweden, neoliberal reformers emerged triumphant from crisis and successfully brought about

---

[87] Berrios (2000).

dramatic changes in the country's political economy. Although there was little opposition to the welfare state's continued financing of social services on the principle of universality, successive Swedish governments vehemently pushed for the creation of markets by setting up private and corporate welfare programmes.[88]

Across many countries, neoliberal reforms have reorganised goods and service delivery away from direct state provision or institutionalised delivery through non-state actors, to a system that facilitates delivery through competitive contracting in an open market. The introduction of managerial practices has led to the introduction of performance frameworks, significantly shortened the time horizons by which aid officials assess the success of aid, and re-oriented evaluation to focus on achieving results in the short-run. The new rules and practices thus entrench neoliberal beliefs by imposing a playbook that limits the delivery choices that are considered rational. And importantly, they affect the behaviour of aid officials well into the future. Even today, many decades after neoliberal reforms reorganised the public sectors of some donor countries, the behaviour of US, UK, or Swedish aid officials, among others, is influenced by institutional legacies, rather than what they may conceive as optimal delivery choices today.

The character of the aid organisation thus explains why the United States, the United Kingdom, and Sweden, more so than Germany or France, are likely to create parallel structures in places where the recipient government poses challenges in implementation. Drawing on the *Varieties of Capitalism* literature as well as public administration studies, I develop a binary donor typology of neoliberal and traditional public sector donors. This typology helps make sense of the empirical puzzles highlighted in the previous section: it explains why the United States and Sweden opt for bypass in Uganda, while France and Germany opt for more government-to-government engagement. In Chapter 3, I elucidate how the neoliberal aid organisation, or the lack thereof, constrains aid delivery decisions in favour of more bypass, while precluding government-to-government delivery. Consistent with institutionalist research, we expect aid delivery patterns to be stable because political actors whose interests are aligned with these arrangements are going to fight to protect them.[89]

---

[88] Micheletti (2000); Molander et al. (2002).   [89] Pierson (1994); Wood (2001).

As a final step, I develop testable hypotheses that link the character of aid organisations to variations in aid delivery. When donor officials work in aid organisations whose bureaucratic structures and rules are of neoliberal character, they will react to the risk of aid capture in aid-receiving countries with a strategy of bypass. I test this key hypothesis at the donor country-level as well as the level of the individual decision-maker.

Before I spell out my empirical strategy for testing these hypotheses, I want to briefly return to my argument. Although my empirical predictions are derived from theorising about aid officials and their different micro-institutional environments today, I want to further develop the idea that these delivery patterns have ideological origins. After all, institutions and their character are not exogenous. They are human creations that reflect a particular way of thinking about societal problems and how they can best be addressed and solved.[90]

Drawing on insights from research on state formation and comparative public administration, I suggest that the organisation and character of state institutions, including national aid organisations, are endogenous to predominant beliefs about the appropriate mode of public sector governance that, at different times in different donor countries, were mobilised to solve important societal challenges. It is about the blend of roles between state and market in public sector governance. As I will show in more detail in Chapter 2, questions about how to best address societal challenges have been answered differently by states across time. Whether governance orientations become consequential for the direction of institutional reform is not because they are compelling. They become consequential because opportune political circumstances favour it.[91] During moments of critical juncture, the mechanisms of institutional reproduction are undermined because old ideas lose legitimacy and/or key political and economic actors form coalitions to promote institutional reforms.[92]

The claim that micro-institutions have ideological origins and that these origins shape the character of the institutional environment plays an important role in my theoretical framework. First, it suggests that today's aid delivery decisions are shaped by institutional legacies, by rules and practices that were put in place many decades earlier and that

---

[90] North (1990).　　[91] Lieberman (2002).　　[92] E.g. Thelen (1999).

serve to lock-in the very ideas that gave rise to the institutions in the first place. I do not argue that the systems and character of national aid organisations lead to organisational pathologies in the sense of Barnett and Finnemore's in *Rules For the World: International Organizations in Global Politics*.[93] Instead, I want to highlight that there is an ideological origin to institutions that shapes how donors deliver aid in developing countries. Past decisions to organise state institutions, including national aid organisations, make it difficult and costly to change aid delivery tactics, even when these policies are considered dysfunctional.

Second, by integrating the ideological origin of bypass or engagement in my analytical framework, I am able to embed micro-institutions in the broader context of important ideological, macro-level transformations that have shaped world politics. As economic historians tell us, we observe swings in dominance of states and markets that go back many centuries. While the industrialisation process of the West in the nineteenth century was characterised by a dominant market and a small government sector, the state gradually took on a more prominent role during the inter-war years, promoted by ideas and beliefs in planning as the best way to promote a stronger economy and a better life for its citizens. Over the course of the twentieth century, neoliberal ideas have proliferated and replaced more statist ones in many countries across the world. This ideological transformation finds its manifestation in the type of rules that make up and organise state organisations.[94] As the ideological character of the institutional environment changes, as goes my argument, I expect aid officials' behaviour to change as well.

To be sure, macro-level constructs such as neoliberalism do not help me specify the constraints mechanism that I suggest creates ordered, regular patterns in aid delivery within aid organisations.[95] Once beliefs are institutionalised and taken for granted, institutional constraints do the heavy-lifting in explaining aid delivery patterns. But, linking institutions to macro-level concepts and phenomena enables me to account for policy change over time. As Schumpeter reminds us in *Capitalism, Socialism, and Democracy*, the ideological origins of

---

[93] Barnett and Finnemore (2004).   [94] Ruggie (1982); Polanyi (2001).
[95] Lieberman (2002).

institutions also carry the seed for 'creative destruction' and, therefore, institutional and policy change.[96]

1.6 Empirical Strategy

A key contribution of this book lies with the wide range of evidence that I leverage to test my argument. To test the cross-sectional variation in aid delivery, some of the evidence comes from statistical analyses of a global sample of twenty-three OECD donors from 2005 to 2015. Other evidence comes from individual-level survey data of sixty-five foreign aid officials who have experience in aid decision-making across six countries, the United States, United Kingdom, Sweden, Germany, France, and Japan, which was collected between 2013 and 2015. I leverage these data to show that my theoretical argument about donor heterogeneity is supported at both the micro- and the country-levels. I directly measure variation in national aid organisations through a binary variable that separates donor countries which organise their public sector governance around neoliberal principles from donor countries whose public sector is underwritten by a more traditional public sector logic.

In the cross-country statistical tests, I assess the effect of national aid structures on aid decision-making, while controlling for important potential confounders. As ample research has demonstrated, systematic determinants of foreign aid levels include donor security and economic interests as well as political and historical ties. I show that, consistent with previous research, these factors also influence donor decisions to bypass or engage but that the effects of micro-organisations prevail across all model specifications. These findings push back against a stream of research that does not attribute attention to the role of domestic politics in aid decision-making. They also push back against research that assumes that aid officials across donor countries are constrained and behave in similar ways.

As I have advocated an empirical focus on aid officials and their decision-making across donor countries, my empirical strategy must directly test my argument at the level of the decision-maker. Because I assume that within the same organisation all decision-makers

---

[96] Schumpeter (1950), p. 83 as cited in Lieberman (2002), p. 704.

respond to the same set of incentives, I expect individual decisions to aggregate up to the donor country level and determine aid delivery budgets across aid delivery channels. My theory generates additional empirical implications at the level of the individual decision-maker, for which I find support. The institutional rules of the game limit aid officials' discretion and thus constrain aid officials in their tactics. When donor officials work in bureaucratic structures and rules are built on more statist conceptions of governance, rules and practices are in place that make government-to-government donor–recipient interactions more likely. They will respond to the risk of aid capture in poor governance environments with more government engagement but will reduce the risk by being more hands-on in the aid delivery process.

In addition, the book is rich with quotes from these aid officials who are the main actors in my theory of decision-making. I collected them, along with other qualitative insights, through extensive open-ended interviews. The broad scope of aid officials from different donor governments is unprecedented for original field research in the study of foreign aid decision-making. In addition, I undertook extensive archival research to document organisational structures of aid organisations across donor countries. In Chapter 3, I use this qualitative evidence to establish variation in my key independent variable: the bureaucratic structures and administrative processes of aid organisations. In addition, I leverage this evidence to elucidate the causal mechanism that links micro-structures and their character to aid delivery: I show that the character of aid organisations determines whether aid officials are more likely to engage with or bypass the recipient government in foreign aid.

My interviews further serve to push back against potential alternative explanations. To convince readers of my argument, I need to show, for example, that aid officials from neoliberal aid organisations do not choose bypass under conditions of poor governance because they believe that it is a more appropriate strategy. Although ideas matter insofar as they shape the rules and character of aid organisations, aid delivery decisions result, so I argue, because aid officials pursue material interests in the context of their institutions. As my interviews revealed time and again, aid officials felt constrained and limited in their ability to respond to high risk in aid-receiving countries. The implication of my argument is that donor–recipient interactions in world politics are first and foremost constrained by the micro-institutional context in which aid officials operate.

Furthermore, I leverage additional interview evidence with officials as well as originally collected public opinion data to push back against claims that the reason why the United States bypasses more under conditions of poor recipient governance than Germany is because the US and German publics want their governments to do more or less bypass, respectively. As my interviews revealed, aid officials across countries asserted that they did not attribute much importance to the public because they did not believe that the public had a position on this particular issue, nor did they think that this issue was salient. On the basis of survey experimental evidence collected in Germany and the United States, I show that differences in aid delivery decisions between the United States and Germany are not consistent with differences between how the two donor publics think about foreign aid delivery.

Finally, my theory also predicts overtime variation. Unfortunately, the kinds of historical data I would need to evaluate the empirical relevance of my argument over time do not exist. However, I will make use of historical sources and my own interviews with aid officials to strengthen the claim that a donor's transitions from traditional public sector to neoliberal models of governance make it more likely that the donor chooses to deliver aid through bypass than government-to-government aid.

1.7 Theoretical Contributions and Policy Implication

In exploring the origins of foreign aid delivery patterns across donor countries, my book highlights the importance of national structures. It illuminates previously unexplored linkages between the organisation of domestic political economies and foreign aid. I show that political economy differences impose important constraints on foreign aid decision-making. Thus, the results of this book directly reinforce and extend a prominent line of work by Katzenstein, Gourevitch, Simmons, Milner, Broz, Pevehouse, and others that emphasises the importance of domestic factors on foreign policy.[97]

---

[97] For example, see Katzenstein (1978); Gourevitch (1986); Simmons (1994); Milner (1997); Broz (2005); Mansfield and Pevehouse (2006), and see Lake (2009a) for a review of this literature.

My argument presents a different lens through which one can understand the role of beliefs and institutions on foreign policy. For all the talk about how neoliberalism as an ideology has transformed world politics, I suggest that aid officials are first and foremost constrained by micro-bureaucratic structures and practices, and it is the institutions that drive aid delivery in a particular direction. Ideology matters for aid delivery because, at different times in different countries, ideas about the appropriate role of the state in public sector governance were mobilised to create new rules and thus reshaped the character of the aid organisation in which foreign aid officials operate. This argument is different from the claim that aid officials are guided by what they feel is the appropriate response. It also differs from arguments that suggest that ideas and beliefs serve as heuristic tools that guide decision-making under conditions of uncertainty. As the theory and evidence of this book reveal, the reason why aid officials deliver aid in the way they do is because they pursue material interests by following rules and practices that underwrite the national aid organisations.

My book contributes to the aid effectiveness debate by suggesting that the proliferation of neoliberal ideas has not led to a convergence in aid delivery across donor countries. Instead, as predicted by scholars in the *Varieties of Capitalism* tradition, donor governments pursue different aid delivery tactics in countries where the risk of aid capture is high; and these differences result from variation in institutional constraints across national aid organisations. These institutional differences also explain why some donor governments more than others want to maximise short-term results, prioritize short-term aid relief over capacity-building, and use different metrics to assess the success of the aid. Any attempt to say which of these regimes may be better is missing the point.

Donor governments that bypass recipient governments by outsourcing foreign aid delivery to non-state actors may achieve greater success in providing immediate relief to the poor through easily implementable health interventions than donor governments that continue to engage in institution building in collaboration with the state. However, outsourcing in foreign aid delivery might hamper or even undermine donor efforts to build up a state capable of managing its own development – an objective which ranks high for donor governments that prefer a tactic of greater engagement with the government in the developing country. Whether aid is delivered through bypass or government-to-government aid, donors and their development tactics have lasting and transformative consequences for recipient country development insofar as for recipients, each tactic implies a particular model of development. While donors often offer a combination of short- and long-term approaches, the results of this study imply that political economies may shape where donor governments come in on this fundamental dilemma in aid provision.

My study also sheds light on potential trade-offs between aid effectiveness and policy influence. By setting up parallel structures, market-oriented donor governments may achieve greater success in providing direct relief to the poor. However, this approach may bring some unintended consequences. By de-emphasising state-building, donor governments may surrender the opportunity to strengthen relationships with state and local authorities. This may undermine donor ability to more directly shape policy and governance processes in aid-receiving countries.

My argument has implications for our understanding of donor coordination – a practice that has long been encouraged by the OECD Development Assistance Committee (DAC), but which has advanced little. If differences in national structures make donor coordination difficult, then we should only expect countries with similar political economies to be able to coordinate successfully. My argument also predicts that as recipient governments improve the quality of their governance, the debate over whether to push for bypass or government-to-government tactics will become increasingly mute, and donor coordination should become easier.

My argument has important policy implications as well. It suggests that over time dominant beliefs about public sector governance have changed, from being more statist in conception during the years of welfare state expansion to a neoliberal view of a more limited role of state involvement. As donor political economies have reorganised their aid bureaucratic structures and processes in line with this new approach to governance, the neoliberal governance model has gained an upper hand over a more statist conception of governance. This matters for aid effectiveness insofar as this dialectic between governance ideas and political economies leads to decisions as to what is the better approach to delivering foreign aid effectively.

1.8 Organisation of the Book

Chapter 2 develops the principal claim of the book, which posits that foreign aid delivery is endogenous to national structures. I start with a brief historical account of how patterns of foreign aid delivery have evolved since the end of World War II. I then flesh out three theoretical and empirically informed observations about aid decision-making: (1) that aid officials, as key decision-makers, seek to minimise risk in aid delivery, that (2) their response to risk is conditional on the rules and practices that make up the national aid organisations in which they operate, and (3) that these rules and practices have ideological origins that inform us about the substance of aid delivery: why it is that aid officials choose to bypass or engage with the recipient government.

In Chapter 3, I focus on elucidating the link between national structures and foreign aid delivery. To that end, I trace how national aid organisations vary in their bureaucratic structures and practices and show that this variation maps onto my binary donor typology of neoliberal and traditional public sector donors. By tracing the link between particular institutional environments and aid delivery decisions, I show how bureaucratic structures and practices influence priorities of aid officials and authorise, enable, and justify particular delivery tactics and donor–recipient interactions, while precluding others. That is, I lay out why and how institutions of different ideological orientation constrain donor officials differently, and how they influence aid officials' decision-making.

I turn to testing my central argument in Chapters 4 and 5. The evidence in Chapter 4 is quantitative and tests the argument at the donor–recipient country level, using a data set of twenty-three OECD donors and their aid-receiving countries between 2005 and 2015.[98] The key independent variable is donor political economy type: whether national aid organisations are organised around neoliberal or traditional public sector principles. If my argument is empirically useful, what I would find is that, after controlling for other factors that are systematically associated with aid delivery decisions, donor governments whose bureaucratic structures and rules are of neoliberal

---

[98] Although I would have preferred to test my argument on a longer temporal timeframe, data for aid delivery have only become available in more recent years.

character are more likely to bypass than their traditional public sector counterparts. I also expect to find that neoliberal donors are more likely to increase bypass tactics when the quality of recipient governance is low.

In Chapter 5, I further probe the substantively and statistically robust relationship between national structures and foreign aid delivery at the level of the individual decision-maker. Because my theory puts the aid official front and centre, I expect aid officials from different political economy types to state different preferences for foreign aid delivery under similar conditions of high risk in recipient countries. To that end, I collected original survey data for sixty-five aid officials from six different donor countries who vary in their political economy type, including, on the neoliberal end, the United States, the United Kingdom, and Sweden, as well as, on the traditional public sector end, France, Germany, and Japan. In addition to quantitative analyses of the survey, I leverage extensive qualitative interview evidence to demonstrate that my central claim and additional empirical implications of my argument find robust empirical support. This chapter also provides further qualitative support for the causal mechanism spelled out in Chapter 3.

In Chapter 6, I shift the focus from explaining why aid officials differ in their aid delivery decisions across different political economies to investigate the extent to which these preferences may be driven by what donor publics want aid officials to do. To that end, I leverage interview evidence with officials as well as originally collected public opinion data to push back against claims that the reason why the United States bypasses more under conditions of poor recipient governance than Germany is because the US and German publics want their governments to do more or less bypass, respectively. Time and time again, my interviews revealed that aid officials across countries did not attribute much importance to the public on aid delivery decisions because they did not believe that the public had a position on this particular issue. On the basis of survey experimental evidence collected in Germany and the United States, I show that differences in aid delivery decisions between US and German aid officials are not consistent with differences between how the two donor publics think about foreign aid delivery.

The final chapter of the book, Chapter 7, considers the implications of my analysis for the study of foreign aid effectiveness as well as policy-making. It has implications because it establishes a link between political economies and the different kinds of outcomes that donor officials prioritise. Donor governments that outsource aid delivery in countries with bad governance may achieve greater success in providing immediate relief to the poor through easily implementable health interventions than donor governments that continue to engage in institution building in collaboration with the state. However, outsourcing in foreign aid delivery might hamper or even undermine donor efforts to build up a state capable of managing its own development – an objective that ranks high for donor governments who prefer a tactic of greater engagement with the government in the developing country. This book also suggests that the proliferation of neoliberal governance beliefs, and its managerial tools like performance indicators, puts increasing pressure on statist regimes to change their metric, a process which may come at the expense of efforts to strengthen the capacity of the state abroad. Finally, my book opens up future avenues for research that seek to explain foreign policy decisions in areas as varied as migration and defence, and research that seeks to understand the downstream effects of donor tactics on the behaviour of implementing actors in development.

2 | How National Structures Shape Foreign Aid Delivery

A Theory

2.1 Introduction

Why do some OECD donor governments choose to bypass recipient authorities in poorly governed recipient countries, while others continue to provide substantial amounts through the government-to-government aid channel? How do national structures influence foreign aid delivery tactics across donor countries and across time? In this chapter, I develop a theoretical argument to answer these questions.

While research on foreign aid has been around for decades, the empirical study of foreign aid delivery, as I pointed out in Chapter 1, is in its infancy. To better understand how aid delivery tactics are made and how they differ across countries, my theory, in the first instance, undertakes an empirical 'shift' away from the more conventional macro-level: I study aid decision-making at the level of the aid official who works in aid organisations across donor countries and who assumes a central role in decisions to deliver aid. The official's world is characterised by risk and rational expectations, where aid officials seek to promote their organisation's development mandate by making decisions about delivery tactics. One of their central concerns is risk of aid capture abroad, and they seek tactics that promise to minimise this risk.

As I noted in Chapter 1, aid officials across donor governments have multiple delivery options. They can work directly with the recipient government or they can bypass it by channelling aid through non-state actors, including international organisations, non-state actors, or private contractors, only to name the most prominent non-state delivery channels. Whether aid officials decide to bypass or engage with the recipient government, or have a tendency to opt for one but not the other, is not decided in a vacuum. The decision hinges on the guidelines that direct aid officials' decisions. As rational actors, aid officials follow formal rules and practices that are set up to advance their aid organisation's goals. My argument distinguishes between rules and practices that are organised around a neoliberal conception of public sector governance and institutions that are built on more traditional public sector principles. While a neoliberal rulebook authorises, enables, and justifies bypass under conditions of poor governance, it precludes government-to-government delivery. At the same time, aid officials from more traditional public sector structures are incentivised to deliver aid through the government-to-government channel under similar conditions. As aid officials learn about risks to aid delivery in poorly governed countries, their choice set is constrained, depending on the character of their institution. Returning to the empirical puzzles presented in Chapter 1, this book explains why the United States, the United Kingdom, and Sweden employ bypass tactics in Sri Lanka, while Germany, France, and Japan take the route of government-to-government aid.

My argument also posits that the core mission or mandate of the aid organisation is not objectively defined. Rather it reflects the ideological context in which it was created, and is therefore endogenous to the organisation of the donor political economy. This implies that aid officials differ in their priorities as to what kind of development outcomes they want to accomplish in the first place, whether it is results on the ground in the short-term or capacity-building and more government ownership over the process. Furthermore, my argument suggests that, depending on their political economy type, aid officials will resort to different metrics to measure aid success. In other words, aid success means different things to aid officials from different political economies. My argument rejects the claim that aid officials can easily optimise aid delivery following whatever tactic appears to be most promising at any given time. I argue that for ideas to be consequential they need to be compatible with the underlying institutional rulebook.

My approach to studying aid delivery relies on an analytical framework that interlocks institutions and beliefs. To be sure, institutional constraints do the heavy lifting in explaining stable and regular patterns of aid delivery across donor governments in the more recent past, for which data are available. The integration of ideas and beliefs, however, allows me to say more about the political dimension of aid delivery. By theorising about the ideological origins of institutions, I provide, as Lieberman would suggest, 'the raw material upon which institutional theory feeds'.[1] I account for the goals and beliefs that led to the creation of the aid organisation and that, through institutional legacies in the form of institutional rulebooks, shape how aid officials think about and respond to risk in foreign aid.

Although this book places a central focus on explaining donor heterogeneity in foreign aid delivery in a post-Cold War context, my argument also predicts variation within donor governments over time. As a result of data constraints, my evidence to assess over-time variation is not quantitative but largely qualitative in nature, drawing on interviews with aid officials and historical sources. In the next section of the book, I provide a brief historical account of aid delivery patterns: Section 2.2 begins with a discussion of foreign aid delivery in the post-World War II years through the 1970s. It documents, albeit impressionistically, a persistent and uniform government-to-government approach to foreign aid delivery across OECD donors that is rooted in then-dominant views about the importance of the state in the economy and development. The predominantly government-to-government tactic also corresponded with security objectives of the Cold War, where the United States, or more broadly, Western foreign policy strategy, directly targeted governments across the developing world to contain the spread of Soviet communism. The section then proceeds to identify the crisis of the welfare state and the global ascendancy of neoliberal doctrine, as a period of critical juncture that set some but not all donor governments onto what then became diverging paths of foreign aid delivery. For countries that undertook reforms, neoliberal doctrine had direct implications for how donor governments structure donor–recipient interactions. Neoliberalism promotes state rationalisation processes that result in large-scale restructuring of public sectors, including aid organisations. A historical perspective on foreign aid delivery enables me to trace the linkages between ideological, macro-level transformations and the ideological origin of aid organisations and their aid delivery tactics.

In Section 2.3, I then make an empirical shift onto the micro-level and explain the micro-foundations of aid delivery tactics. I explain why neoliberal restructuring of aid organisations incentivises individual aid officials to select bypass tactics under conditions of poor recipient governance. My micro-institutional argument also explains why aid

---

[1] Lieberman (2002), p. 697.

officials who work in traditional public sector economies tend to choose government-to-government tactics under similar conditions. Finally, the chapter spells out the testable implications of my framework that I will evaluate against quantitative and qualitative evidence in subsequent chapters. I expect aid delivery decisions to be endogenous to donor political economy type: When donor officials work in aid organisations whose bureaucratic structures and rules are of neoliberal character, they will react to the risk of aid capture in aid-receiving countries with more bypass. When donor officials work with structures and rules that are built on more traditional public sector principles, they are less likely to engage in bypass tactics and more in government-to-government delivery.

2.2 A Historical Perspective of Foreign Aid Delivery

Foreign aid scholars often reference the Marshall Plan and Point Four of the Truman Doctrine as the start of modern foreign development assistance as we know it today.[2] It marked the beginning of a sustained effort by the United States government to help rebuild Europe and modernise poor countries around the world. In the eyes of many, the Marshall Plan was a bold model of international cooperation, as it represented a departure from American attitudes of retreat after World War I.

In its scope and mode of delivery, however, the Marshall Plan, a vast government stimulus programme that placed European governments at the centre of foreign aid delivery efforts, very much reflected dominant economic ideas at the time. As World War II came to an end, the experience of the Great Depression had already unravelled trust in the ability of markets to coordinate economic activity. Led by influential figures in international economics, including Keynes, Myrdal, Lewis, Gerschenkron, and Galbraith, a post-war consensus emerged that put the state at the centre of the economy and development efforts abroad.[3] Walter Lippmann describes the growing appetite for statist governance throughout the 1930s and 1940s to transcend ideologies thus: 'Throughout the world, in the name of progress, men who call

---

[2] See Lancaster (2007); Bermeo (2018).
[3] Blyth (2002); Swank (2002); Ekblad (2011).

themselves communists, socialists, fascists, nationalists, progressives and even liberals, are unanimous in holding that government with its instruments of coercion must, by commanding the people how they should live, direct the course of civilization and fix the shape of things to come.'[4] Along similar lines, sociologist Karl Mannheim asserted that there was 'no longer any choice between planning and laissez-faire, but only between good planning and bad'.[5]

Because this book is interested in explaining foreign aid delivery tactics, I stress that the responsibility of implementing the Marshall Plan was squarely in the hands of European governments. In April 1948, Congress approved the Economic Cooperation Act authorising the Marshall Plan, which poured more than $100 billion at today's dollar price into the economies of Western Europe over the course of four years.[6] This assistance was delivered in annual instalments, as cash support without a lending component.[7] Congress placed the distribution of the ERP funds in the hands of the Economic Cooperation Agency (ECA), which was created in 1948. The agency reported to the U.S. State Department and the Department of Commerce but was based throughout all sixteen capitals of countries participating in the Marshall Plan.[8]

In Europe, governments requested cash payments from the ECA for the delivery of goods in industrial and agricultural commodities and food, to only name the three largest payment sectors, among others.[9] As Dean Acheson later recalled in his *Homage to General Marshall*, the Plan was built on George Marshall's conviction that European recovery had to originate with and be devised by the European governments themselves. He noted that Marshall believed that the United States should deliver the means that Europe could not supply but that it should not offer or impose an American plan. Rather the role of the United States would be to 'help those who energetically and cooperatively helped themselves'.[10]

By 1949, President Truman's vision of modernisation had expanded beyond Europe to include 'under-developed' countries in the world,

---

[4] Lippmann (1937), pp. 3–4. Cited in Ekblad (2011).
[5] Mannheim and Shils (1940), p. 6. Cited in Ekblad (2011).   [6] Judt (2001).
[7] Behrman (2008).   [8] Economic Cooperation Administration (1951).
[9] Economic Cooperation Administration (1951).   [10] Acheson (1959), p. 25.

whose emergence from the historical status of 'underdevelopment' was presumed to result from American assistance. In Truman's words,

We must embark on a bold new program for making the benefits of our scientific advances and industrial progress available for the improvement and growth of underdeveloped areas. More than half the people of the world are living in conditions approaching misery. Their food is inadequate. They are victims of disease. Their economic life is primitive and stagnant. Their poverty is a handicap and a threat both to them and to more prosperous areas. For the first time in history, humanity possesses the knowledge and skill to relieve suffering of these people. The United States is pre-eminent among nations in the development of industrial and scientific techniques. The material resources which we can afford to use for assistance of other peoples are limited. But our imponderable resources in technical knowledge are constantly growing and are inexhaustible.[11]

Like the Marshall Plan, Truman's Point Four placed government at the centre of development. It called for the United States to share its 'know-how' and help nations gain prosperity with foreign aid delivered through the government-to-government channel. For example, the United States provided foreign assistance in the form of extensive technical assistance and capital projects through several agencies, including the Mutual Security Agency, Foreign Operations Administration, and the International Cooperation Administration.[12] After Congress approved Point Four in 1950, Truman established the Technical Cooperation Administration (TCA) within the State Department whose goal was to promote centralised policy-making and provide technical knowledge to countries.[13]

This government-to-government approach to foreign aid delivery had ideological roots insofar as it was embedded in national structures that were created in a statist image a decade earlier. Then, the collapse of world trade and the economic challenges of the Great Depression had created an opportune political moment, a critical juncture, during which economic ideas about a more interventionist state found persuasive expression among political actors, including, but not limited to, President Roosevelt and a largely Democratic Congress.[14] These actors promoted significant restructuring of the public sector, including an

---

[11] United States, Department of State Bulletin (1949), p. 123.
[12] USAID (2019).   [13] USAID (2019), p. 10.
[14] Blyth (2002); Ekblad (2011).

expansion of the bureaucracy and its management by experts.[15] These institutional changes laid the institutional foundations for a more expansive welfare state that lasted a generation, enabling the implementation of domestic social programmes like the New Deal as well as future Presidential initiatives like John F. Kennedy's New Frontier, Lyndon Johnson's Great Society, and Richard Nixon's New Federalism.[16]

Importantly, the reorganisation of the public sector in a more statist image also influenced the delivery of national aid programmes. As the historian David Ekblad notes in *The Great American Mission: Modernization and the Construction of an American World Order*, the scope of US foreign aid programmes from the Marshall Plan throughout the Eisenhower, Kennedy, and Johnson administrations reflected beliefs in the virtues of the state as an important actor in the economy.[17] These beliefs were locked in through national aid organisations that had the capacity to directly implement projects and maintain regular contacts and interactions with recipient government officials, civil society leaders, or business, even in remote areas.

When discussing the creation of USAID in 1961, for example, President Kennedy re-emphasised the government-to-government character of aid, while demanding sufficient capacity to implement it. He notes that US aid programmes require 'a highly professional skilled service, attracting substantial numbers of high-caliber men and women capable of sensitive dealing with other governments, and with a deep understanding of the process of economic development'.[18] Under the Kennedy and Johnson administrations, USAID personnel increased significantly. As a former USAID administrator, Andrew Natsios, suggests in a cunning assessment of the early days of USAID,

The daily business practice of this new aid agency was manifold and required complex negotiations with the recipient government. For example, the agency insisted on vetting school building proposals with community groups, obtaining approval of the local schools by the Education Ministry, helping build ministry capacity to staff, equip and meet the recurrent costs of the education system. USAID also required its primary contractors to work with local companies to build indigenous capacity across sectors.[19]

---

[15] Yoo (2018).   [16] Lynn (2006); Ekblad (2011).   [17] Ekblad (2011).
[18] Cited in Radelet (2003) , p. 110.   [19] Natsios (2010), p. 25.

This kind of government-to-government engagement was only possible because USAID had the in-house expertise and capacity to implement projects and influence policy-making. It was set up to produce development outcomes in the long run. This state-centred approach not only required technical capacity. It also made regular interactions and exchanges with foreign government elites a necessity.

Of course, the emphasis on government-to-government foreign aid at the time coincided with the overarching ideological battle between democracy and communism during the Cold War. As many scholars have noted, throughout the Cold War, the United States used foreign aid as a tool to contain the spread of Soviet-influenced communism.[20] For example, economic recovery in post-World War II Europe was seen as key to strengthening democratic forces against communist parties. It was in the interest of the United States to build up a strong Europe insofar as strong allies would make a superior bulwark against the Soviet Union. Government-to-government aid programmes were also enlisted in counter-insurgency efforts in Vietnam, for example. To promote democracy in South Vietnam and convince insurgents of the American cause, USAID not only built many schools, hospitals, and roads. It also sent a great number of technical experts, engineers, and civilian advisors to facilitate the implementation of aid projects and engage in policy dialogue with the South Vietnamese government.[21] Between 1962 and 1975, South Vietnam received more US aid than any other developing country: in 1967 alone the agency's budget allocated more than one-quarter of its USD 2 billion to a country of some 17 million people.[22] This example suggests that government-to-government aid delivery tactics derived their rationale not only from economic beliefs but also from geostrategic efforts to enlist governments abroad to join the US cause.

Outside the US context, once Western governments had transitioned from being beneficiaries of the Marshall Plan to assuming their own responsibilities as donor governments, they, too, pursued a government-to-government approach to foreign aid delivery. As my argument suggests, donor governments did so in part because at the time their national structures were set up to promote government-to-government

---

[20] Baldwin (1985); Morgenthau (1993).   [21] Ekblad (2011), p. 9.
[22] Leepson (2000).

aid. Across the board, staff in domestic and international agencies fulfilled multiple functions and had responsibility for a great number of tasks, including planning and budgeting as well as policy analysis and evaluation.[23] They delivered aid projects directly and in close cooperation with recipient governments.

In the 1970s, as a result of economic crises and fiscal scarcity the credibility and legitimacy of domestic welfare state expansion came under siege. Influential intellectuals such as Hayek and Friedman, among others, claimed that national governments had lost control over their economic policies. Weighed down by tedious and heavy bureaucracy, national governments were no longer considered capable of providing solutions to challenges in an increasingly globalised world where competition had become more intense.[24]

Osborne and Gaebler articulate a fairly typical critique of the welfare state

The kind of governments that developed during the industrial era, with their sluggish, centralised bureaucracies, their preoccupation with rules and regulations, and their hierarchical chains of command, no longer work very well. They accomplished great things in their time, but somewhere along the line they got away from us. They became bloated, wasteful, ineffective. And when the world began to change, they failed to change with it. Hierarchical, centralised bureaucracies designed in the 1930s or 1940s simply do not function well in the rapidly-changing, information-rich, knowledge-intensive society and economy.[25]

In an ever more globalised world, traditional public sector structures and their mechanisms of reproduction were not only perceived as outdated but as undermining national competitiveness. The collapse of the Soviet Union further underscored this concern, as it signalled to the world that communism had failed to promote national economic and security interests.

Akin to domestic developments, the crisis of the welfare state laid bare inefficiencies of delivering foreign aid through the government channel. By the end of the Cold War, many of the world's poorest countries had not improved in spite of decades worth of development assistance; while, increasingly, studies revealed that aid may not only exacerbate

---

[23] Raadschelders and Toonen (1999); Lynn (2006), pp. 54–55.
[24] Dalton (2013).   [25] Osborne and Gaebler (1992), pp. 11–12.

corruption or worsen governance[26] but also prop up dictators,[27] among other negative outcomes that donors care about. Across donor countries, aid critics tapped into contemporary, anti-government sentiment that portrayed the state as inefficient, non-transparent, and out of tune with what citizens wanted. The infamous critique of US foreign aid efforts by the US Republican senator Jesse Helms, who likened foreign aid to throwing "tax dollars down a foreign rat hole",[28] was an open attack on foreign aid. It only reinforced perceptions that foreign aid was wasteful and superfluous, that it did not deliver what it promised, and that the public sector was part of the problem.[29] This tune was remarkably similar to more general critics of the welfare state.

As the earlier period of economic stability came to an end, neoliberal doctrine promised a particular solution to concerns over competitiveness in the global economy by promoting a new blended role between the state and the market. It saw market liberalisation, government retrenchment, and state rationalisation as a panacea for achieving better outcomes. In the United States, neoliberal doctrine emerged victorious over statist governance thinking in the 1970s; during this historical period, existing statist structures had lost their legitimacy and grip on state agents and enabled political and economic neoliberal reformers to pursue policies that dramatically reorganised the public sector and the economy.[30] During this period, the seeds were sown that would transform USAID from an organisation that was set up to promote government-to-government aid and that had the manpower and budget to implement aid abroad to a dismantled government agency that assumed managerial responsibilities and outsourced aid implementation to non-state actors. Similar transformations occurred in other Western donor governments, where neoliberal reforms occurred on a grand scale. Although I will shed more light on why and how these organisational changes have long-term and transformative effects on donor–recipient interactions in Section 2.5 as well as Chapter 3, this brief and impressionistic historical account serves to build the intuition that national structures provide a potential answer as to why donor governments of a particular type pursue particular aid delivery tactics.

---

[26] Bates (2001); Knack (2001); Remmer (2004); Weinstein (2005).
[27] Kono and Montinola (2009).   [28] Cited in Natsios (2010), p. 22.
[29] Mawdsley et al. (2014).   [30] Osborne and Gaebler (1992).

2.3 The Rise of Neoliberalism, National Structures, and Divergence in Foreign Aid Delivery

Since the 1970s, neoliberal doctrine has transformed the global landscape. It is associated with a range of economic policies such as fiscal discipline achieved through government spending cuts, outsourcing, as well as trade and financial liberalisation. As an order of markets and enterprise, neoliberalism is inherently distrustful of the state and propagates market liberalisation and government retrenchment as a panacea for achieving more frugal, efficient, and effective policy outcomes.[31] Like classical liberalism, neoliberalism argues against coordinated political economies and towards dispersed competition in a free market.[32] Unlike classical liberal theory, as Baccaro and Howell remind us, neoliberalism posits that the state has an important role to play insofar as its role is to support the free functioning of markets by making rules as well as monitoring and enforcing them.[33] If markets do not exist, the state is expected to intervene and create them. Incentives within public or non-profit sectors should mimic competitive production in the private sector.[34] This new order not only separates demand from supply. It also requires the state to actively create and maintain the market. This new blend of roles has been captured as 'steering not rowing', or 'entrepreneurial government'.[35] Yet others talk in terms of 'regulatory state',[36] 'government at a distance',[37] or the state's 'privatization'.[38]

Of significance to my theory, neoliberalism promotes a particular form of public sector governance.[39] As Foucault points out, the character of the neoliberal order is inherently 'private' insofar as norms, rules, and procedures that underwrite it stem from the market and private enterprise.[40] As a government rationality, neoliberalism structures and organises the actions and interactions of the state and society

---

[31] Dardot and Laval (2009). [32] Streeck (2010), p. 149.
[33] Baccaro and Howell (2017), p. 16.
[34] Le Grand and Bartlett (1993); Gingrich (2011).
[35] Osborne and Gaebler (1992). [36] Amann and Baer (2005); Yeung (2010).
[37] Rose and Mille (2008). [38] Hibou (2015).
[39] Peters (1996) provides an excellent overview of changes in governance beginning in the 1970s. Also see: Benz (1995).
[40] Foucault (2004). See also Hibou (2015) on the organization of the neoliberal bureaucracy.

in accordance with the principle of competition.[41] The neoliberal state breaks with the traditional public sector order insofar as it replaces authoritative coordination and control with dispersed competition. It emphasises individual over collective action. The neoliberal order derives its basis of legitimation from its output, which some have associated with effectiveness and efficiency in achieving results.[42] A regime that disappoints in terms of results delivery or performance becomes vulnerable to attacks on its legitimacy.[43]

I thus conceive of neoliberalism as a form of government that internalises a market-based rationality and creates rules and practices that reflect the culture of private firms and that, once imposed, govern the behaviour of state agents and contractors on the principle of competition. This order has straightforward organisational implications insofar as neoliberal doctrine motivates processes of state rationalisation. First, it prescribes a significant reduction in the scale of the state, including aid organisations. It also entails that the traditional mechanism of goods and service delivery, which organises delivery via institutionalised or direct goods and service provision, be replaced by a mechanism of competitive contracting, requiring officials to select delivery channels in an open market.[44] However, as scholarship of delegation and principal–agent relations has noted, the process of delegation or contracting out is not without risk.[45] If the agent has interests and incentives that are not perfectly compatible with those of the official, as is assumed by scholars who contribute to this literature, delegation can generate agency problems.[46] In most situations, it is difficult for state officials to know whether the agents are slacking or whether their actions are consistent with what the state desires, and the agents can exploit this informational asymmetry to their advantage.[47] To ensure that the use of competitive contracting yields expected

---

[41] See Dardot and Laval (2009) for an excellent overview of the political and economic circumstances of neoliberalism.
[42] Scharpf (1997a).   [43] Tallberg et al. (2018).
[44] Peters and Pierre (1998); Pollitt and Boukhaert (2011); Bertelli (2012).
[45] Goodsell (1981), Kumlin and Rothstein (2005); see Pepinski et al. (2017) for a review.
[46] Snyder and Weingast (2000); Dixit (2002); Nielson and Tierney (2003); Whitford (2005).
[47] Dixit (2002).

efficiency gains and pre-specified results are delivered, the state needs to reduce agent shirking and keep the agent honest and accountable. Second, neoliberal doctrine promotes a particular solution to accountability, which, again, borrows directly from the private sector: it promotes the imposition of managerial practices that enable monitoring and control of agent behaviour through sanctions and incentives on a frequent and regular basis. It requires, for example, the set up of extensive monitoring and reporting systems. These systems allow state officials, in their role as principals, to know what happens with the contract and whether the agent fulfils its contractual obligations by delivering on results. To be able to control production, the state requires the capacity to clearly specify outcomes and to monitor the performance of providers and discipline non-compliant producers.[48]

As a process, performance monitoring includes the specification of clear and measurable organisational objectives to promote strategic steering within the organisation as well as provide public accounts of state performance. Performance monitoring helps the state keep tabs on processes and outputs for which it is responsible in its role as agent of citizens.[49] It does so in the short-run, often annually, to feed data for yearly performance reports. Compared to evaluation practices in the traditional public sector, evaluations of performance or success are conducted under greater time pressure and shorter time horizons.[50] To incentivise performance-orientation among officials, the state rewards exceptional efforts through performance pay, among other measures.[51] Neoliberal doctrine thus gives rise to a particular institutional rulebook, bureaucratic structures, and practices that constrain aid officials in a particular policy direction.

Since Thatcher and Reagan took office, neoliberal doctrine has guided many state rationalisation processes around the world, encapsulated as reinventing government, modernising governance, and reengineering public service.[52] Initially, reforms took place in Anglo-Saxon countries in the 1970s. There and then several factors came together

---

[48] Kiewiet and McCubbins (1991); Olken and Pande (2012).
[49] Pollitt and Boukhaert (2011).   [50] van Dooren et al. (2010).
[51] Dixit (2002); Pollitt and Bouckaert (2011). This claim is relatively uncontested, although debates exist about the mechanisms through which institutional rules influence behaviour.
[52] Campbell and Pedersen (2001); Blyth (2002); Campbell (2004).

that led to a break with a statist past and a comprehensive neoliberal reorganisation of the public sector. As I noted in the previous section, the welfare state had been under attack by intellectuals and reformers. As the legitimacy of statist ideas eroded, the very structures that ensured their reproduction and endurance lost their grip on state agents, enabling them to consider and make alternative choices that had previously been closed to them. At the same time, coalitions of political and economic actors were well positioned to promote neoliberal doctrine as competitive or an even better alternative.[53] As historical institutionalists have done before me, I conceive of this historical period as a 'critical' juncture. Consistent with Mahoney, I define a critical juncture as 'choice point[s] when a particular option is adopted among two or more alternatives.'[54] What makes junctures critical is that the choices made during this historical period are of momentous importance insofar as they have long-term and transformative effects on a country's development.[55]

In foreign aid, the reforms that were undertaken to restructure USAID, for example, transformed the agency from an organisation that was set up to promote government-to-government interaction and that had the manpower and budget to implement aid abroad to an agency that holds managerial responsibilities and manages aid delivery through non-state actors.[56] The reform was momentous insofar as its consequences are transformative and lasting. The reorganisation of USAID produced stable preferences for bypass. It also shaped how development takes place in aid recipient countries today. Another legacy of neoliberal reforms was the empowerment of vested interests. As USAID was successively dismantled, non-state actors gained influence and worked towards making bypass endure and remain a stable tactic over time.

By the late 1980s, economic crises in Scandinavia represented opportune political moments for neoliberal doctrine to bring about dramatic changes in the institutional rulebook, especially in the delivery of goods and services. The state was labelled, by some, the private sector's 'poor cousin' or the 'ugly duckling'.[57] Although there was little opposition to the welfare state's continued financing of social services on the

---

[53] Blyth (2002).   [54] Mahoney (2002), p. 6.
[55] Mahoney (2002); Capoccia and Kelemen (2007).   [56] Natsios (2010).
[57] Ehn et al. (2003).

principle of universality, the state created markets by setting up private and corporate welfare programmes.[58] By introducing a voucher system, for example, the Swedish state restructured goods and service provision around market-type mechanisms, requiring, for example, parents of children to make individual choices among privately run schools and kindergartens, or choose among corporate health providers.[59] This kind of delivery modus is neoliberal in character insofar as it organises delivery around the principles of competitive contracting and individual choice.[60] To some scholars this institutional rupture, among others, signifies that Sweden had arrived 'at the end of the Third Road'.[61] Some reacted to this rupture with concerns that the neoliberal turn in goods and service provision might lead to greater levels of inequality.[62] The *Economist*, on the other hand, likened these public sector transformations to encapsulating the 'next supermodel', and devoted an entire 2013 issue on discussing the advantages of curbing government spending, rationalising government, and allowing private firms to run a large share of publicly funded goods and services.[63] Milton Friedman, as one issue contributor put it, 'would be more at home in Stockholm than in Washington D.C., when it comes down to individual choice'.[64]

Yet for all the talk about neoliberal dominance, not all political economies have embarked on large-scale restructuring of their public sectors. Instead, as the authors of *Varieties of Capitalism* and *Public Management Reform: A Comparative Analysis*, among others, show, we continue to see a variety of states, which have staked out their own national responses to globalisation pressures.[65] In Germany or France, for example, the state continues to assume an important role in industrial development or innovation. In public sector governance, we observe that, contrary to those who have argued that all states, as a result of globalisation, are being hollowed out, weakened, or 'privatized',[66] many political economies continue to provide goods and services by way of extensive bureaucratic structures or non-competitive, institutionalised

---

[58] Micheletti (2000); Molander et al. (2002).   [59] *Economist* (2013).
[60] Esping-Andersen (1999); Blomquist (2004); see also Micheletti (2000); Molander et al. (2002).
[61] Pontusson (1992); Gould (1993).   [62] Olson (1996), p. 9.
[63] *Economist* (2013).   [64] *Economist* (2013), p. 3.
[65] Soskice and Hall (2011); Pollitt and Boukhaert (2011).
[66] Peters (2012); Hermann (2014); Baccaro and Howell (2017).

means. The corresponding institutional rulebooks correspond with more statist or neo-corporatist conceptions about the role of the state in public sector governance that were locked in many decades earlier and that to this day remain largely intact, thus shaping state responses to globalisation.

Although ample research has shown that neoliberal doctrine has significantly altered the character of domestic goods and service provision in countries that undertook large-scale reforms,[67] what remains less understood is whether neoliberal doctrine encroaches on foreign policy; or, whether it influences donor–recipient interactions in foreign aid. Simultaneously, we want to know whether or how state structures that are built around traditional public sector principles shape foreign aid; and whether and how the two types of political economy produce systematically different delivery patterns.

It is the central objective of this book to establish a causal link between a donor country's political economy and foreign aid. In doing so, I deviate from the view that foreign policy decision-making follows a different logic than decision-making on domestic issues, as, for example, proponents of the 'two-presidencies' thesis in American Politics have suggested.[68] Although it would be unreasonable to insist that decisions on foreign policy issues come about in the exact same way as decisions about domestic policy issues, I stress the fact that donor aid organisations are at heart national organisations, and, as such, are embedded in state bureaucratic structures and practices that pervade both domestic and foreign policy areas. Whether donors bypass or engage with recipient countries under similar international economic and recipient country conditions is a function of how their institutions are set up and where donors come down on the ideological question of more states or markets in public sector governance.

Consider the following remark from a former high-ranking Swedish government official that was expressed during an author interview,

Swedish aid policy today stresses results-based management, and therefore resembles British aid policy a lot more than it used to in the 1980s or 1990s. Results orientation starts under the Social Democrats in the wake of the real estate crisis in the 1990s when the government begins to liberalize the economy to enhance the efficiency of the welfare state. The budget is tight

---

[67] Hood (1991); Osborne and Gaebler (1992); Christensen and Lagreid (2002).
[68] Wildavsky (1966); O'Sullivan (1991); Peterson (1994).

and there is pressure on the government to justify the aid expense. But results orientation is by no means unique to foreign aid. When you look at other policy areas such as the social transfer system, education, and child care you see similar practices. Today we have an open market in all areas of public goods in Sweden, and the Ministry of Foreign Affairs is developing a so called 'results-based strategy' for foreign aid. They want to make results more visible to the taxpayer. They want results in the short term.[69]

I also diverge from a view that likens donor aid organisations and their structures, including, e.g. the U.S. State Department or USAID, Sida, the German Ministry of Development among others, to those of the World Bank or other international organisations.[70] The implication here would be that they shape world politics in their own right, as independent actors, and detached from domestic politics. As the previous quote illustrates, aid organisations need to be understood in a national context: although their mandate requires them to interact directly with foreign governments, aid organisations are, as I indicated earlier, embedded in a much larger context of national structures that share similar institutional rulebooks. They are at heart national organisations and are thus shaped by domestic politics.

Of course, the claim that domestic politics matters for foreign aid is not novel. As I show in Chapter 1, there is a considerable empirical literature that links variation in foreign aid to domestic political factors. However, much of the work in this tradition suggests that positions on foreign aid are linked to beliefs and values about redistribution that indicate support or opposition to foreign aid. This is at odds with how I theorise the role of ideology. In my theoretical framework, beliefs influence foreign aid delivery by shaping the character of bureaucratic structures and practices, the formal rules of the game that organise the environment in which aid officials operate. Beliefs in the appropriate role of states or markets in public sector governance are consequential for aid politics because they produce institutional rulebooks, or legacies, that limit contingency or choice and that guide the behaviour of aid officials into the future.

[69] Author interview with former senior government official from the Ministry of Foreign Affairs, 17 June 2013, Stockholm, Sweden. See Bjerninger (2013) for an excellent exposition of how Swedish aid has changed over time.

[70] This challenges existing assumptions that define donor aid agencies as international organisations that all share a similar bureaucratic set up, as suggested by Honig (2018).

My argument also deviates from the view that aid officials can interact with recipient governments strategically, without constraints; or, that they can take up any new aid delivery tactic that the market of ideas might view as being better than existing practices. Consider a Swedish aid official during an author interview: 'Here in Sweden, but elsewhere too, the aid community thinks a lot about how to make things better. There are many new ideas that we discuss and debate internally. At the end of the day, though, many of these ideas, however good we might consider them to be, never quite make it. They do not fit into our practices and how we are expected to deliver aid.'[71] Although it would be unhelpful to suggest that beliefs per se never matter for aid decision-making, my research emphasises that, first and foremost, aid officials feel constrained by organisational rulebooks. Beliefs per se do not steer donor decision-making in a robust way. Rather, it is the formal rules and practices that create incentives for action, prescribe how aid officials deal with aid delivery risks in aid receiving countries, and account for observed heterogeneity in aid delivery across donor governments – the central puzzle of this book.

Finally, my argument about the ideological origins of aid delivery tactics can integrate what others might consider an alternative explanation for the observed variation in aid delivery across donor countries. It could be, as Milner and Tingley might argue,[72] that the United Kingdom and the United States do more bypass aid because the non-state actors through which the aid is channelled have more influence in foreign aid decision-making than their counterparts in more traditional public sector economies. In other words, what drives bypass propensity is interest group influence and not institutional rules and practices. In lieu of a competing explanation, however, I conceive of greater levels of interest-group influence as broadly originating in neoliberalism and its corresponding policy choices. As I will show in more detail in Chapter 3, neoliberal restructuring did not only incentivise aid officials to work more closely with non-state actors; the process also dismantled the aid bureaucracy in ways that made aid officials more dependent on outside implementers. As I already noted earlier in the chapter, USAID, at the time of its creation, had plenty of capacity to implement aid projects abroad. Then, only few of the actors existed that populate

---

[71] Author interview with a senior Swedish aid official, June, 2015.
[72] Milner and Tingley (2015).

today's development scene in Washington.[73] Yet, as successive US governments dismantled the US aid bureaucracy, new actors positioned themselves inside of the beltway and have gradually worked to expand their influence. Today, US NGOs or private contractors wield influence in Washington. Firms like Chemonics and DAI are called 'beltway bandits' for good reason insofar as their political activities fully reflect their entrenched and ongoing pecuniary interests: they seek to acquire more and larger contracts or grants.[74] They pursue this interest by donating to political campaigns. They rotate personnel into and out of USAID. Thus, interest groups reinforce the effect of neoliberal institutional rules and practices on aid delivery by pulling aid officials towards more bypass and closing off alternative development trajectories. Through their politics, interest groups make it even less likely that the United States will return to more statist practices of aid delivery.

2.4 Why Donors Respond Differently to Risk

My theory starts by identifying key actors and their institutional environments. In my argument, senior officials in aid organisations are the central actors who make decisions about how to promote international development; and, more specifically, who decide about how to deliver aid in developing countries. My theory posits that aid officials seek to contribute to the goals of the aid organisation and want to help promote prosperity in poor countries. While this may not be their only objective, my argument hinges on the assertion that aid officials consider development abroad a central objective. In *Targeted Development*, Sarah Bermeo shows that over time international development has even become a self-interest to all industrialised states insofar as development abroad keeps problems associated with underdevelopment at bay, including illegal immigration, political instability, spread of diseases, to name only some of the challenges that are not confined within national borders.

I further argue that the world of aid officials is characterised by risk and rational expectations. As my field interviews across several donor countries revealed, aid officials were concerned about risks in the

[73] Roberts (2014).   [74] Berrios (2000).

process of aid implementation. First and foremost, they worried about the risk of aid capture through recipient authorities. To them, decisions about how to deliver aid abroad were made to minimise risks and make aid efforts successful. As analytical and empirical work on aid implementation shows, aid transfers between donor and recipient governments are at great risk of aid capture through agency problems.[75] I define aid capture broadly as resulting from the mismanagement of aid in the recipient country, either by intentional diversion through corrupt authorities or the waste of aid due to weak institutions and/or lack of absorptive capacity.[76]

Thus, the quality of recipient governance becomes a key factor in aid decision-making. To minimise risks, aid officials screen and evaluate potential aid delivery channels for risk and efficiency. To them, a key dimension in the screening process are the risks associated with aid delivery in the recipient country. To proxy this risk they resort to governance indicators. Good governance implies to donors that the recipient government and its institutions do well on things that matter for aid implementation, including the rule of law, corruption control, government effectiveness, and regulatory quality. They matter insofar as indigenous institutions are in place that can constrain recipient governments to divert foreign aid for private gain and to facilitate project delivery to intended beneficiaries. Bad governance, on the other hand, implies that recipient governments cannot or may not want to ensure that foreign aid gets delivered as intended. In poorly governed countries, institutions fail to provide minimal levels of corruption control, rule of law, government effectiveness, and regulatory quality. Alternatively, state institutions may simply lack the capacity to absorb aid flows. When making decisions about aid delivery, aid officials seek out information about risks associated with aid implementation and turn to measures that proxy the quality of governance in aid-receiving countries.

When recipient corruption is high and state institutions are weak, donor officials face a real conundrum. How to respond in a situation

---

[75] Svensson (2000); Brautigam and Knack (2004); Reinikka and Svensson (2004); Gibson et al. (2005); Djankov et al. (2008).

[76] See Dietrich (2013, 2016). This definition differs from the following authors, who define aid capture solely as acts of corruption. Svensson (2000); Jablonski (2014); Winters (2014).

where the risk of aid capture by recipient governments is high? To understand how aid officials approach this question, I turn to micro-institutional constraints. Drawing on decades' worth of research on institutions, I argue that aid officials across aid organisations are motivated to follow institutional rules that channel their behaviour towards organisational goals. Among other things, these institutional rules prescribe how aid officials minimise risk in foreign aid delivery. By following the rules, aid officials can optimise professional gains, such as career promotions or bigger budgets. Formal rules ensure that aid officials of the same organisation face the same incentives, pursue the same interests, and thus respond to aid delivery challenges in similar ways.[77]

Yet, a focus on institutional constraints only tells part of the story. Institutional constraints create stable patterns of behaviour and exert a powerful influence on donor–recipient relations. They do not, however, answer the questions of 'why bypass?' or 'why engage', or why, for that matter, aid officials from different donor countries opt for different aid delivery tactics. I need to understand why aid officials constitute themselves around a particular aid delivery tactic, while rejecting the other.[78]

To get at the origin of aid delivery tactics, my analytical framework accounts for marked differences in how donor aid organisations are organised. Or, as Lieberman puts it, I need to account for the 'substantive course of politics', including the goals, desires, and beliefs that bring about the institutions in the first place.[79] Beliefs are important insofar as they inspired the creation of institutions many decades ago and, once locked in, give them a lasting orientation or ideological character. Today, aid organisations vary markedly in character. Their rulebooks have ideological origins insofar as they promote different approaches to risk and governance.

In this book, I make a broad distinction between two types of approaches. I distinguish between national aid organisations that are neoliberal in character and aid organisations that follow a traditional public sector logic. As I have argued previously, neoliberal doctrine promotes a form of governance that internalises a market-based rationality. It seeks to reorganise public sectors to mimic private sector

---

[77] Within any organisation, it may occur that a minority do not conform to institutional incentives, as found, for example, in Auteresse (2014).
[78] Fearon and Wendt (2002).   [79] Lieberman (2002), p. 697.

governance, emphasising incentives, competition, and performance. Its rules and practices, once imposed, thus promote a particular approach to governing. In the context of aid, the neoliberal rulebook authorises, enables, and justifies bypass as an aid delivery tactic under conditions of poor recipient governance, while precluding government-to-government aid.

How are neoliberal rulebooks consequential for purposeful aid officials? For example, neoliberal organisational rules prescribe that aid officials, in their role as managers of public resources, select the foreign aid delivery channel based on the logic of competitive contracts and thus target actors who are relatively more efficient and effective at delivering foreign aid. To determine this, officials rely on benchmarking practices insofar as they compare the government as a delivery channel to its non-state competition, using criteria of timeliness and cost-effectiveness, among others. They ask: How is the recipient country's delivery effort doing in comparison with that of non-state aid actors such as international organisations, non-profit organisations, public–private partnerships, and for-profit actors? How efficiently is the money translated into a given set of tangible, pre-specified results? A quick indicator for this comparison could be how long it takes the recipient government to develop a plan for project implementation, compared to the non-state development actor.

In poorly governed countries, where fiduciary concerns over government-to-government aid delivery are paramount, neoliberal norms advocate outsourcing of aid to non-state actors and the bypass of the recipient country public sector. Through bypass, donor governments can effectively minimise fiduciary risks ex ante. As a senior official from the U.S. State Department suggests,

Governance is a big issue for us. We always care about it. When we learn of severe corruption in government we turn to our NGOs to deliver our assistance. Or, alternatively, we work with multilateral organizations like the UN Office for Drugs and Crimes [in Central Asia] by funding individual activities because they are well placed and they can deliver for us. We need to make sure that people get our help. If we continued working with the government we would not get anywhere.[80]

---

[80] Author interview with senior US State Department official, 9 June 2009, Washington, DC.

The impetus for bypassing under conditions of poor governance is reinforced by managerial practices that enable aid organisations to monitor and control the delivery of aid ex post. It is difficult to hold governments accountable, especially when their quality of governance is low. When contracting out to an international organisation, an NGO, or a private firm, the donor agency typically retains close contact with the implementer or its representative on the ground and is thus in a relatively better position to control, incentivise, and punish the provider, should they underperform. As a USAID official suggested during an author interview,

When USAID's assistance is delivered through an NGO or a private firm, who are based in the US or who have a more direct connection with us. That way, we are in a better position to catch them and hold them accountable when we are not happy with the work they do. Because USAID is not managing projects directly, they want to have the ability to go after those who do and get their money back if something is wrong; or to discipline them when they do not behave properly.[81]

What is more, managerial practices require aid officials to monitor performance and results of any agent frequently, and on the basis of yearly, and thus relatively short, time horizons. These practices make it more likely that aid officials select non-state bypass channels, especially under conditions of poor recipient governance.

More broadly, aid organisations of neoliberal character prioritise aid tactics that allow them to document accountability or 'being seen as doing the right thing' by a critical domestic audience. After all, reverberations of the welfare state crisis had led to a decline in public support for foreign aid across donors countries. If only the aid bureaucracy created markets and managed for results, as champions of neoliberal reforms suggested, the legitimacy of the aid organisation and the state would be strengthened. To illustrate how these accountability concerns translate into foreign aid programming it is worth briefly turning our attention to the US government's multi-billion dollar President's Emergency Program for Aids Relief (PEPFAR). As an inter-agency initiative, PEPFAR was created in 2003 by President George W. Bush to help countries in Africa and the Caribbean that faced an HIV/AIDS epidemic. With more countries added over the years,

---

[81] Author interviews with former senior US government official, 25 September 2013, Paris, France.

PEPFAR programmes have, according to US government reports, helped 13 million HIV-infected people with antiretroviral therapy. It also prevented around 2 million perinatal HIV infections, among other achievements.[82] Since its creation, PEPFAR has been considered a 'golden goose' of US foreign aid. Unlike other foreign aid programmes in the United States, PEPFAR has not only received strong bi-partisan support in Congress but it has also been continuously funded above the levels requested by government.[83] In principal–agent terms, this suggests that the principal, in other words Congress, felt that PEPFAR was sufficiently robust in terms of accountability.

A closer look at the implementation of the programme suggests just that: In its implementation, PEPFAR has traditionally relied on non-state actors such as the Global Fund to Fight AIDS, Tuberculosis, and Malaria, US-based or international NGOs, public–private partnerships, and private contractors. These non-state actors are expected to get treatments to the people on the ground and are held to account for that by the US government. Because PEPFAR is targeted at saving individual lives, measures that document impact are easy to come by, including, for example, mortality or infection rates.[84] Over the years, however, the vertical scale-up of PEPFAR did little to strengthen local health systems. According to a recent study of the effects of PEPFAR in Uganda, the programme's single focus on treatment and prevention of HIV/AIDS even led to a decline in service for non-HIV care insofar as, for example, local doctors preferred to work for well-funded PEPFAR clinics.[85] This suggests that aid organisations of neoliberal character put emphasis on achieving pre-specified targets or output and focus on organisational performance.

Today, Anglo-Saxon and Scandinavian donors fall under the neoliberal conception of public sector governance. These political economies have, at different points in time, undertaken reform processes that have dramatically reorganised their public sectors, including aid organisations, by imposing rulebooks that promote a neoliberal approach to governance. These reforms have reorganised goods and service delivery away from direct provision or institutional-ised delivery through non-state actors, to one that facilitates delivery

---

[82] Eisinger et al. (2019).
[83] Author interview with senior US government official, 9 October, 2013, Washington, DC.
[84] Natsios (2010), p. 28.   [85] Luboga et al. (2016).

through competitive contracting in an open market. Further, the introduction of managerial practices has led to the introduction of performance frameworks, significantly shortened the time horizons by which aid officials assess the success of aid, and re-oriented evaluation to focus on achieving results in the short run. The new rules and practices thus entrench neoliberal beliefs by imposing a playbook that limits the delivery choices that are considered rational. Even today, many years after neoliberal reforms reorganised aid organisations, the behaviour of aid officials is influenced by institutional legacies, rather than what aid officials may conceive as optimal delivery choices. In Chapter 3, I map out these institutional changes and link them to aid delivery patterns for select cases, including the United States, the United Kingdom, and Sweden.

At the same time, donor regimes whose state structures are underwritten by institutional rulebooks that embrace a traditional public sector logic, and reaffirm the state as the central actor in dealing with risks in aid delivery, will follow a different course of action when the quality of governance is low in recipient countries. To mitigate risks of aid capture, aid officials will work to increase the degree of oversight and control but they will do so in the context of government-to-government relations. That is, they will bypass less and work with the public sector more but do so in a more 'hands on' fashion. This tactic involves more frequent communication and staff exchanges to address capacity problems, as well as more frequent auditing.

As a senior French AFD official suggests,

If we discover some corruption in our own projects we have an armed response for that. The first could be to discuss our due diligence procedures and then we have some strong decision from the government in changing the structure, making more audits, strengthening the project audit. [...] If we discover a huge scandal in the education sector for example then, if you are working as we are working, which means through the local administrations, you will be fully aware that the local administrations are very weak. If they are weak, we are going to work very cautiously by increasing technical assistance to strengthen their institutions, to strengthen their auditing system and so on. We do not avoid the government.[86]

---

[86] Author interview with senior official at the Agence Française de Développement (AFD), Paris, 10 July 2013.

Advocates of such 'hands-on' delivery tactics in poorly governed countries repeatedly stressed the importance of continued state engagement. This pro-state orientation also indicates that donor governments attach significance to building up the capacity of the recipient government so that eventually government authorities can assume more responsibility and ownership. A senior Japanese government official expressed this pro-state orientation in foreign aid during an author interview, while drawing interesting parallels to domestic experience,

The philosophy of Japanese aid is, in part, based on our own development after the World War II where we had a very strong state leadership and state capacity. In essence, Japan's growth was led by the state. We were not a socialist country but it was civil servants who planned development and led the country and this was successful to a certain extent. And, we believe that in developing countries there should be a capacity on the state-side to be able to plan ahead and manage resources and allocate them adequately and properly. We place a lot of emphasis on working with the recipient state, working with public servants to realize a collective solution to development, just like we do at home.[87]

The Japanese official then encouraged me to study one particular aid project in Cambodia that, in his opinion, serves well to illustrate Japan's governance orientation, which emphasises the importance of long-term institution-building. In this particular aid project, the aid official described aid efforts to build the capacity of the Phnom Penh Water supply authority (PPWS). There, Japan and France disbursed bilateral aid in the form of capital, projects, and technical assistance targeting public servants and local experts with the objective of transferring knowledge and expertise to develop sustainable water supply systems. They also provided an additional oversight function to ensure that the aid was effectively implemented. According to the Asian Development Bank, the PPWSA is rightfully considered a foreign aid success story, as the authority was able to increase water supply coverage in Phnom Penh from 25 per cent in 1993 to 90 per cent in 2006.[88] This example emphasises long-term capacity building efforts, and contrasts with the increasing tendency to bypass the state to deliver aid.

---

[87] Author interview with senior Japanese official, 12 August 2013, Paris.
[88] Asian Development Bank (2009).

This example illustrates that donors resort to different tactics to mitigate the risk of aid capture in recipient countries, and that, consistent with my argument, the choice of delivery mechanism is conditional on the institutional rulebook or the character of the aid organisation. While aid officials in the United States, the United Kingdom, and Sweden are incentivised to utilise bypass tactics in poorly governed countries to maximise performance and results in aid delivery, and to do so in the short run, Germany, France, and Japan, exhibit different tendencies. Their action is incentivised by rules that reflect the importance of continued state engagement and working with local institutions to ensure sustainable development in the long run.

My argument further predicts that aid officials, regardless of political economy type, converge towards government-to-government delivery in better governed countries. In these contexts, risks of aid delivery are low. And even aid officials from organisations of neoliberal character are going to embrace better governed recipient government for two reasons: First, while well-governed governments may not be as efficient as non-state actors, they do represent a credible alternative insofar as authorities hold important knowledge of needs, demands, and local customs that can contribute to more effective aid implementation. Second, foreign aid, as a government-to-government affair, allows aid officials to form and strengthen bilateral partnerships with recipient countries. As long as the risk of aid capture is sufficiently low, I would expect aid officials to prefer the government-to-government channel. After all, state-to-state interactions are a direct way to promote donor interests and influence world politics. The logic of selectivity in aid delivery is best illustrated by examining the mandate and institutional set up of the Millennium Challenge Corporation (MCC), an important US foreign aid agency created in 2003 by George W. Bush.[89] As an institution, the MCC is set up to deliver aid government-to-government but its underlying principle of aid disbursement is to pick winners, or countries that are well-governed and trustworthy and have a good track record in implementing foreign aid.[90] So, even in neoliberal aid organisations, aid officials

---

[89] For thoughtful discussions of the MCA in the context of a larger foreign policy strategy, see Girod et al. (2009).
[90] Mawdsley (2007), p. 494.

have a preference for government-to-government aid, but only when risks are considered manageable.

Understanding how aid systems differ in their institutional environment across donors enables me to hypothesise about the effects that national structures have on world politics. My argument leads to one general expectation: the nature of interactions between donor and recipient countries is predicated on the organisation of donor political economies. When donor officials work in aid organisations whose bureaucratic structures and rules are of neoliberal character, they will react to the risk of aid capture in aid-receiving countries with a strategy of bypass. The institutional rules of the game limit aid officials' discretion and thus constrain aid officials in their tactics. When donor officials work in bureaucratic structures and rules are built on more statist conceptions of governance, they have rules and practices in place that make government-to-government donor–recipient interactions relatively more likely. They will respond to risk of aid capture in poor governance environments with more government engagement but will reduce the risk by being more hands-on in the aid delivery process.

If we now wanted to make comparisons across different types of donor governments, we expect political economies to produce different aid delivery tactics in similar environments. I expect the proportion of bypass to be highest when aid officials work for a neoliberal aid organisation and the recipient country's quality of governance is low. A traditional public sector donor, facing similarly poor governance conditions, is expected to bypass less; and I expect this difference to be statistically significant. I do not expect donor governments to exhibit statistically different delivery tactics when the quality of governance is high; although I do expect neoliberal aid organizations to exhibit bypass at higher levels, all else equal.

Importantly, my argument does not suggest that aid officials of neoliberal aid organisations never promote government-to-government aid under poor recipient conditions. Nor am I saying that Germany or France never bypasses recipient governments when the quality of governance is low. Donors of all stripes combine different aid delivery tactics. Yet, my argument makes predictions about where donor governments stand on the fundamental question of aid provision, whether to bypass or engage with recipient governments. They do more or less of one or the other, depending on their national structures.

In Chapter 3, I elucidate the link between national structures and aid delivery across five donor countries. I show that these structures shape aid officials' behaviour and determine what particular course of action aid officials are more likely to take; whether they bypass or engage with the recipient government under conditions of poor governance. In Chapter 4, I test my argument at the country level. In Chapter 5, I test the same hypothesis at the level of the individual donor official across six donor governments, the United States, the United Kingdom, Sweden, France, and Germany.

More broadly, my argument suggests that governance beliefs also shape what donors seek to maximise with their aid. As I have said earlier, neoliberal doctrine promotes an institutional order that reflects the culture of private firms.[91] As such, it breaks with the traditional public sector order by replacing authoritative coordination and control with dispersed competition, and emphasising individual over collective action and accountability. This order not only has organisational implications, as I argued previously. It also has implications for organisational goals and the objectives that aid officials pursue and prioritise in foreign aid.

Because, as scholars of public administration have argued, neoliberal reforms reorganise public sectors to mimic private sector governance by emphasising incentives, competition, and performance, the basis of legitimation of a neoliberal institution is in large part derived from its output, its ability to deliver on the results that it had promised, in the most efficient way possible. Any regime that disappoints in terms of results delivery or performance becomes vulnerable to attacks on its legitimacy.[92] The neoliberal value for money calculus implies, for example, that aid organisations assess the cost and quality trade-off to determine the viability of a potential aid project in terms of its pre-specified objectives. For example, if aid officials can buy the installation of water taps cheaper through one particular company compared to others, or the recipient government, for the same 10 per cent promised increase in people having access to clean water, they are incentivised do it. Their rulebooks are set up to reach results that were specified in the delivery contract, while saving valuable taxpayer dollars, whenever possible. Time and again, my interviewees from

---

[91] Foucault (2004); Hibou (2015).
[92] Scharpf (1999), p. 17; Van de Walle et al. (2008).

neoliberal aid organisations suggested that this particular approach to aid delivery was particularly useful for persuading aid critics or donor publics that foreign aid can be successful.

At the same time, a major counter-argument to this approach is 'what happens when this project comes to an end?' 'What system is left behind?' These latter questions arose consistently in interviews with aid officials in more traditional public sector aid organisations who took a more long-term view on foreign aid, emphasising the importance of strengthening the recipient state. While I do not wish to make normative claims about which approach is better suited to promote prosperity in developing countries, one important contribution of this book is to show that the core mission or mandate of the aid organisation, or what aid officials perceive as successful aid, is not objectively defined. It is endogenous to the organisation of the donor political economy.

One empirical implication of this argument is that, for example, donor officials of different political economies have different aid priorities. We would expect aid officials who follow neoliberal rulebooks to prioritise accountability-enhancing projects that focus on the provision of water taps and getting water directly to the people. More generally, they will prioritise short-term basic needs delivery over long-run capacity building efforts. At the same time, aid officials that are incentivised by traditional public sector rulebooks prioritise continued state engagement and support of the government's capacity to provide clean water access by training water supply engineers or statisticians. In Chapter 5, I test these empirical implications of the argument at the level of the aid official across donor countries.

2.5 Why Aid Delivery Must Be Understood in a Historical Context

Before I proceed to test the book's central argument in subsequent chapters, I want to return to my assertion that national aid organisations have ideological origins. This is an important part of the argument for several reasons. First, the claim that preferences for bypass and engage can be found in the character of the institution and its formal rulebook pushes back against research suggesting that heterogeneity in aid delivery across donors reflects differences in opinion about what the more appropriate aid delivery channel under conditions of poor governance should be, what the right objectives of aid should be, and how one best measures aid success. Instead, preferences for bypass and engage, and differences therein, follow rational, materialist behaviour of aid officials who are constrained to follow a particular aid tactic.

Second, my argument suggests that, today, aid officials are tied to rules and practices that were locked in many decades before and have shaped the organisation and character of the countries' aid organisations to this day. Drawing on insights from research on state formation and comparative public administration, I suggest that institutions and their rulebooks are endogenous to predominant beliefs in public sector governance that have, at different times in different countries, been mobilised to solve important societal challenges.[93] After all, institutions are human creations that reflect a particular way of thinking about societal problems and how they can best be addressed and solved.[94]

Historically, these approaches promoted a particular blend of roles between states and markets in public sector governance.[95] While nineteenth-century industrialisation processes were characterised by a dominant market and a small government sector, the interwar years saw the state gradually taking on a more prominent role. At the time, a more state-centric view of governance was widely perceived as the best solution to achieve optimal social outcomes. This view was based on the premise that governments should actively interfere in the economy because a free market was perceived as inherently unstable and not able to address social challenges. Over the course of the twentieth century, neoliberal doctrine rose to replace beliefs in statist governance and, where systematically adopted, reconfigured political economies, finding its bureaucratic manifestation in state-wide rationalisation processes. Once locked in, neoliberal rules and practices created path dependency. In the context of foreign aid, past decisions to change the aid organisation's character from traditional public sector to neoliberal make it difficult and costly to change aid delivery tactics from bypass to engagement today, even when bypass may be considered dysfunctional. This ideological origin of the institution, coupled with

[93] For example, Dobbin (1994).   [94] North (1990).   [95] Evans (1995).

the constraining effect of institutional rules and practices, makes it difficult and costly to change aid priorities away from results-orientation and towards the strengthening of the recipient government.

More broadly, whether governance beliefs become consequential for the direction of aid delivery is not because they are compelling at the moment an aid official makes decisions about aid delivery. They are consequential because, at different times in different donor countries, opportune political circumstances favoured the adoption of governance beliefs that assigned different roles to states and markets in public sector governance.[96] As ample research on critical junctures has demonstrated, mechanisms of institutional reproduction can lose their grip on political actors during extraordinary historical moments.[97] During these moments, beliefs that had formerly prevailed are no longer able to resolve the problems they were set up to address. However, as Lieberman claims new beliefs can only replace old doctrine and its institutional rulebook when they find "persuasive expression among actors whose institutional position gives them both the motive and the opportunity to promote institutional change."[98] Only then can new beliefs promote institutional and policy change.

In my theory, ideological and institutional elements thus overlap and interact, and, together, explain donor–recipient interactions.[99] Understanding the ways in which ideology and institutions interact also explains change in state or aid institutions. In the United States, as the historical overview at the beginning of this chapter illuminates, the critical juncture of the 1970s opened the door for neoliberal reformers to push institutional change. In the United Kingdom, institutional change was similarly possible because, during the critical juncture of the 1970s, statist beliefs had lost their appeal and key political actors in the right institutional positions embraced neoliberalism. In his review of the UK experience, public administration scholar Rhodes points to three important factors that jointly helped bring about large-scale institutional change,

---

[96] Lieberman (2002). [97] Thelen (2003); Capoccia (2015).
[98] Blyth (2002); Lieberman (2002), p. 709.
[99] Katznelson (1997), p. 99 reminds us not to try to determine whether ideas or institutions matter more or less but rather how the variables are joined together in specific historical circumstances.

First, Margaret Thatcher pushed through reform of the civil service. The phrase political will is commonly used to explain the government's determination. Strong, directive and above all persistent, executive leadership is longer but more accurate. Second, there are few constitutional constraints on that leadership, especially when the government has a majority in Parliament. Central administrative reform in Britain does not require a statute, only the exercise of Crown Prerogative, or executive powers. Finally, the government evolved a clear ideological strategy to justify and sell its various reform packages. It attacked big government and waste, used markets to create more individual choice and campaigned for the consumer.[100]

What makes this particular juncture critical is that the outcomes generated in this particular historical moment persist over time and shape, among other things, how the United Kingdom delivers foreign aid abroad, what motives it pursues in international development, and how it measures aid success. I will elucidate the link between aid organisational changes and aid delivery tactics in the subsequent chapter.

In Sweden, international economic shocks rippled through the economy in the 1970s and 1980s and laid bare the difficulties of a growing welfare state to deal with dramatic changes in the international economic environment. Around 1990, the burst of a housing bubble plunged the country into a severe financial crisis. To many, the crisis suggested that existing governance models and structures had failed to provide adequate solutions to secure Sweden's economic security. In response, the state decided to break with the past and embrace neoliberal doctrine. The state cut spending and replaced existing structures with a new set of streamlined institutions that were set up to improve the country's competitiveness.[101] Among the many wide-reaching efforts to put budgets back into balance, Sweden reorganised its public sector around incentives, competition, and performance.[102]

To be able to prevail in a globalised world, neoliberal reformers made efforts to make the state more business-like and create and maintain open markets for goods and service delivery. This vision

---

[100] Rhodes (1997), p. 44.
[101] Iversen et al. (2000); Rothstein (1998); Ryner (2004).
[102] OECD (1996), p. 245.

had numerous organisational implications. As in the United States and the United Kingdom, the Swedish government pushed streamlining and rationalisation programmes through the public sector. For example, and as I will show in more detail in Chapter 3 of this book, the government increased individual accountability in corporate fashion by restructuring a traditional public sector model to one that shifts responsibility for staffing and organisational resources from central personnel offices of line departments to line managers.[103] In addition, the Swedish aid system put incentive structures in place to increase performance and productivity. Reforms in the Swedish International Development Agency (Sida) entailed, among other things, the tight setting of parameters within which officials undertook their work, with a view towards optimising individual productivity.[104]

Even more striking than the government's commitment to streamlining the public sector was the voracity with which the political economy was restructured from institutionalised goods and service provision to competitive contracting. In the domestic sphere, the Swedish state allowed private companies to compete with government bodies for goods and service delivery. For some time now, the lion's share of new health clinics and kindergartens in Sweden is being built and run by private companies, requesting citizens to shop around for the best services and take their money with them.[105] In the foreign aid sector, the government made extensive efforts to ensure wider use of competitive contracting as coordinating mechanism for aid delivery. Where there were no markets, the Swedish state created them.

Unlike the United Kingdom, however, Sweden did not discard the welfare model entirely. It did not launch an all-out attack on the state. Much like its Scandinavian neighbours, Sweden continues to be a welfare state. To this day, the Swedish state continues to rank among the most generous in the world in terms of spending, and about 30 per cent of its labour force works in the public sector.[106] In foreign aid, Sweden, alongside other Nordic countries, leads the world in terms of aid effort. As a country, Swedes pride themselves on their generosity towards the poor.

---

[103] OECD (1996), p. 245.   [104] Holmgren and Svensson (2005).
[105] *Economist* (2013).   [106] OECD (2017).

Across time, questions about how to best address societal challenges have thus been answered differently by states. In Germany or France, neoliberal doctrine at best inspired select and punctuated reform, which pales in comparison to the comprehensive restructuring efforts that we observe in Anglo-Saxon or Scandinavian countries.[107] While it is outside of the scope of this book to explain why some countries adopted large-scale reform while other regimes stayed largely intact, I draw on research that has proffered explanations for individual countries, placing them into their historical contexts.

In France, for example, scholars of public administration have traditionally associated the country with a strong state tradition, where the state assumes a range of roles, including sovereign functions as well as industrial and commercial activities.[108] Broadly, the structural features of the French state have to be understood in their historical context insofar as they are shaped by institutional legacies of the different successive regimes since the French revolution. They anchor the state and its component parts. As research of the French administrative system highlights, the French civil service enjoys relatively high levels of autonomy vis-à-vis other institutions,[109] is differentiated around administrative law, and is highly fragmented through its division into corps and ministries.[110] As members of the *grands corps*, French state officials enjoy high social prestige and significant political power, insofar as they feature prominently in any proposals that address institutional reform.[111] This structural set up makes the French state relatively robust to institutional rupture, insofar as political actors who are in key positions to influence reform have been shown to protect their interests and combat reform proposals that upend the very arrangements that protect them. This includes aid organisations that are set up to promote government-to-government aid.

In a similar fashion, the German state exhibits continuity of structure, as scholars have noted, and needs to be understood in a historical context.[112] In Germany, the military and moral defeat in World War II represented a critical juncture. During this time, key political actors

---

[107] Schröter and Wollmann (1997); Jann (2003); Pollitt and Bouckaert (2003); Lynn (2006); Pollitt and Boukhaert (2011).
[108] Bezes and Gilles (2011).   [109] Quermonne and Rouban (1986).
[110] Bezes and Gilles (2011).   [111] Bezes and Gilles (2011).
[112] Benz and Gotz (1996); Bach and Jann (2010); Pollitt and Boukhaert (2011); Kindermann (2005).

formed coalitions to set up an institutional structure that would prevent the resurgence of radical forces. Although post-war institutional change did not entail a radical break with the past insofar as it retained its traditional public sector structure, changes to the constitution strengthened existing federalist elements to guarantee a more effective balance of power.[113] Instead of promoting autonomous policy-making, the constitutional reforms made consensus-based policy-making central by emphasising power-sharing arrangements between the different government branches.[114]

As scholars of German politics have noted, the perhaps unintended side effect of post-war reform, which aimed to prevent the rise of radical forces, was that the new consensus-based German federal system became more rigid than ever before, making future institutional reform even more difficult.[115] Already, as public administration scholars have argued, state structures that are built on a *Rechtsstaat* regime are 'stickier' than public interest regimes insofar as any changes in administrative practices, such as one would require for the imposition of managerial practices, require changes in law.[116] Existing structures also make it more difficult for state officials who have traditionally been trained in administrative law to shift to a 'managerial' or 'performance-oriented' perspective.[117] As a result of these inherited politico-administrative features, among others, the German state has proven to be quite resilient to large-scale reform processes.[118] In foreign aid, the public sector has been structured government-to-government, with state agencies implementing aid in cooperation with aid-receiving governments. Ultimately, as these examples illustrate, institutional change is shaped by how political struggles play out in particular historical and institutional contexts that shape political power as well as the options and channels through which economic beliefs can translate into institutional reform.[119]

By emphasising a variety of ideological origins in my analytical framework, I am able to embed micro-institutions in the broader context of important ideological, macro-level transformations that have shaped world politics over time. These ideological transformations have resulted in different types of rules that make up and shape

---

[113] Benz (2003).   [114] Kuhlmann et al. (2021).   [115] Broschek (2010).
[116] Schröter and Wollmann (1997).   [117] Pollitt and Boukhaert (2011).
[118] Soifer (2012).   [119] Steinmo et al. (1992); Thelen (2003).

the organisation of national or international organisations. As I have suggested, these different rulebooks reflect different conceptions about the role of states and markets that have been advanced to solve societal challenges at different times, across countries. These beliefs also carry the seed for policy change insofar as ideological changes in institutional environments make for different rulebooks.[120] And, as the ideological character of the institutional environment changes, as per my argument, I expect aid officials' priorities and behaviour to change as well.

2.6 Conclusion

In this chapter, I have presented the theoretical framework of this book. My principal claim states that national structures shape donor–recipient interactions. While neoliberal governance structures authorise, enable, and justify bypass under conditions of poor governance, they preclude government-to-government delivery. At the same time, traditional public sector models incentivise aid delivery through the government-to-government channel under similar conditions. My argument also posits that donor priorities in foreign aid are endogenous to the organisation of the donor political economy. Whether donors prioritise short-term relief or capacity-building in the recipient country depends on whether organisational objectives seek to maximise results in the short run or more government ownership over the process.

An important insight of my argument is that institutional constraints do the heavy lifting in explaining the link between national structures and aid delivery. For neoliberal donors, this means that economic management principles drive donor–recipient interactions. For traditional public sector donors, organisational characteristics and their constraining effects ensure that aid officials stick to government-to-government interaction, even if they considered bypass a better strategy.

Before I go on to test the empirical usefulness of this theoretical framework in Chapters 4–6, I want to first examine the causal mechanism more closely in Chapter 3. In particular, I will establish empirically, for a select number of donors, including the United States, the

---

[120] Schumpeter (1950).

United Kingdom, Sweden, Germany, and France, that national aid systems are organised in markedly different ways. I distinguish between donor organisations that have neoliberal attributes (United States, United Kingdom, and Sweden) and ones that are organised around a traditional public sector logic (Germany and France). Most importantly, the next chapter will elucidate how these institutional differences lead to different behaviour among aid officials of different political economies. Or, why and how institutions of different ideological orientation constrain donor officials differently in aid delivery, my dependent variable.

3 Examining the Causal Mechanism across Donors

The United States, the United Kingdom, Sweden, Germany, and France

3.1 Introduction

Why do countries make different foreign aid delivery choices under similar international economic and recipient country conditions? Why are donors like the United States and the United Kingdom more likely to bypass under conditions of poor recipient governments than peers like Germany or France? The previous chapter provided the theoretical framework that explains marked cross-national variation in foreign aid delivery tactics. It is the principal claim of this book that the nature of interactions between donor and recipient countries is predicated on the organisation of donor political economies. I argue that the origin of bypass or engagement with recipient authorities can be found inside aid organisations, or more specifically in the character of the institution's rules and practices, which incentivise aid officials to deliver aid in particular ways. These rules also determine priorities in aid, what outcomes should be realised, and how one best measures aid success.

One key insight of my theoretical argument is that aid organisations, like state organisations, are, at heart, ideological institutions, or institutions of a particular character, that were set up at critical junctures, at different times in different countries, to serve common goals and norms. They lock in preponderant beliefs about the role of markets and states in public sector governance through rules and practices. As I argued in Chapter 2, neoliberal doctrine, as a global trend, inspired bureaucratic reforms and state rationalisation processes in those countries where neoliberal reformers seized on opportune political moments to turn state agents into economic managers. This insight matters because it suggests that today's approaches in aid delivery are part of an institutional legacy.

Another important insight of my argument is that institutional constraints do the heavy lifting in explaining the link between national structures and aid delivery. It is not that aid officials do not care when they make aid delivery decisions even when evidence stacks up against a particular aid delivery tactic. They measure consequences but they are not able to change the incentive structures inside the institution. For neoliberal donors, this means that economic management principles drive donor–recipient interactions. For traditional public sector donors, organisational characteristics and their constraining effects ensure that aid officials stick to government-to-government aid.

In this chapter, I develop the causal mechanism that links the institutional environment to foreign aid delivery. My analytical focus on aid decision-makers encourages me to study micro-level rules and practices within institutions, and how they vary across donor governments. I want to show how the institutional context affects aid decision-making; and how different rules and practices lead to different donor–recipient interaction.

Because variation in the character of aid organisations is my key independent variable, I need to first establish empirically that, today, bureaucratic structures in which aid officials work are organised in markedly different ways. As per my theoretical argument, I seek to distinguish between donor organisations that have neoliberal attributes and ones that are organised around a traditional public sector logic. As I compare aid systems across donor countries, I focus on institutional differences in the organisation's bureaucratic structures and their administrative practices, which represent the institutional backbone of an organisation. They represent the institutional rulebook that reinforces and reproduces the logic on which the institution is built.

To keep the comparisons of aid structures manageable, I select five donor countries as my cases, the United States, the United Kingdom, Sweden, Germany, and France. I focus on these five donor countries because they offer variation in micro-structures; four of them are major donors in terms of absolute contributions. Sweden is a leading donor in terms of foreign aid effort and has, from the early 1990s, alongside other Scandinavian countries, significantly restructured its public sector in a neoliberal image. Although the foreign aid systems across these donors involve more than one organisation, I focus on the key ministries and organisations in charge of foreign aid.

As an evidence base, I draw on multiple sources of data, including reports from state agencies, peer review assessments from the OECD DAC, and other historical sources up to 2015. In addition, I leverage insights from originally collected survey data with aid officials across the five donor cases from 2013–2015, the data collection strategy for which I describe in detail in Chapter 5. Finally, I benefit from insights generated by scholars of public administration who have extensively analysed variation in bureaucratic structures. From them we know, for example, that Anglophone countries, including the United States, United Kingdom, Australia, and New Zealand, are leaders in implementing the neoliberal reform agenda and have dramatically restructured the provision of goods and service delivery across domestic policy sectors. I also build on a rich *Varieties of Capitalism* (*VoC*) literature that explains how and why advanced industrial democracies have organised their economy in different ways. While public administration and *VoC* scholarship focus on policy and outcomes in the domestic sphere, what remains less understood is whether and how neoliberal reforms have encroached on the foreign aid sector. In this book I show that political economy goes a long way in explaining foreign economic policy-making and, in particular, the nature of donor–recipient interactions.

Of course, it is difficult to map the diffusion of neoliberal norms and their organisational prescriptions with precision across countries over time. As comparative public administration experts Christopher Pollitt and Geert Bouckaert have noted, these kinds of data are difficult to gather systematically.[1] To date, there is no database that systematically tracks reform activities across different donors over time. Laws like the Government Performance and Results Act (GPRA) in the United States make reform mandatory and lead to government announcements about what they are going to do. However, as Pollitt and Boukhaert argue, the mere presence of laws does not tell us everything about levels of implementation. What is more, they suggest that governments may be reluctant to share details of how the process of implementation is going; and there may be even greater reluctance to share this information for foreign aid organisations that serve at the intersection of domestic and international interests.

What we can see from the outside, however, is a broad pattern regarding the direction and extent to which neoliberal reforms influence bureaucratic structures and management practices across aid agencies. To document organisational variation across aid systems,

---

[1] Pollitt and Bouckaert (2011).

the devil may not be in the detail, as Pollitt and Bouckaert remind us.[2] I look for rough patterns that capture the extent to which aid bureaucracies, in the form of their structures and practices, have acquired a neoliberal character. In this chapter, I provide diagnostic evidence that the character of the institutional environment, my hypothesised explanation, varies markedly in organisations across donor governments. I show that, today, aid systems in the United States, the United Kingdom, and Sweden are on a neoliberal trajectory, as their aid systems exhibit large and pervasive neoliberal footprints.

Aid structures in France and Germany, on the other hand, despite exhibiting some neoliberal reform efforts, continue to be on a public sector trajectory that reaffirms a more traditional role of the state in public sector governance. This pushes back against research suggesting that institutional environments are similar across donor countries and that aid organisations share the same objectives with aid.[3] By accounting for substantive differences in the direction of constraints and shedding more light on what motivates and drives aid officials' behaviour across donor countries, my research adds an important comparative lens to an already rich body of principal–agent studies that examine how organisational controls constrain agents.[4]

A second crucial task of this chapter is to establish that these institutional differences lead to different behaviour among aid officials of different political economies. That is, I elucidate why and how institutions of different ideological orientation constrain donor officials differently, and how they influence aid officials' decision-making, my dependent variable. I show how an aid organisation of neoliberal character, with its particular rules of the game, as manifested in bureaucratic structures and administrative practices, leads aid officials to prioritise bypass, especially under conditions of poor recipient governments, while precluding greater levels of government-to-government engagement. At the same time, I show how aid organisations that are

---

[2] Pollitt and Bouckaert (2011).

[3] To say that bureaucratic structures and rules influence foreign aid decision-making matters is not new. As I note in Chapter 1, there are recent studies that link foreign aid decisions to institutional environments (Swedlund 2017; Honig 2018). Much of this work, however, assumes that donor aid organisations or aid bureaucracies, like international organisations more broadly, are similar in their organisation, producing expectations that aid officials across aid organisations should converge on similar delivery policy under similar conditions.

[4] Hawkins and Jacoby (2006).

structured according to the traditional public sector logic constrain aid officials to prioritise government-to-government aid delivery, while precluding greater levels of aid that bypass recipient governments, under similar conditions in aid-receiving countries. This suggests that donor preferences for more bypass or engagement have their origin in a variety of institutional forms.

By laying out the mechanics that link the character of aid organisations and aid delivery, I show that, ultimately, it is institutional rulebooks and their ideological origin that influence priorities and authorise, enable, and justify particular delivery tactics and donor–recipient interactions. This part of the analysis draws from archival sources as well as evidence from author interviews from aid officials across countries. From my field visits and conversations with aid officials from the United States, the United Kingdom, Sweden, Germany, and France, I learned that aid officials are driven by the desire to promote their aid organisation's goal of helping bring about development. But what development looks like, what they consider successful aid efforts, and how they go about helping development depend on the organisation's bureaucratic structures and practices, which create incentives, motivate, and prescribe behaviour. In the next section, I present the organisational dimensions across which I will make comparisons among five donor countries.

3.2 Tracing Neoliberal Footprints across Aid Organisations in the United States, the United Kingdom, Sweden, Germany, and France

To study neoliberal footprints across aid systems, I draw on scholarly practices in the study of public administration. In this subfield of political science, neoliberal governance reforms have been studied under the label of new public management (NPM) or deviants of it.[5] As an approach to studying public sector organisations, NPM is rooted in neoliberal doctrine and consists of assumptions and value statements about how public sector organisations can be made more 'businesslike' and efficient by using private sector management tools.[6]

[5] Pollitt (1990); Hood (1991).
[6] As its theoretical base, NPM draws on public choice theory, new institutional economics, principal–agent theory, and managerialism. See, for example, Kaboolian (1998); Batley and Larbi (2004); Diefenbach (2009).

Building on the approach employed by Christopher Pollitt and Geert Bouckhaert in *Public Management Reform: A Comparative Analysis*, I identified bureaucratic structures and administrative practices as broad organisational dimensions across which I can trace neoliberal reforms among aid systems. Under the rubric *Organisational Patterns*, I examined the scale of bureaucratic structures and the principle by which foreign aid delivery was coordinated. *Under Managerial Patterns*, I examined the extent to which processes and behaviour, both within the aid organisation and its relations with aid implementation partners, are governed by managerial practices.

Of course, neoliberal reforms come in different shapes and forms, with governments adopting different reform instruments, or variants thereof, to achieve similar goals. As Pollitt and Bouckaert have argued, these reform variants depend on many factors, including existing organisational features of the state, the administrative context, as well as political and international factors. These factors all contribute to explaining why governments adopt particular reform variants or why reform processes may change, be altered, and, in the end, produce considerable national diversity.[7] For example, political economies of the same neoliberal type, such as the United States or the United Kingdom, can differ in the voracity with which governments have dismantled aid bureaucracies over time, or have imposed managerial systems of governance to manage aid operations. Alternatively, within the same donor country, political change can bring about different ideas and visions for the future that react to the existing order of its political economy. With the arrival of President Obama, for example, as expressed in his 2010 Policy Directive, the government placed more emphasis on government engagement with aid-receiving governments than George W. Bush, and, consequently, de-emphasised processes of downsizing and outsourcing.[8] There was recognition in the administration that a more complex approach to development was needed, one that paid more attention to local solutions that engaged donor and recipient state structures.

For this political idea to become reality, the administration, under the umbrella of the USAID FORWARD initiative, pushed through rule changes that would enable new practices that, in the absence of the rule

---

[7] Pollitt and Bouckaert (2011), pp. 71; 94–95.
[8] Presidential Directive on Global Development (2010).

change, would have not been authorised. Importantly, however, these rule changes were not only marginal but they were accompanied by efforts that doubled-down on results and performance-based planning. As I will discuss in more detail later, such marginal shifts merely indicate movement from the minimalist end of the neoliberal trajectory to a modernising one.[9] It does not signify a paradigmatic transformation of the public sector. In the end, the Obama administration continued the contracting-out policies of the previous administrations, relying extensively on contractors in the delivery of foreign aid.[10] On its face, the occurrence of marginal policy changes within political economy types might make a typology less tidy. The important point is, however, that such changes fall short of the kind of institutional rupture that would signal a change in trajectory. Marginal, system-friendly change that keeps inside the outer bounds of a neoliberal or traditional public sector trajectory indicates that material incentive structures can be adjusted to incorporate different, even conflicting, governance ideas. In what remains of this chapter, I compare organisational patterns across aid systems. I structure the discussion by political economy type and then individual donor country.

3.3 Organisational Patterns and Foreign Aid Delivery in the United States, United Kingdom, and Sweden

As I have argued throughout this book, the primary division among political economies is the blend of roles between the state and the market in public sector governance. As an ideology, neoliberalism is inherently distrustful of the state. Neoliberal governance reforms signify a change of decision-making context from one of routine, institutionalised bureaucratic response to public demands to one of an enterprise where individuals engage in discretionary decision-making based on incentives and performance. As developed in more detail in the preceding chapter, accountability is organised at the level of the individual, around efficiency, effectiveness, and productivity criteria, which makes it possible to monitor the state through the individuals that work within it.

This significantly deviates from more traditional public administration systems where accountability is organised hierarchically around criteria such as legality, fairness, integrity, and procedural

[9] Gingrich (2011).   [10] OECD DAC Peer Review US (2011), p. 55.

correctness.[11] In the context of foreign aid delivery, this implies that parliament or the executive government hold aid organisations accountable for how they manage foreign aid, how they use public funds abroad. Correspondingly, aid organisations hold their providers accountable for what is in the sphere of their responsibility. Actual development outcomes or impact are not in focus insofar as they depend on a number of different factors.

Before I discuss how neoliberal doctrine has motivated the restructuring of aid systems across the United States, the United Kingdom, and Sweden at different points in time, I want to present a broad overview. As a broad generalisation, I find that across all three country cases, neoliberal reforms have imposed competitive contracting as the central coordinating principle in foreign aid delivery.[12] In foreign aid, aid officials largely select aid delivery channels in an open market. Further, I find that reforms have significantly reduced the scale of aid bureaucracy in the United States and the United Kingdom, with less marked changes in Sweden. These organisational changes, once imposed, make up a markedly neoliberal rulebook that compels aid officials to bypass recipient governments in poorly governed recipient countries, while closing off government-to-government interactions that reflect a major alternative public sector trajectory.

United States. As I documented in Chapter 2, the scope of US foreign aid programmes from the Marshall Plan throughout the 1970s placed beliefs in the virtues of the state front and centre. These beliefs were locked in by national aid organisations that had the capacity to directly implement projects and maintain regular contacts and interactions with recipient government officials, civil society leaders, or business even in remote areas.[13] At its creation in 1961, USAID was set up as a large organisation, counting just shy of 7,000 direct hires and a total staff count of 15,000. As the central aid agency, USAID had extensive field presence, which was perceived as one of USAID's most important assets.[14] For example, USAID officials were traditionally involved in the design and implementation of aid projects and programmes. They had technical experience in responding to evolving foreign policy priorities and emerging crises. Officials were experienced in assuming

[11] Hibou (2015) p. 89.
[12] Peters and Pierre (1998); Pollitt and Boukhaert (2011); Bertelli (2012).
[13] Raadschelders and Toonen (1999); Lynn (2006), pp. 54–55.
[14] Essex (2013), p. 70.

multiple functions, including the production and training of in house expertise, the direct delivery of foreign aid, as well as policy-making.[15] Officials engaged in extensive policy dialogue with local authorities. By the mid-1970s, recessions in much of the Western world had put a halt to post-WW II economic stability and expansion. High unemployment and high inflation directly challenged the suitability of the old economic order to deal with challenges arising in an increasingly globalised world. According to Blyth, the historical juncture of the 1970s was critical in the United States insofar as it loosened existing statist structures and allowed reform-minded influential political actors, often in coalitions with business leaders, to promote neoliberal forms across the board as the best solution to resolving the crisis and to deal with future societal challenges.[16]

As a result, since the mid-1970s, USAID's bureaucratic structure has undergone numerous rounds of 'streamlining', cuts, and reorganisation.[17] By the end of the Reagan administration the overall number of direct hires was reduced by half to approximately 3,500 and the total staff count was at approximately 8,000. At that time USAID had eighty-three missions abroad.[18] The 1980s were also marked by the Reagan Administration's efforts to support private enterprise in developing countries as well as policies, such as the Private Enterprise Initiative, that promoted greater reliance on the private sector in implementing US aid programmes, raising the private sector's profile and influence in international development.[19] During the Clinton administration, USAID personnel cuts continued under the motto of reinvigorating operations as part of the Reinventing Government movement. As one of a few so-called reinvention laboratories, USAID further dismantled in house capacities by eliminating ninety units in USAID headquarters[20] and closed twenty-one missions on account of cost-saving and efficiency measures.[21] As per the 1994 Federal Workforce Restructuring Act, the government required the civil service to become more flexible and responsive, more focused on getting results, and

---

[15] Natsios (2010).
[16] Blyth (2002). Pollitt (1990) suggests that, at the beginning of his presidency, President Reagan asked 2,000 business leaders to propose changes to the state structures in the context of the Grace Commission.
[17] Essex (2013), p. 94.   [18] OECD Aid Review – USA (1989/90), p. 29.
[19] Lawson (2011).   [20] OECD Aid Review – USA (1994/95), pp. 9; 23; 61.
[21] OECD Aid Review – USA (1994/95), p. 29.

more like 'normal' private sector jobs that lacked the kind of 'feather bed' and overprotection that the civil service traditionally had. The orientation was to attain a larger proportion of employees who had experience in the private sector and to hire them on performance-related contracts.[22] By the end of the Clinton administration USAID only counted approximately 2,000 direct hire employees, and a total staff count of approximately 7,500.[23] When George W. Bush took office in 2000, we observe a halt in the uninterrupted trend of personnel cuts, and even note a small uptick in direct hires by 10 per cent. Between 1970 and 2008, USAID thus exhibits a dramatic 70 per cent reduction of its direct hires.

After decades of sustained and deliberate government efforts to downsize staff and reform the civil service in the image of private sector jobs, USAID today is no longer able to fulfil many of the functions it had previously carried out. Importantly, the government no longer expected the agency to fulfil them. Instead, USAID was going to outsource to NGOs, international organisations, and private contractors to fulfil some of the functions it had hitherto assumed, including programme design, training and monitoring functions, or expertise.[24] USAID's dismantlement was consistent with the neoliberal vision of a limited state: USAID's role was going to be more limited. With fewer and less experienced staff, USAID's ability to oversee the delivery of foreign assistance was becoming increasingly stifled.[25]

This pattern of state dismantlement in the spirit of efficiency and cost-effectiveness was lauded by neoliberal reformers. But it also received criticism. Among the more frequently cited reactions to this development is Defense Secretary Robert Gates' statement during a 2008 speech in Washington DC, in which he noted,

It has become clear that America's civilian institutions of diplomacy and development have been chronically undermanned and underfunded for far too long – relative to what we spend on the military, and more important, relative to the responsibilities and challenges our nation has around the world. I cannot pretend to know the right dollar amount – I know it's a good deal more than the one percent of the federal budget that it is right

---

[22] Pollitt and Boukhaert (2011), p. 73.
[23] USAID (2007), p. 1, cited in Essex (2013).
[24] Essex (2013), p. 95; GAO (2003), p. 2, cited in Essex (2013), p. 110.
[25] GAO (2003).

now. But the budgets we are talking about are relatively small compared to the rest of government, a steep increase of these capabilities is well within reach – as long as there is the political will and wisdom to do it. But even as we agree that more resources are needed, I believe that there is more to this problem than how much money is in the 150 Account. The challenge we face is how best to integrate these tools of statecraft with the military, international partners, and the private sector.[26]

Carol Lancaster, who served as USAID Administrator from 1993–1996, criticised that 'USAID has left the re-tail game and become a wholesaler. In fact, it has become a wholesaler to wholesalers.'[27] In 2009, before being sworn in as Secretary of State, Hillary Rodham Clinton remarked, 'I think it is fair to say that USAID, our premier aid agency, has been decimated. It has half the staff it used to have. It's turned into more of a contracting agency than an operational agency with the ability to deliver.' She added that 'even when there are not headline-grabbing abuses, there has been a steady transfer of authority and resources from government employees and a chain of accountability to contractors'.[28]

The reduction in overall, and particularly experienced, staff numbers are only half of the story. The loss in staff might have been less detrimental if aid spending had gone down alongside it. Instead, since the end of the Cold War, USAID had begun to operate in more countries and managed foreign aid programmes in nearly 160 countries by the end of the 1990s.[29] Since the mid-1990s, the number of country programmes and funding had continually increased from approximately $8 billion in 1995 to approximately $10 billion in 2005.[30] By the time the Obama administration took office, programme responsibility surpassed $13 billion. Although USAID had set a target of contracting officers managing a range of $10–14 million per year, the 2008 level was at an average of $57 million.[31] The surge in spending, coupled with a reduction in scale, meant that USAID often even lacked the capability to execute its primary duty: to effectively manage and oversee the delivery of assistance in more countries.[32] USAID, therefore, needed to contract out administrative and oversight duties with programme funds, in addition to contracting out delivery functions.[33]

---

[26] Gates (2008).   [27] As cited in Roberts (2014), p. 6.
[28] As cited in Roberts (2014), p. 6.   [29] Essex (2013), p. 95.
[30] GAO (2003).   [31] Spero (2010).   [32] GAO (2003); Natsios (2010).
[33] GAO (2003).

This transformation in USAID's bureaucratic structures has produced a slimmed down and streamlined bureaucratic structure that today relies more extensively on non-state actors than before. Under the Obama administration, there was a recognition that the dependence on non-state actors had become too pronounced, and that international development was more complex than what was possible through economic management. Under the USAID Forward initiative, USAID reprioritised the rebuilding of its human resource base, instituting programmes such as the New Entry Professional or the Development Leadership Initiative to attract and retain talent. By 2012, some 800 new direct hires had been brought on board.[34] These efforts were broadly welcomed to address chronic shortages of in house expertise, to regain public sector capabilities. As one senior USAID official suggested during an author interview,

Our (then) USAID administrator, Ravi Shah, stands for a new development model for the 21st century, one that modernizes foreign aid by spelling out targets and indicators but also by focusing more on local solutions. USAID Forward is one initiative that reflects this focus. It also emphasizes more capacity-building and state-strengthening. We need to be more present in the ministries abroad, we need to scale up to analyze their public financial management system. We need to help them improve their own performance and deliver aid.[35]

In the end, however, this uptick in hiring remained limited and did not entail a significant return to a more robust reinforcement of capacity that would move USAID off its neoliberal trajectory. As a senior USAID official concedes during the author interview, 'Our latest hiring did not dramatically change the situation, unfortunately. We continue to be dependent on other actors. For us it is inconceivable that, at this point, even if we wanted to, we can make a case to the American people to ramp up our capacity to levels that we knew thirty or forty years ago.'[36] There is, of course, an element of path dependence in this process. As bureaucratic structures become more and more dismantled in terms of their capabilities and expertise, it becomes more politically probative for governments to back away from the neoliberal governance model. A dismantled aid bureaucracy thus implies that non-state

---

[34] Dunning and Leo (2016), p. 4.
[35] Author interview with senior USAID official, Washington DC, 10 August 2013.
[36] Author interview with senior USAID official, Washington DC, 10 October 2013.

development actors have become critical actors in US foreign aid. In such an environment of dependence, non-state actors are well positioned to articulate and defend their interests by lobbying for more or larger aid contracts or grants. Although outsourcing to private actors has its origin in the orienting neoliberal ideology and was pursued because of an ideologically inspired faith in the superiority of private actors, interest group politics render aid delivery tactics expressly political insofar as contracting firms or NGOs will go a long way to promote their interests through direct lobbying of aid officials. As Milner and Tingley have shown, interest groups systematically influence US foreign aid.[37] Such a confluence of ideology, institutional constraints, and interest group pressure makes it more likely that aid officials in neoliberal political economies choose to bypass rather than engage with the recipient government in foreign aid.

United Kingdom. When we compare the United Kingdom with the United States, we observe similar patterns of dismantlement of the foreign aid bureaucracy in the late 1970s and 1980s. When Margaret Thatcher came into office in 1979, her government spearheaded significant reforms in public administration. As I suggested in Chapter 2, economic turmoil in the 1970s helped loosen the constraints of existing statist structures by delegitimising the institutional mechanisms of reproduction that had, until then, locked in statist policies. This vacuum of political ideas enabled reform-minded actors, such as Thatcher and other key political and economic actors, to push for transformative and long-lasting neoliberal changes that not only broke with the old public sector order but also prescribed dramatically divergent action in domestic and foreign policy. As Thatcher famously declared, 'There Is No Alternative' to welfare state retrenchment and a leaner social economic model.

Throughout the 1980s, the neoliberal view of management as key to better government became, as Christopher Pollitt characterises it, a dominant ideology for the public services of the United Kingdom.[38] Hood and Dixon go as far as labelling the United Kingdom a 'poster child' and a 'vanguard state' of the managerial movement.[39]

---

[37] Milner and Tingley (2015).   [38] Pollitt (1990).
[39] Hood and Dixon (2015).

Thatcher's policies of fiscal tightening alongside her visions for a 'leaner' and more business-like civil service came with considerable reductions in foreign aid staff.[40] According to the OECD Aid Review of 1984/85, staff numbers in the Overseas Development Administration initially fell by 25 per cent, from 2,285 staff members to 1,717 between 1979 and 1984, with additional, sustained staff cuts in headquarters and in the field over the following ten years. What is more, traditional mechanisms of aid delivery, which organise delivery via institutionalised or direct goods and service provision, were increasingly replaced by a mechanism of competitive contracting, requiring officials to select delivery channels in an open market.

In 1997, the incoming Labour government, who placed greater importance on overseas development than the Conservative administration, undertook initial steps to rebuild a severely weakened bureaucracy. It re-established a separate ministry for aid, the Department for International Development (DFID), whose goal it was to make foreign aid focused on poverty reduction and to shun any use of aid for national interests, as was common under the previous Conservative government.[41] By December 2000, the 2001 OECD DAC Peer Review reports a DFID total staff figure of 2,259 and the DAC Peer Review of 2006 states that staff numbers nearly doubled between 1997 and 2005 to a total staff figure of 2,853.[42] These developments were, in part, attributed to Labour's strong commitment to international development.[43] It was also attributed to robust leadership of senior development figures, including Barbara Castle, Judith Hart, and Clare Short, who believed that the state was an important agent of change, yet acknowledged the need to show the connection between what DFID was doing in terms of development funding and its impact on poverty reduction around the world.[44]

---

[40] Ireton (2013), pp. 71; 234; OECD DAC Peer Review – UK (2001), p. 52.
[41] Barder (2005); Ireton (2013), p. 50; Valters and Whitty (2017) p. 8.
[42] OECD DAC Peer Review – UK (2001), p. 53; OECD DAC Peer Review – UK (2006), p. 62.
[43] OECD DAC Peer Review – UK (2001), p. 17; Ireton (2013), p. 1.
[44] Ireton (2013), p. 65.

However, because DFID had to fit within New Labour's vision for modern government, leadership had to make drastic changes to how foreign aid was managed. DFID adopted a corporate management system that would be used to track objectives set by central management, to demonstrate results, and to manage performance, which I will discuss in more detail in Section 5.4.[45] Government-wide streamlining efforts and efficiency targets under the Brown government soon chipped away at gains that had been made earlier. Between 2005 and 2008, DFID, like other government departments, needed to cut administrative costs by 10 per cent, which led to staff cuts across the board, but particularly in overseas offices. This led to country office closures in thirty-six countries between 2002 and 2008 and a concentration of 90 per cent of DFID's bilateral programmes on only twenty-three countries.[46]

As in the United States, staff cuts went hand in hand with a significant increase in foreign aid levels.[47] In 2004, Prime Minister Blair committed to a timetable to reach the 0.7 per cent of gross national income target by 2013, a commitment that remained throughout the Brown and Cameron administrations. In 2004, UK aid stood at 0.36 per cent, rising to 0.57 per cent by the time Labour left office.[48] Under Cameron the aid budget continued to grow, reaching the 0.7 per cent norm for the first time in 2013. Simultaneously, administrative costs including staff were reduced by a third between 2009 and 2013.[49]

As in the United States, government-wide reinvention efforts chipped away at certainties associated with civil service jobs, by making them more like private sector jobs; by making it more difficult that lasting fiefdoms could be created. For example, the 2012 Civil Service Reform requests that DFID's senior positions require previous commercial and/or corporate management experience.[50] In addition, even Whitehall permanent secretaries and director generals need to compete for their own jobs after three to four

---

[45] OECD DAC Peer Review – UK (2006), p. 56, Valters and Whitty (2017), p. 19.
[46] OECD DAC Peer Review – UK (2010), p. 50.
[47] OECD DAC Peer Review – UK (2006), p. 16.
[48] Randel and German (2015).
[49] OECD DAC Peer Review – UK (2014), p. 59, Ireton (2013), p. 57.
[50] Veillette (2007), p. 15.

years. As in the United States, DFID offset staff reductions with more outsourcing through contractual arrangements. In the context of New Labour's efforts to enhance value for money, DFID pushed towards competitive bidding among NGOs to become standard practice for commissioned work.[51] Having crossed the 0.7 per cent threshold in 2013, DFID took advantage of economies of scale by significantly increasing contracting with international organisations for delivery of its bilateral aid, while keeping tight tabs on accountability and control. Since 2012, DFID has also invested in strengthening the role of private finance and, in particular, UK-based private contractors.[52]

As a former DFID official suggested during an author interview,

The contracting out has definitely become stronger. This trend brings our overseas development assistance closer to the transatlantic view of what makes international development effective. It implies that we reduce the power of the state when administering public services. So, there is now a bit of a flutter of interest. You talk to people at DFID now. They are creatively spinning off all manner of joint venture type vehicles with private sector agencies to the point that there is a DFID and, then, there is a satellite mass of things. This includes seeding private sector initiatives and hoping that the big construction companies will come in to complete large-scale infrastructure projects abroad. People associate this contracting-out and private sector frenzy with the Conservatives in particular who they view as more comfortable with private equity perspective, but this approach is likely to and has already survived any change of government. It fits into the larger picture of celebrating a private sector approach to international development.[53]

Today, the institutional environment of the UK aid system is characterised by slimmed down and streamlined structures as well as a reliance on market-type mechanisms for the delivery of foreign aid. As in the United States, another 'legacy' of neoliberal reforms was the

---

[51] The practice of working with non-state actors in aid delivery went back to the 1980s, where British aid administration began to direct more financing towards NGOs; but not through contractual arrangements. Ireton (2013), p. 236.
[52] Valters and Whitty (2017), p. 9.
[53] Author interview with former DFID official, London, 24 June 2014.

empowerment of vested interests. As the UK aid system was successively dismantled and streamlined, non-state actors gained influence and worked actively to make bypass a stable tactic that persists over time. Aid officials who work in this environment are encouraged to base their aid delivery decisions on evaluations about the efficiency and effectiveness of aid implementers. When the quality of recipient governance is low, aid officials are incentivised to bypass the recipient government. This development also implies that both the logic of economic management and capability are more likely to promote bypass than government-to-government delivery in foreign aid.

Sweden. Throughout the post-World War II era, political economists have characterised Sweden's political economy as an extensive welfare state, which functions on the basis of closed and institutionalised cooperation between government, labour unions, the non-profit sector, and corporations.[54] As economic turmoil rocked Sweden's economy in the 1980s and early 1990s, policy-makers turned to economic management as a solution to the welfare state crisis. To bring the state back from the economic brink, Sweden's government cut spending and set into motion a number of reforms, including a reorganisation of its public sector around incentives, competition, and performance.[55] Supported by both left- and right-leaning political parties, public administration reform 'became a tool' in fighting the fiscal crisis and set the stage for a new mode of governance that differed significantly from the past.[56] Under the responsibility of the Ministry of Finance, public administration reforms aimed to make the state and the public aid system more business-like. These forms required public officials to create and maintain markets for goods and service delivery. The conventional neo-corporatist mechanism of goods and service provision was gradually replaced with competitive contracting.[57] In addition, the Swedish bureaucracy, including its aid system, reformed political control of public authorities by implementing what was then known as management by objectives.[58] This structural shift put an incentive system in place that would emphasise results, performance, and productivity, which included, for example, tight regulatory control over how officials responded to risk; all with a view towards

---

[54] Pontusson (1992); Schnyder (2012). [55] OECD (1996).
[56] Esping-Andersen (1999); Blomquist (2004).
[57] Lewin (1994); Ehn et al. (2003). [58] Ehn et al. (2003).

optimising individual performance and aid results.[59] While the state continues to play a large role in terms of funding levels for goods and services, governments choose to modernise it by creating internal markets for goods and service delivery, leading to significant increases in outsourcing.[60]

Although Swedish aid, compared to its domestic policy counterparts, is a laggard in adopting and implementing neoliberal reforms, the last thirty years have seen numerous reform efforts that seek to place results-orientation at the heart of aid policy.[61] In 1995 the Swedish government merged existing aid organisations and set up the Swedish International Development Agency (Sida) as the central Swedish actor responsible for foreign aid.[62] In 2003, the Swedish government adopted a new Swedish Policy for Global Development that established new goals for development cooperation and required Sida to work out a methodology that would allow those goals to be obtained, with a particular focus on demonstrating results of Swedish development assistance. Swedish aid experts,[63] as well as the aid officials whom I interviewed, indicate that the most drastic organisational changes occurred when the Moderate Party assumed governing responsibilities in 2006 and Gunilla Carlsson became Minister of Development. Carlsson focused, first and foremost, on performance aspects related to Swedish aid, especially in more difficult recipient country environments. In a 2012 speech she remarked,

The Swedish Government has increasingly focused development cooperation on 'fragile and conflict states'. Yet these are, for obvious reasons, the hardest places of all to make aid work. If we cannot transparently and systematically report on how our aid budget is spent, and what is achieved in the form of results, the credibility of development cooperation itself will be undermined. Mutual accountability is only possible if transparency is our guiding star and results our foremost ambition. Consequently, results are, by definition, at the very heart of aid effectiveness.[64]

Throughout Carlson's tenure, Sida was heavily scrutinised by the Swedish National Audit Office and pressured to improve its results reporting.[65] In 2010, the Swedish Government Bill redefined Sida's

---

[59] Holmgren and Svensson (2005).   [60] Belfrage and Kallifatides (2018).
[61] Vähämäki (2017).   [62] Bjerninger (2013).
[63] Bjerninger (2013); Wohlgemuth and Odén (2013), p. 30.
[64] Carlsson (2012).   [65] Vähämäki (2017), p. 173.

role, making it more similar to peer agencies such as USAID that assume largely managerial functions. Aid policy-making and international representation were now left to the Ministry of Foreign Affairs.[66]

Such organisational changes have direct implications on how Swedish aid officials approach aid under conditions of poor governance. When risks of aid capture through recipient governments are high, economic management dictates that aid officials prefer to deliver aid through non-state actors. Consider a remark from a Sida official during an author interview,

The Sida official position here (on corrupt recipient governments, *added by author*) would be to abandon governments because of the risks posed by corruption and weak state institutions. We tend to be a bit afraid of being involved with these kinds of governments these days and would work more through NGOs for service delivery and to strengthen their watch dog function vis-à-vis the government.[67]

This same Sida official, like several others whom I interviewed, then went on to place current aid delivery tactics into a historical context, pointing out that Swedish development assistance had changed significantly over recent decades,

Sida's position on corrupt or weak governments is different today than what it used to be. Today, the official position would be to abandon governments because of the risks posed by bad governance, like corruption. We have become more afraid of being involved with corrupt governments and therefore work more with NGOs or IOs for service delivery. We have become too short-sighted and do permit ourselves less to the long-term relations and operations that build up the capacity of the state. Sida used to think of Swedish aid as making changes in the long-term, in dialogue with the recipient government. But this has changed. Thanks to transitioning from a welfare state model to a system that is outsourcing-oriented, with a short-term focus in the implementation of public goods.[68]

This contrasts with Sweden's traditional aid approach from earlier decades, which was more accepting of direct recipient government engagement.[69] Then, collaboration with Swedish or international

---

[66] Vähämäki (2017), p. 170.
[67] Author interview with senior Sida official, Stockholm, 25 June 2013.
[68] Author interview with senior Sida official, Stockholm, 25 June 2013.
[69] Wohlgemuth and Odén (2013).

NGOs was largely institutionalised with a view towards promoting good governance abroad.[70]

Because organisational reforms had moved markets as well as the state's managerial role in creating enabling environments into focus, interactions between aid officials and implementing partners, especially the private sector, have been increasingly embedded in policy and strategic frameworks.[71] For example, Sida provides support to market development through its Business for Development programme, which invites companies to compete for funding to deliver results that include, for example, 'access to more affordable essential products and services for people living in poverty'.[72] Although Swedish development cooperation has always relied on non-state actors for its implementation, neoliberal organisational reforms have gradually heightened the influence of non-state actors on foreign aid decision-making.[73] Overall, I note that the United States, the United Kingdom, and Sweden have significantly reorganised their aid structures. Although Sweden trails the United States and the United Kingdom in how far it has downsized the aid bureaucracy, Swedish leaders have aggressively streamlined the public sector and invested much political capital in making competitive contracting become the primary mechanism of coordinating foreign aid delivery. These institutional changes prioritise bypass over government-to-government delivery when the quality of recipient governance is low. The effect of these micro-institutional changes on aid delivery implies that today's aid delivery decisions in these three countries are systematically shaped by institutional legacies, by rules and practices that were put in place decades ago; since the 1970s in the United States and the United Kingdom, and a about a decade later in Sweden. These past decisions to organise state institutions, including national aid organisations, make it difficult and costly to change aid delivery tactics, even when these policies are considered dysfunctional.

---

[70] For an excellent discussion of the role of civil society in Sweden see Micheletti (1995).
[71] Billing et al. (2012), pp. 26–27.   [72] Billing et al. (2012), p. 30.
[73] Billing et al. (2012).

3.4 Organisational Patterns and Foreign Aid Delivery in Germany and France

In this section, I show that German and French aid delivery is also influenced by institutional legacies that organise their national aid organisations. Yet, the direction of the constraints differs insofar as past decisions to organise institutions have reaffirmed the importance of the state for solving societal challenges or, more specifically, for reducing risk in aid delivery abroad.

Although, over the past four decades, neoliberal doctrine has found its way into the German and French state and their aid systems, reforms have been at best incremental. As political economy and public administration scholars have noted, institutional changes within the two political economies fell short of the kind of institutional rupture that we observe among Anglo-Saxon and Scandinavian countries.[74] To this day, the German and French public sectors remain centred on a traditional public sector model. The state remains an important actor with its own standards and scripts for practices, including, for example, that authority be exercised through a disciplined hierarchy of impartial officials rather than a devolved system of individuals.[75] The state is not reduced to a steering function.

As I noted in Chapter 2, comparative scholarship has tried to explain why countries like Germany and France but also others have not undergone large-scale institutional reform. They have pointed to a number of politico-administrative factors, or prohibitory antecedent conditions, including relatively rigid institutional structures that have made neoliberal reforms difficult in Germany and France. Further, scholars have suggested that governments were less enthusiastic about dismantling and rationalising state organisations than their US and UK counterparts during the economic downturn of the 1970s that affected all OECD countries. This lack of enthusiasm was not because 'big government' was not considered problematic. But rather, the neoliberal credo of dismantling the state and making it more business like was not believed to hold all the answers for addressing the challenges associated with globalisation.[76]

---

[74] Kinderman (2008); Streek (2010); Pollitt and Boukhaert (2011); Thelen (2014).
[75] Pollitt and Boukhaert (2011).   [76] Streek (2010).

Over recent decades, public sector cuts and streamlining efforts took place but were relatively mild. In Germany, the tightening of the government budget in the wake of Germany's reunification required the BMZ, Germany's development ministry, to cut staff by 1.5 per cent annually until 2005; and another 0.6 per cent annually until 2009.[77] During these years, the BMZ was able to compensate for loss of staff by transferring and drawing on personnel from its two implementing agencies, the GIZ, which is in charge of technical cooperation, and the KfW, which is in charge of financial cooperation, for advisory work, the review of tasks, adjustments to human resource management, and changes in procedures.[78,79] Between 2009 and 2014, the data show that the BMZ made important gains in field staff levels to ensure policy dialogue and increase the monitoring capacities of its implementing agencies as well at the local level.[80] There was also a nearly 30 per cent increase in BMZ headquarters staff, which is largely based in Bonn but has one-third of its staff based in Berlin. In 2016, the BMZ has approximately 1,000 staff members, of which two-thirds are based at BMZ headquarters, and one-third are based in Berlin.[81]

In France, it is more challenging to analyse human resource patterns within the aid system because foreign aid is not the exclusive function of any of the principal institutions.[82] Overall, there has been some staff reduction at several points in time for certain posts, but these cuts are often closely linked to changing priorities and areas of focus in French development cooperation, rather than displaying a link to sustained efforts at dismantling the structure of French development cooperation. Across French ministries that partake in development cooperation, cuts in staff with technical expertise have been most pronounced over recent years.[83] A glance at developments within the Agency for French Development, the financial cooperation agency of the French

---

[77] Ashoff (2009), p. 2.
[78] Ashoff et al. (2008), pp. 61–64, as cited in Ashoff (2009), p. 2.
[79] The KfW also streamlined its headquarters operations in Frankfurt, downsizing its staff by 15 per cent. In 2011, Germany completed a large institutional reform project by incorporating technical cooperation agencies under GIZ.
[80] DAC Peer Review – GER (2015), p. 56.
[81] OECD DAC Peer Review – GER (1998), p. 15; OECD DAC Peer Review – GER (2001), p. 60; OECD DAC Peer Review – GER (2010), p. 65; OECD DAC Peer Review GER (2015), pp. 5, 8.
[82] OECD DAC Peer Review – FRA (2004), p. 58.
[83] OECD DAC Peer Review – FRA (2013), pp. 31; 62; 65.

government, suggests that from the 1990s to 2004, staff in headquarters have slightly increased to around 700, while overseas staff has been slightly reduced to around 550.[84] Until 2012, staff numbers grew by another 35 per cent, largely in the agency's Paris headquarters.[85]

Since the mid-2000s, we note that mounting pressure on public expenditure and government-wide cost-saving measures have resulted in lower staffing levels across the board.[86] More recently, we observe a decline in direct hires and rise in fixed term contracts in the Ministry of Foreign Affairs and the Ministry of Finance,[87] which has increased staff turnover rates and, according to the OECD donor peer review report, makes it difficult to capitalise on expertise and makes the effective administration of aid programmes more challenging.[88] What is more, the skill base seems to be changing insofar as more recent recruitment has brought in new people with skills in various professional areas.[89] More than in Germany, where civil servants remain 'mandarins' with long experience and well-established personal networks, we observe that members of the French *grands corps* frequently move in and out of jobs in the private sector.[90] In spite of these changes, the OECD notes that the staffing structure is still largely dominated by technical categories and that France's ample technical expertise is 'recognized and appreciated by governments no less than by other partners'.[91]

Unlike in DFID and USAID, accountability in Germany and France is organised hierarchically, although networking mechanisms have been introduced to soften the hierarchical top-down structure. While employment in the aid bureaucracies in the United States and the United Kingdom became more like 'normal' jobs in the private sector, with less security of tenure and promotion tied to job performance criteria, the majority of civil servants have long experience and established personal networks.[92] In France, recent trends to streamline the

---

[84] OECD DAC Peer Review – FRA (2004), p. 59.
[85] OECD DAC Peer Review – FRA (2013), pp. 19; 66.   [86] Amable (2017).
[87] OECD DAC Peer Review – FRA (2013), p. 19.
[88] OECD DAC Peer Review – FRA (2013), p. 66.
[89] OECD DAC Peer Review – FRA (2004), p. 59.
[90] Pollitt and Boukhaert (2011).
[91] OECD DAC Peer Review – FRA (2013), p. 19.
[92] Pollitt and Boukhaert (2011).

public sector have led to movements towards this kind of 'normalising' trajectory, where the civil service is 'deprivileged' and increasingly treated on the same fragmented and locally varying terms as private sector employment.[93] Relative to the United States and the United Kingdom, however, this trend is mild. In France and Germany, the state apparatus may undergo changes but there remains a conviction that traditional bureaucracy has its virtues, which should be preserved. The key to success, so goes the view, would be to combine these virtues with more efficient procedures.

German and French development cooperation shows little appetite for outsourcing. Nor is the predominant mechanism for coordinating implementation one of competitive contracting. Of the small number of programmes that are channelled to German-based or international NGOs for implementation, institutional arrangements often serve as a mechanism for awarding actors, rather than competitive contracting, as is the custom with DFID and USAID. Less than 10 per cent of German and French aid is channelled through non-state actors.[94]

The following quotes from senior aid officials are useful for elucidating the effect of structures on aid delivery in poor governance environments. Consider first this remark from a German official,

We are required to use local systems, to work with the public sector in developing countries, as much as possible. If state structures are weak, we need to make an extra effort to assist in the implementation, we need to be more hands-on and build capacity, while trying to ensure project outcomes. We are similar to our French counterparts for wanting to work with the recipient government. The Kreditanstalt für Wiederaufbau (KfW) is much like the Agence Française du Développement (AFD) in this regard. For the procurement of goods, the Gesellschaft für Internationale Zusammenarbeit (GIZ), our implementing partner, controls the process more heavily when local systems are not fit to ensure that the process is not corrupted. The GIZ sends experts and training staff that assist and monitor the local governments so that the implementation of the project works as desired. The role

---

[93] OECD DAC Peer Review – FRA (2000), p. 54; OECD DAC Peer Review – FRA (2004), pp. 59; 68f; OECD DAC Peer Review – FRA (2013), pp. 19; 64; 66.
[94] OECD DAC Peer Review – GER (2015), p. 19.

of the government is very important here because it sets the objectives the projects, and is involved in the process of implementation.[95]

In a similar vein, a senior French official remarks,

In France we respond to and penalize corrupt practices in the public sector but not by cutting aid to the government and shifting it to NGOs. We mitigate corruption through our strong due diligence process within the AFD [Agence Française de Développement]. In fact, France is at the maximum of government- to-government cooperation where we work closely with the institutions of our partners. If they have weak institutions we need to continue working with them, and accompany them with our capacity. We give them frequent advice where needed. We have almost daily dialogue with our partners on sector program choices and on the implementation of the projects. In fact we have offices of the AFD with experts in almost every country in which we work. We consider that it is not a good way to accept project implementation from an agency outside their own local structure.[96]

In both cases, aid officials work in a bureaucratic structure that is set up to be government-centred and makes it more likely that donor officials work with government under conditions of poor governance.

In Table 3.1, I summarise the differences in organisational structures between donors from different political economy types and document, again, marked differences in institutional environments that incentivise aid officials from different political economies into different directions in aid delivery.

3.5 Managerial Practices in the United States, the United Kingdom, and Sweden

In this section, I compare the same donors but focus on tracing the extent to which neoliberal managerial practices pervade organisations. My argument highlights marked variation in administrative practices across donor political economies, and suggests that Anglo-Saxon and Scandinavian donors impose private sector practices to manage agents within the organisation as well as interactions with recipient governments and non-state delivery actors.

---

[95] Author interview with senior German official, Paris, 17 July 2013.
[96] Author interview with senior French government official, 3 July 2013, Paris.

Table 3.1. *Summary of select neoliberal reforms and their outcomes across donor countries since 1980*

	United States	United Kingdom	Sweden	Germany	France
Major and sustained personnel cuts	yes	yes	no	no	no
Major streamlining reforms	yes	yes	yes	no	no
Making civil service jobs more like private sector jobs	yes	yes	yes	no	no
Extensive Outsourcing	yes	yes	yes	no	no
Aid agency (or part of it) is reinvention laboratory	yes	yes	no	no	no

As the principal–agent literature has shown, the process of contracting out goods and service delivery can be challenging. If the agent has interests and incentives that are not perfectly compatible with those of the official, the delegation of goods and service production may generate agency problems. In most situations, it is difficult for officials to know whether their agents are slacking or whether the agents' actions are consistent with the state's desires. The agent therefore can exploit this informational asymmetry to its advantage.[97] To ensure that the use of competitive contracting yields expected efficiency gains or value for money, aid agencies, when executing their function as facilitator, need to control the activities of goods and service providers. They need to be able to keep the agent honest and accountable and ensure that results, as specified in the contract, are delivered.

One common private sector approach to reduce agent shirking is to set up extensive monitoring and reporting systems that allow contract managers, in their role as principals, to know what happens with the contract and whether the agent fulfils its contractual obligations by delivering on results. To be able to control production the aid

---

[97] Kiewiet and McCubbins (1991); Tallberg (2002); Strøm et al. (2003); Hawkins et al. (2006); Conceição-Heldt (2013).

organisation requires the capacity to clearly specify outcomes and to monitor the performance of providers and discipline non-compliant producers.[98] Performance monitoring is at the heart of managerial practices. It is used internally to understand how the individual aid organisation delivers aid and whether it is done well and has achieved pre-specified targets and results.[99]

Performance monitoring, more than other systems of evaluation, allows aid organisations to document success in delivering foreign aid. It keeps tabs on processes and outputs for which the aid agency is responsible. For example, it includes the specification of clear and measurable organisational objectives to promote strategic steering within the organisation. It entails the systematic use of indicators and measures of organisational performance to assess organisational output. It also entails the application of performance appraisal of individual employees to assist in harmonising their efforts and focusing them towards organisational objectives. It also includes the use of performance incentives, such as performance pay to reward exceptional personal efforts towards organisational goals, among other measures.

Extensive scrutiny of these processes and outputs through independent arm's length auditing organisations reinforces a focus on organisational effectiveness. However, performance monitoring may not provide information about whether aid has contributed to development in the recipient country. An aid intervention may achieve all its targets regarding the delivery of goods and services, but not be effective at the outcome or impact level. As aid agencies introduce performance monitoring, 'being seen to do the right thing' becomes a stronger, if not dominating, motive for foreign aid delivery. Because the primary consumers of performance information are domestic actors, consisting of a critical parliament and taxpayers, aid organisations 'turn inward' in several ways. They set up performance frameworks that work for them across a variety of management purposes, including the benchmarking of organisations or functions, budgetary decisions, and determining budget allocation, as well as decisions regarding career development and the promotion of individuals.[100] The required information about performance is produced in short intervals, at multiple levels of

---

[98] Kiewiet and McCubbins (1991).   [99] Van Dooren et al. (2010).
[100] Pollitt and Boukhaert (2011); Holzapfel (2016).

aggregation, is publicly available, and is easily accessible online. I observe this pattern in the United States, the United Kingdom, and Sweden, but not in Germany and France.

United States. In the United States, the aid system has always pursued a target-driven approach to managing foreign aid. In the 1960s, USAID invented the logical framework to set realistic, specific, and measurable objectives for foreign aid, distinguishing between inputs, outputs, and then specified outcomes. By the 1980s, USAID had instituted the use of the logical framework to improve planning processes and clearly demonstrate who benefits from USAID assistance. Since the 1980s, USAID has gradually set up metrics that would allow aid organisations to demonstrate their performance. I note a significant shift towards performance-oriented evaluation in the 1990s, propelled by the Reinventing Government movement. Under the National Performance Review, USAID, alongside other federal agencies, was required to identify policies and organisational processes that would help improve its organisational effectiveness.[101] As a 'reinvention laboratory' under the Clinton administration, USAID invested a large share of its budget in identifying new ways of doing business. The credo here was to do more for less, and it led to a series of streamlining measures that transformed USAID's bureaucratic structure and imposed private sector tools to improve the performance of USAID in managing personnel, the budget, and contracting.[102]

Through the Government Performance and Results Act (GPRA), performance measurement and management become a legal requirement. As cross-cutting legislation, GPRA represents a comprehensive government effort to organise and manage the public sector around performance criteria.[103] It reflects the neoliberal orientation of the United States across four administrations insofar as the legislation was drafted under G. H. Bush, signed by Clinton, strengthened under G. W. Bush, and, finally, updated with slight revisions by Obama in 2010.[104] As a management system, GPRA anchors the 'three M's' – markets, managers, and measurement – in public sector governance.[105] It seeks to tie performance results to budgetary and staffing

[101] OECD Aid Review – USA (1994/95), p. 9; Essex (2013), p. 92.
[102] GAO (1996).   [103] Radin (1998).
[104] US Office of Management and Budget (1993, 2011) and Lynn (2006).
[105] Ferlie et al (1996).

decisions. It required all federal agencies, including USAID, to produce a strategic plan with organisational goals and objectives; a performance plan including measurement and data on meeting objectives; and a performance report including actual performance data.[106] GPRA's administrative expectations have direct effects on how foreign aid agencies, including USAID, conduct their daily business. The legislation increased pressure across all agencies to carefully benchmark and manage for efficiency and effectiveness by managing goods and service delivery through competitive contracts.[107]

Throughout the 1990s, USAID introduced different management programmes and systems centering on performance measurement to improve practices in accounting, budgeting, human resource management, planning, and procurement assistance.[108] Examples include the New Management System (NMS) and the Performance of Routine Information System Management (PRISM), which gave USAID managers and policy-makers private sector tools for results planning and tracking, reporting performance of aid programmes, and minimising risks in acquisition and foreign aid delivery.[109] Since 1992, USAID has compiled and published agency-wide annual performance reports.[110] Since 1995, individual country missions have been required to report annually on results and performance.[111] The OECD notes in the context of a donor peer review that USAID has come a long way in development performance monitoring and management.[112] In 1997, USAID issued its first multi-year strategic plan to manage for results and improved performance, as directed by GPRA.[113] In addition, USAID produced, at the level of each operational unit, a forward-looking performance plan that outlined performance goals and expected results as well as a backward-looking annual performance report that compared actual performance with expected results.[114] Performance assessments begin in the field but

---

[106] Dietrich (2016), p. 72.   [107] Dietrich (2016), p. 72.
[108] OECD Aid Review – USA (1994/95), pp. 21; 22.
[109] OECD DAC Peer Review – USA (1998), pp. 13; 48.
[110] OECD DAC Peer Review – USA (1998), p. 20.   [111] Natsios (2010), p. 23.
[112] OECD Aid Review – USA (1994/95), p. 10.
[113] OECD DAC Peer Review – USA (1998), pp. 10; 13; 20; 48.
[114] OECD DAC Peer Review – USA (1998), p. 66.

then get aggregated and analysed with reference to strategic object-ives. Assessments can be based on quarterly reporting from the field as well as annual reporting at the level of the recipient country and USAID headquarters.[115]

The agency's strategic objectives approach to implementation requires that USAID headquarters as well as field missions, which are at the lowest level of performance and results aggregation, engage in strategic results monitoring and detailed measurement and reporting that goes into the production of the performance plan and the performance report. The focus here is on measuring outputs through pre-specified, often standardised, indicators that are quanti-fiable and measurable.[116] USAID regularly updates guidance and trains its staff in improving the agency's performance measurement and monitoring practices as performance frameworks change, includ-ing, e.g., the selection of new indicators.[117] For example, in 2006, 400 indicators served as the basis for assessing the efficiency and effectiveness of USAID programmes.[118] By 2010, this number had nearly tripled to 1,100, stoking concerns over the ability to meaning-fully integrate such a high number of indicators for assessments.[119] In the context of an OECD DAC peer review of US foreign aid, the OECD reports scepticism among US senior government officials about the quality of outcome assessments of foreign aid. They felt that too much time was spent 'ticking boxes' rather than invested in assessing the relative importance of different performance indicators, or improving the quality of the underlying data and how it was put to use.[120]

This development also sparked debates over how to best use human resources within USAID, as performance monitoring is onerous insofar as it requires extensive data collection, paperwork, and a detailed classification of activities funded by USAID.[121] As Andrew Natsios illustrates,

---

[115] OECD DAC Peer Review – USA (2002), p. 66.
[116] Holzapfel (2016), p. 22, finds that USAID uses standardised indicators at multiple levels of the results chain (activities, outputs, short-term outcomes, and medium-term outcomes and impacts).
[117] Natsios (2010), p. 23; OECD DAC Peer Review – USA (1998), p. 47.
[118] Natsios (2010), p. 33.
[119] Criticised by OECD DAC Peer Review – USA (2011).
[120] OECD DAC Peer Review – USA (2006), p. 52.   [121] Natsios (2010), p. 33.

From the perspective of the officers running programs in the field, two months (October and November) are devoted to reviewing and reporting on past performance; the next four months (December through April) are pretty much devoted to budget and implementation proposals: Preparing the Congressional Budget Justification for the coming year, preparing Mission Strategic Plans for the future year, and preparing Operational Plans for the current year. And, of course the final two months of each fiscal year (August and September) are devoted to preparation and signing of contracts and grants to obligate newly appropriated funds that have finally been made available. Almost eight months of every fiscal year are dominated by reporting and budget processes, leaving program and technical experts precious little time to design new programs and monitor the implementation of ongoing programs.[122]

The preoccupation with performance measurement and monitoring of output led USAID to move away from traditional evaluation practices. During the 1980s and early 1990s, USAID had evaluated the impact of their aid policy on a large scale. By 1994, the number of evaluations submitted to the Development Experience Clearing House was just shy of 500. Between 1994 and 2001, however, the number of evaluations carried out fell by 80 per cent.[123] Because departments, missions, and projects had to carry out their own evaluations and performance assessments, greater emphasis on 'being seen to do the right thing' led to a shift in resources towards performance monitoring and away from evaluation that would measure outcomes and impact. The incoming Obama administration promised a better balance between performance monitoring and evaluation for impact across programmes, introducing 'performance evaluation', a mixed approach that aimed to evaluate performance in terms of achieving actual outcomes rather than outputs.[124] This led to a significant reduction in indicators on which USAID needed to report. The Obama administration also established more centralised evaluation functions within USAID's bureau for Policy, Planning, and Learning in 2010, which led to an uptick in

---

[122] Natsios (2010), p. 26.   [123] OECD DAC Peer Review – USA (2006), p. 53.
[124] OECD DAC Peer Review – USA (2011), pp. 17; 59; Natsios (2010), p. 27; OECD DAC Peer Review – USA (2002), p. 73; OECD DAC Peer Review – USA (2011), pp. 17; 59.

outcome evaluations.[125] Importantly, however, performance monitoring remained dominant insofar as units are required to extensively track outputs and, whenever possible, attribute progress on output or impact directly to US funding.[126]

Extensive public sector auditing through arms' length institutions ensures that USAID does not lose focus on domestic accountability. Multiple agencies exist that scrutinise USAID. For example, the USAID Office of the Inspector General (IG), created in 1980, is there to undertake hundreds of audits and inspections of aid programmes in USAID headquarters and field mission.[127] Key questions of interest to auditors address efficiency and effectiveness. For example, auditors assess whether vaccines for children in need have been purchased at unnecessary expense or whether vaccines, though perfectly legally purchased, do not reach the intended beneficiaries within the planned time frame. Or, auditors evaluate the quality of management systems that are in place. Or, they undertake audits of management systems.

Then there is the General Accounting Office (GAO). Like the OIG the GAO consists of government-wide agents of the executive government and Congress that set government-wide standards and regulations for USAID and other federal agencies. GAO also engages in auditing activities, and conducts about half a dozen or so audits on USAID's programmes every year. In these audits, GAO points out agency failings to adopt managerial practices as required by law through GPRA, including, for example, USAID's achievements as well as shortcomings in adopting strategic plans, annual performance plans and goals, performance measures, or reporting mechanisms. The Office of Management and Budget (OMB) also ensures that performance measurement and monitoring is properly enforced.

For example, the OMB has chief performance officers in every agency that are linked by the Performance Improvement Council (PIC), which supports inter-agency collaboration and best practice sharing on management methods. The PIC meets once a month with all the agencies' performance officers to discuss new guidance. The PIC sees itself as 'the heartbeat of government performance management'. Aside from these governmental agencies and Congress, the US

---

[125] OECD DAC Peer Review – USA (2011), p. 59.
[126] OECD DAC Peer Review – USA (2011), p. 71; Holzapfel (2016), p. 22.
[127] USAID (2019).

taxpayer has full access to findings related to agency performance or more traditional evaluations that focus on wider developmental impact. At USAID, all performance reports and evaluations are publicly available. Under the Development Clearing House database, USAID makes available all studies that were ever done or commissioned by USAID.

The managerial practices and external oversight make aid officials more risk averse: when they evaluate aid delivery channels, the rulebook incentivises them to play it safe and select aid delivery channels that are more likely to deliver on results, and that enable aid officials to document that they, themselves, performed well in their position; that they selected the most efficient and productive aid delivery channel that was more likely to deliver on the output, for which they are responsible. Andrew Natsios, a former USAID Administrator and outspoken critic of the neoliberal turn inside USAID, observed that efforts to observe and measure inputs, outputs, and outcomes had turned USAID into a risk-averse 'production agency'.[128]

As per my theory, under conditions of high risk through aid capture, I expect aid officials who work in neoliberal organisations to bypass more than their counterparts from traditional public sector economies. Consider the remark by a US senior official during an author interview,

If donors like us care a lot about trying to guarantee results and they view that governance of the country is not sufficient in terms of governance, like their procurement systems or the budgetary planning, or the audit or execution systems, they are going to be more inclined to use either international NGOs or international contractors to implement it. If donors belong to a different spectrum, one that is less focused on results than ours, they might be more willing to work with the government, or even give sectoral budget support. So foreign aid delivery are related to these different beliefs. They are related to how much pressure is on aid bureaucrats to track and monitor the use of funds, to have the ability to go after them and legally get their money back if something is wrong. Needless to say, it is much more difficult to hold a corrupt government accountable.[129]

United Kingdom. In the United Kingdom, we observe a similar trend. Under Thatcher, government organisations, including the foreign aid

---

[128] Natsios (2010) p. 6.
[129] Author interview with senior US government official, Washington DC, 26 September 2013.

department, came under increasing scrutiny over their organisational effectiveness. In 1979, for example, an efficiency unit was created to scrutinise activities across Whitehall departments and to report inefficiencies directly to the Prime Minister. This government unit recommended a drastic 35 per cent in cost reduction measures for the aid department, which were gradually implemented in subsequent years. As Ireton notes, these cuts relegated the aid department's role to that of monitoring the implementation of projects.[130] In the 1980s, the Foreign Aid Department followed in the footsteps of USAID and adopted the use of logical frameworks for its project-cycle management and project completion reports.[131] In 1983, the National Audit Office Act empowered the National Audit Office to undertake value for money studies of expenditures incurred by government departments, including foreign aid.[132] Only a few years later, the UK aid bureaucracy introduced the systematic use of Logical Frameworks and Project Completion Reports designed to assess aid success.[133]

The government-wide UK Citizen's Charter initiative from 1991, among other government initiatives in the early 1990s, pushed departments towards systematic adoption of results-based management and performance monitoring systems.[134] In 1995, the Conservative government required Whitehall departments, including the aid system, to undertake Fundamental Expenditure Reviews.[135] In 1997, the incoming Labour Government created the Department for International Development (DFID) as a separate foreign aid agency, moving foreign aid policy and spending more into the spotlight.[136] To fit with New Labour's vision of modern government, one that prioritised tracking objectives set by central government, DFID leadership needed to chart an overall approach to provide quality assurance over its bilateral investment cycle.

To this end, previous expenditure reviews were replaced by government-wide Comprehensive Spending Reviews (CSRs) and Public Service Agreements (PSAs). The implementation of government-wide Comprehensive Spending Reviews (CSRs) and Public Service Agreements (PSAs) require DFID to translate policy objectives into specific, time-bound objectives and targets.[137] Service Delivery

---

[130] Ireton (2013), p. 240.   [131] Ireton (2013), p. 240.
[132] Ireton (2013), p. 260.   [133] Ireton (2013), p. 241.   [134] Holzapfel (2016).
[135] Ireton (2013), pp. 48; 252.   [136] Valters and Whitty (2017), p. 8.
[137] Valters and Whitty (2017), p. 19.

Agreements (SDAs) explain how DFID would deliver these targets and how progress would be measured.[138] Value for money featured prominently in each PSA. According to Michael Barber, who spearheaded the Prime Minister's Delivery Unit at the time, the Blair government was the first to systematically integrate targets into its administrative culture.[139] Like USAID, DFID makes use of a corporate development results framework. It makes use of performance management tools like PRISM and ARIES[140] and regularly trains its staff on performance monitoring by establishing the Performance Assessment Resource Centre (PARC).[141] DFID produces annual performance reviews, end-of-cycle-reviews, and an institutional performance review.

By the early 2000s, DFID's evaluation system had evolved significantly, indicating a clear shift towards performance monitoring. Under the Cameron government, value for money concerns became DFID's top priority in aid management.[142] As in the United States, the growing influence of the value for money focus was reinforced by arms-length institutions such as the National Audit Office and DFID's its own Internal Audit Department, who scrutinise programmes and make recommendations about how to improve organisational effectiveness.[143] Since 2005, all project and programme documents have been made available to the public under the UK's Freedom of Information Act.[144] In 2010, the Cameron government went a step further to create an independent aid commission that would further scrutinise DFID's foreign aid delivery. In a press release to unveil the commission, DFID Secretary, Andrew Mitchell, underscores the importance of the value for money mantra,

The UK Government is dispensing with the power to sweep things under the carpet. The Commission will shine a light on where aid works and where improvements are needed. We will lead other donors in opening our books

---

[138] OECD DAC Peer Review – UK (2001), p. 55.
[139] As cited in Valters & Whitty (2017), p. 19.
[140] Aries was a new management system that integrated financial accounting, project databases, statistical and management reporting, budgeting and expenditure forecasting, and procurement. It helped measure and evaluate progress and increased the focus on the achievement of specific quantifiable goals; OECD DAC Peer Review – UK (2010), p. 59.
[141] OECD DAC Peer Review – UK (2001), p. 56.
[142] Valters and Whitty (2017), p. 9.   [143] Valters and Whitty (2017), p. 19.
[144] Barder (2005).

to independent scrutiny. We have a duty to squeeze 100 pence of value from every pound. (...) Results, transparency and accountability will be our watchwords and will define everything we do. The new Commission has the power to scale up the projects that have proved their success. It will be there to ensure we deliver on our promises.[145]

In 2014, we note that DFID has somewhat softened its domestic accountability focus to allow for more context-dependent accounting by adoption of so-called Smart Rules.

Overall, the economic management trajectory is broadly similar to that which we observe in the United States, although differences exist in the use and application of management tools, reporting procedures, and project design processes.[146] Overall evaluation focuses more on performance than traditional evaluation methods, and this share has increased over time.[147] Although the OECD DAC notes that DFID has managed to more clearly separate performance monitoring from evaluation, in the United States performance spills more into other forms of evaluation.[148] As in the case of the United States, the imposition of performance frameworks incentivises aid officials to select aid delivery channels that increase the probability that output will be in the form of pre-specified development results. These practices prescribe bypass under conditions of poor recipient governance. They also disincentivise aid officials from prioritising institution-building, which is more difficult to measure and requires longer time horizons for assessing aid success.

As a former DFID official suggested during an author interview,

The good side of having a performance system in place is that it pushes people to document the cost-effectiveness of the intervention. It exerts a relentless pressure to measure things, like governance, that DFID staff previously thought was unmeasurable. They now ask 'what particular indicator can you deliver me that Yemen is less of a basket case tomorrow than today?' This requires a lot of ingenuity and imagination, and people have been pushing the envelope of framing metrics. In the end, though, on balance, this pressure has pushed people to do more readily measurable things, like the bednet model in the health sector. There people would have a 100 million project for health and they would quote the most recent cost-effectiveness

---

[145] DFID (2010).   [146] Honig (2019).
[147] OECD DAC Peer Review – UK (2001), p. 56.
[148] OECD DAC Peer Review – UK (2006), p. 60.

RCT data on bednets, but when you look at what percentage of the total project was allocated to bednets, it was tiny. But, if you focus on the bits that are measurable, you naturally gloss over the much needed systems expenditure for which it is incredibly hard to demonstrate results.[149]

Sweden. Since the late 1980s, Sweden has pursued a managerial trajectory where organisational performance assumes a high place on the reform agenda.[150] In 1988, Parliament requested that the Swedish aid system adopt a system of management by objectives to improve its effectiveness in delivering foreign aid.[151] In the 1992/1993 Budget bill, Parliament demanded the introduction of management by results to further control aid organisations. In subsequent years, Sida has promoted an agency-wide effort to improve management practices in the agency, including new guidelines for managers. 'Sida at Work' recommended, for example, the use of logical frameworks as were in use at USAID and DFID to monitor progress and evaluate impact on a frequent basis.[152] From 1997 onward, Sida was required to submit yearly reports to Parliament on the level of target achievement and operational efficiency.[153] In 2003, the government presented its new 'Policy for Global Development', which calls for more careful monitoring and evaluation, and more results-based management in Swedish aid.[154] By 2005 performance monitoring was accepted as a concept, although an audit report on Sida's performance management found that the agency still needed to extend the use of the logical framework approach and that some uncertainty existed within Sida as to what the goals really are and how results should be measured.[155]

This requirement to measure and report frequently has implications for donor–recipient interactions insofar as it produces incentives for aid officials to prioritise projects that are more likely to deliver on the output and to generate results in the short run. Consider the following remark by a Swedish aid official during an author interview,

Our government is thinking in ever shorter time frames. If we were to build capacity in the recipient country, like for example a public accounting

---

[149] Interview with former DFID official, London, 24 June 2014.
[150] Hammerschmid et al. (2016), p. 162.
[151] Holmgren and Svensson (2005), p. 25.
[152] Holmgren and Svensson (2005), p. 5.　　　[153] Poate (1997), p. 18.
[154] OECD DAC Peer Review – SWE (2005), p. 52.
[155] Holmgren and Svensson (2005).

system, we would face difficulty in measuring progress in the short-run, and not be able to report much in one, two, or three years. In Swedish aid, we now have an extreme situation where we become obsessed with results and measuring results and in a way this may actually turn out to be harmful for what we do. We tend to choose the results and indicators that are easy to communicate and that are easily quantifiable and measured. There is a temptation to become short-sighted and not permit ourselves the long-term relations, and operations that are necessary for achieving the kind of results that we intend to achieve in the long-run. So, we end up doing things that we think are the best ones to do given the pressure on us to report and communicate, but it was not always so.[156]

Over the years, arms-length independent agencies like the Agency for Public Management and the National Financial Management Authority have played important roles in enforcing public management reforms across domestic and foreign policy areas, including foreign aid. In the context of neoliberal reforms, they have stepped up their auditing rates of Sida. To diffuse management ideas, government-wide associations such as the Swedish Directors-General Association bring together senior officials from Swedish state agencies for joint seminars on managerial practices and study abroad tours to learn from neighbouring countries' state management practices.[157]

When the Moderate Party took office in 2006, Sida's managerial trajectory that had begun in earnest under the Social Democratic Government advanced more quickly. In the context of government-wide reforms, the creation of a results-based management system became a top priority.[158] By 2009, domestic accountability concerns had moved centre stage. Through a series of measures, Sida had adopted a more corporate character, with much inspiration coming from how aid was managed at USAID.[159] For example, Sida had established, among other things, a Quality Assurance Committee to review each new proposal over USD 15 million for results orientation. Sida's new three-year operational planning tool required annual reviews of progress, rather than just a completion report. Sida had introduced a country reporting matrix that compelled country teams to identify indicators to assess progress at both country and sector levels and to monitor them annually. Sida introduced results objectives for

---

[156] Author interview with senior Sida official, 12 June 2013.
[157] Hammerschmid et al. (2016), p. 167.
[158] OECD DAC Peer Review – SWE (2009), p. 58.   [159] Vähämäki (2017).

both individuals and teams that link to corporate objectives.[160] In 2013, the OECD highlighted Sida's developments in the context of a donor peer review for having 'a strong culture of program monitoring in the field, which is appropriately budgeted for and undertaken in a timely manner'.[161]

In spite of Sweden's neoliberal trajectory in foreign aid, it is important to note that, in comparison with the United States and the United Kingdom, managerial reforms were not quite as far reaching.[162] For example, Swedish aid did not impose management tools or technologies to the same degree as in the United States and the United Kingdom. Nor did Sweden adopt standardised indicators in an attempt to generate generalised knowledge that is applicable across developing countries, without paying attention to contextual or particularistic concerns.[163] Several reasons come to mind that may have contributed to Swedish reluctance to promote wholesale change. It is possible, for example, that aid officials perceived managerialism as a threat to the Swedish administrative cultural tradition, which emphasises Weberian values, corporatism, and equality, while de-emphasising economic considerations.[164] Further, it is possible that officials considered wholesale managerial reforms as not equally applicable across government ministries and agencies; that, in the world of foreign aid, too much emphasis on organisational management techniques can produce pathologies that jeopardise the very objectives of reform. While propagated because of their supposed rationality, in practice, the introduction and maintenance of reporting and monitoring systems not only requires a significant commitment of human and financial resources but it can also at times be self-defeating insofar as the complexity of measuring, standardising, and reporting aid success through numbers fails to capture important nuances in development.[165] Or, a focus on economic management can undermine all important policy dialogue between aid officials and their partner governments that would advance reform and policy changes. The managerial gaze and its respective practices can even alienate governments because it treats their needs and interests as inferior to organisational demands. More recently, Sida has made a case that managerial techniques need to be

160 OECD DAC Peer Review – SWE (2009), p. 59.
161 OECD DAC Peer Review – SWE (2013), p. 124.   162 Vähämäki (2017).
163 Vähämäki (2017), p. 3.   164 Dahlström and Lapuente (2017).
165 Birdsall and Kharas (2010).

adjusted so that trust can grow between the aid agency and its developing country partners.[166] In spite of these propositions for how management concepts and techniques could be modified, performance and results remain a central focus in Swedish aid.

3.6 Managerial Practices in Germany and France

Although managerial practices bring private sector practices to the state, they can be used in a less command-and-control fashion. For example, the use of performance indicators can serve officials to assess risk in aid delivery ex ante and help evaluate whether government-to-government aid delivery was timely and efficient. The use of indicators can help orient foreign aid away from an input focus towards the more important question of achievement. They help orient governments away from focusing too much on following ex ante procedural rules, but do not necessarily lead to their abandonment. Employed in a more selective fashion, performance indicators can, in fact, be compatible with traditional public sector governance.[167]

In the 1990s, when the development of performance monitoring was in full swing in the United States, a 1993 BMZ summary analysis of programmes and projects revealed serious 'deficiencies in the definition of funding objectives' in about a quarter of the evaluated projects.[168] In 1994, 1998, and 2001 donor peer reviews, the OECD criticised the German aid system for doing too little from an accountability perspective; for doing too little to adapt to new directions set by the OECD and World Bank for aid management.[169] For example, it lacked training opportunities for civil servants on the systematic take up of management tools.[170] In 1998, the OECD wrote,

While project implementation is generally considered to be a strength of German development co-operation, problems are encountered regarding the definition of objectives and project planning. Although some improvements are reported, much remains to be done, in particular regarding targeting and setting up the conceptual base of the projects.[171]

---

[166] Vähämäki (2017), p. 205.   [167] Pollitt and Boukhaert (2011).
[168] OECD Aid Review – GER (1995), p. 8.
[169] OECD DAC Peer Review – GER (2001), p. 40.
[170] OECD DAC Peer Review – GER (2001), p. 34.
[171] OECD DAC Peer Review – GER (1998), p. 28.

Throughout the 2000s, the German aid system gradually introduced performance indicators in the planning, implementation, and monitoring of its foreign aid to modernise its foreign aid system.[172] For example, in 2002, the BMZ and GIZ agreed to adopt a new Development Policy Framework for Contracts and Cooperation (AURA), which requires GIZ to specify objectives, means, and expected results in contracting across the board.[173] It is also expected to monitor contract performance. By 2008, the BMZ, GIZ, and KfW had introduced individual staff performance targets within their organisations, although their application remains spotty, with variation across sectors.[174] Traditionally, the German auditing landscape has focused their evaluation efforts on the effect of funding on institution-building and living conditions in aid recipients, in spite of methodological challenges of demonstrating impact for measures that capture capacity gains and low evaluation budgets.[175]

In 2012, the creation of the German Institute for Development Evaluation (DEval) represents another step in modernising the German aid system. Up until then, select performance assessments were done for internal purposes only and not often shared beyond the project manager. Although reporting on performance has become more frequent over time, the DEval now serves as an important independent agency whose mission it is to evaluate the effectiveness of foreign aid. It does so alongside the BMZ and the National Audit office, who, compared to their counterparts in the United States, focus their auditing activities more on compliance and financial auditing.[176] Unlike independent auditing agencies in the United States, the United Kingdom, and Sweden, the DEval does not really serve the same watchdog function. Nor does it pursue stringent performance assessments of the kind that we note in the United Kingdom or the United States. Instead, the DEval is considered an independent actor that, through recommendations, contributes to learning and better strategy and policy-making. What is more, the DEval devotes substantial resources to helping partner countries develop evaluation capacities.[177]

---

[172] OECD DAC Peer Review – GER (2001), p. 40.
[173] OECD DAC Peer Review – GER (2005), p. 54.   [174] BMZ (2008), p. 70.
[175] OECD Aid Review – GER (1995), p. 28.   [176] Pollitt and Boukhaert (2011).
[177] DEval (2020).

In its 2010 and 2015 donor peer reviews, the OECD notes that managerial practices are only used selectively in Germany's aid system.[178] For example, the OECD notes,

Germany has gone some way towards linking its country programming and resources to results and aligning them with effective partner country performance assessment frameworks, where these exist. Germany's implementing agencies are using performance indicators that are broadly consistent with partners' national development strategies and partner countries' own results-oriented reporting and monitoring frameworks. Where Germany is providing support to program-based approaches it is harmonizing its monitoring and reporting requirements to a large extent.[179]

However, compared to developments in the United States and the United Kingdom, the use of performance indicators and efforts to monitor them remain incomplete and inconsistently implemented. Nor do these efforts push the aid system's capacity to its limits, as threatens to be the case in the United States.

Instead, the German aid bureaucracy has championed a more flexible approach that combines ex post and ex ante controls. It has done so to be able to take advantage of 'political windows of opportunity' at home and abroad.[180] Or, put differently, to be able to pursue more 'risky' financing, such as supporting state structures or finance policy change in aid recipients. A more balanced approach to aid administration reinforces statist tendencies insofar as the focus on showing short-run results is less pronounced. For example, the OECD notes that the share of German foreign aid that includes projects with activities that could generate easily measurable objectives targeted at identifiable target groups remained rather small. Instead, Germany largely pursues an indirect approach through comprehensive interventions on the macro and sectoral level. Measures falling into this category include, for example, support for policy change, institutional capacity building, and large infrastructural projects.[181] This is a pattern that contrasts with the pattern we observe in USAID and DFID.

Overall, I note that, since the 1990s, the German government has gradually reoriented its aid administration to become more

---

[178] OECD DAC Peer Review – GER (2015), pp. 20; 73.
[179] OECD DAC Peer Review – GER (2010), p. 79.
[180] OECD DAC Peer Review – GER (2005), p. 36.
[181] OECD DAC Peer Review – GER (2001), p. 34.

accountability-oriented. To that end, the German aid system has introduced some managerial practices, or better variants of it, to reform its aid system. But, unlike their neoliberal counterparts, the German government never considered managerial reforms to be the only game in town, and, consequently, managerial practices have never been as broad or far reaching. Instead, the donor continues to place value in legality, compliance, fairness, and other values inherent in traditional public sector governance. The role, not the individual, continues to be the basic organisational unit and bureaucrats follow rules and orders 'because they are given by officeholders as trustees of a legitimate and impersonal rational-legal order'.[182]

In France, we also observe a lukewarm reception for managerial practices but, as of the mid-2000s, managerial reforms have picked up steam and have led to a more comprehensive adoption of performance monitoring than we see in the German aid system. Unlike in Germany, France has pursued government-wide administrative reform at the federal level, mandated by the 2001 Institutional Act on Finance Legislation, the so-called LOLF. The bill required that all government agencies implement target-related programmes and budgets underpinned by the production of daily numerical targets and measurement indicators.[183] But, unlike in the United States, the adoption of managerial practices was not done with the same disruptive intention, nor with the objective of paradigmatic change in public administration. Instead, the link to performance was made selectively. For example, the OECD notes that the French aid system only uses project results and the monitoring of performance to better understand resource allocation but not to steer in other areas.[184]

Notably, the proposed shift in managerial culture as mandated by the LOLF clashed with beliefs that reaffirmed the role of the state in public sector governance and that did not believe that private sector management systems were the only answer to problems associated with foreign aid effectiveness. The passing of the LOLF led to widespread protests and implementation delays across French ministries, with notable resistance in ministries that promoted French foreign policy.[185] In a 2004 donor peer review, the OECD notes, 'There will

---

[182] Olsen (2008).   [183] COCOPS report by Bezes and Jeannot (2013).
[184] OECD DAC Peer Review – FRA (2008), p. 26; OECD DAC Peer Review – FRA (2013), p. 82.
[185] Boussard and Loriol (2008).

have to be some major shifts in mentality. The widespread strike that hit the MAE at the end of 2003, and the delays experienced in implementing the LOLF show just how much distance is yet to be covered.'[186]

By the end of the 2000s, the monitoring and evaluation systems had been overhauled to reflect a greater focus on ex post controls consistent with performance monitoring but remain limited to the budgetary context. A French strategy document of 2011 documents a further shift towards performance in budgetary terms. It documents that projects are subject to annual performance analysis and reporting, which compare forecasts and execution in budgetary and full cost terms as well as with respect to the objectives, indicators, and targets contained in the annual performance plan.[187]

The same strategy document also raises concerns over managerial reforms leading too far in a technocratic direction, where recipient governance problems are circumvented. It states that cooperation policy 'should avoid short-circuiting legitimate governmental and administrative bodies on the pretext of short-term aid effectiveness, as this might well undermine them.'[188] By reaffirming the importance of the state in public sector governance, the French aid system indicates its support for recipient state engagement and scepticism towards managerial practices that emphasise short-term results over long-run developmental impact. Overall, the French aid system remains far less codified in terms of targets and objectives than in the United States and the United Kingdom (Table 3.2).

3.7 Conclusion

In this chapter, I provided an in-depth study of my hypothesised institutional constraints mechanism across five donor countries. In doing so, I documented that aid systems not differ markedly in their institutional rulebooks across my cases. Under the rubric *Organisational Patterns*, I examined the scale of bureaucratic structures and the

---

[186] OECD DAC Peer Review – FRA (2004), p. 57.
[187] Directorate-General of Global Affairs, Development and Partnership (2011), p. 52, 56.
[188] Directorate-General of Global Affairs, Development and Partnership (2011), p. 33.

Table 3.2. *Summary of managerial practices in the management of foreign aid*

	United States	United Kingdom	Sweden	Germany	France
Financial resources devoted to performance and impact evaluation (as % of total programme)	>3%	1.5–3%	No info	<1.5%	no info
Comprehensive performance monitoring of projects and programmes	yes	yes	no	no	no
Institutionalised, comprehensive Performance Auditing	yes	yes	yes	no	no
Use of corporate results framework for aggregating results	yes	yes	no	no	no
Number of reports evaluating performance, progress and functions per year	>100	>100	>100	50–100	50–100
Requires accountability through direct attribution of results	yes	yes	no	no	no

principle by which foreign aid delivery was coordinated. Under *Managerial Patterns*, I examined the extent to which processes and behaviour, both within aid organisations and their relations with aid implementation partners, are governed by managerial practices.

Importantly, I elucidated how these different rulebooks incentivise aid officials to select different forms of donor–recipient engagement under similar international economic and poor recipient governance conditions. That is, how aid officials from neoliberal donors are more likely to select bypass, while their peers from traditional public sector donors continue to engage directly with recipient authorities in the implementation of aid. Furthermore, I elucidate how the different rulebooks lead to different aid priorities among OECD donor countries.

This chapter also elaborated on the origin of national structures by putting institutional developments in a historical context across my five cases. Drawing on research from historical institutionalists and public administration scholars, I document how, in the United States, United Kingdom, and Sweden, during critical historical junctures at different points in time, neoliberal reformers were able to loosen the constraints of existing structures and advance large-scale rationalisation and streamlining processes. I use my own qualitative data to show how these reforms affected national aid organisations in similar ways. At the same time, I show that Germany and France did not undergo similarly dramatic public sector reforms and maintained aid structures that reaffirm the role of the state in public sector governance. This implies that today, as for the many previous decades, German and French aid systems are set up to promote government-to-government aid, prescribing similar action moving forward.

In subsequent empirical chapters, I now put my argument to a series of empirical tests. As I suggested in Chapter 1, I leverage both quantitative and qualitative data tests for the cross-sectional dimension of my argument, which explains why marked heterogeneity exists in how donor governments deliver aid. Because of the lack of systematic data over time, I employ qualitative data from historical sources and interviews with aid officials to support the over-time dimension of my argument, which suggests that, as a donor transitions from traditional public sector to neoliberal forms of governance, the new institutional rulebook prescribes divergent action moving forward, and increases a donor government's propensity to bypass, all else being equal.

4 | Country-Level Evidence Linking Donor Political Economies to Variation in Aid Delivery

4.1 Introduction

The previous two chapters presented the theoretical framework and the causal mechanism that explain cross-national variation in foreign aid delivery tactics. My argument asserts that national structures, or the organisation of national aid systems in donor countries, encroach on donor–recipient interactions by imposing institutional constraints that authorise, enable, and justify particular aid delivery tactics while precluding others. In my theory, the causal mechanism has institutional origins. Yet, the constraining effects of institutions only tell part of the story. As I argued in Chapter 1, recent micro-institutional analyses of aid organisations have linked organisational constraints to aid decision-making; and, in doing so, they have theorised about or explained an ordered regularity in decisions within and across aid organisations.[1] They explain why rational, incentive-oriented aid officials behave the way they do given constraints that arise from formal rules of the game.

What I add to this debate is that, across donor governments, the character and direction of constraints vary markedly insofar as they reflect dominant beliefs about the role of states and markets in public sector governance at the time when institutions were created. Neoliberal doctrine is consequential for aid delivery in the United Kingdom and the United States because its rules prescribe and incentivise aid officials to select bypass under conditions of poor recipient governance. More traditional public sector beliefs are consequential for aid delivery in Germany and France, because their national aid organisations were set up to promote government-to-government aid delivery. My argument suggests that today's aid delivery decisions are shaped by institutional legacies that affect how aid officials choose to

---

[1] Martens et al. (2002); Honig (2018).

negotiate and interact with recipient countries; they influence the goals that aid officials prioritise in foreign aid, and how regimes think and measure aid success.

This chapter is the first of three empirical chapters, in which I assess the empirical utility of my theoretical framework. I begin my empirical testing at the macro-level, where I compare the impact of national structures on donor decisions to deliver aid to developing countries. Although I have specified my theory at the level of the individual aid official, my argument has implications for the country level insofar as I expect aid officials within the same aid organisation to follow institutional rules and practices. If the majority of aid officials engage in optimising behaviour in line with their aid organisation's objectives I expect individual aid decisions to aggregate up to the donor country level.

Specifically, I will analyse the main outcome of interest, foreign aid delivery decisions at the country level, across twenty-three OECD DAC donor countries. Although my central actors are aid officials within aid organisations, my institutional constraints mechanism suggests that, within the same organisation, formal rules and practices constrain officials to act in similar ways, and towards the goal of the organisation. If we can expect, as I do, that a majority of aid officials behaves in similar ways then we can expect individual decisions to aggregate up to the country level. The universe of recipient countries includes foreign aid eligible countries as defined by the OECD. I define foreign aid as public funding that donor governments use to promote development abroad that includes at least a 25 per cent grant element.[2]

As I will discuss later, the data for aid delivery channels are a relatively recent addition to the OECD CRS database. The temporal domain of the study ranges from 2005 to 2015. My statistical analyses show that robust support exists for the main hypothesis advanced in this book. I show that donor countries of neoliberal structures employ significantly different aid delivery tactics from their counterparts from traditional public sector economies under conditions of poor

---

[2] My definition of private aid excludes charitable giving. Although global philanthropy has increased over the years and has become an important pillar of international development, my research question explicitly focuses on the interaction between donor and recipient states. For recent studies that examine the drivers of private aid flows see Büthe, Solomon, and Mello e Souza (2012). Metzger, Nunnenkamp, Mahmoud (2010). Fuchs and Öhler (2021).

governance in the aid-receiving country. I begin this chapter by describing the foreign aid delivery measure, before turning to my key measures, whose interaction in the analysis enables me to directly test my argument: donor political economy type and the quality of recipient governance.

4.2 Measuring Foreign Aid Delivery: Between Bypass and Government Engagement

The outcome variable in this study is foreign aid delivery. As I argued in Chapter 1, political scientists and economists have only recently begun to study the different ways in which donor governments can go about delivering their aid. I seek to understand the factors that incentivise donors to be more likely to embrace bypass or engagement with recipient governments as their preferred aid delivery channel. I conceptualise government-to-government aid as any aid activity that involves the recipient government as an implementing partner. Examples of this type of aid delivery can include project and programmable aid or technical assistance.

In contrast, aid delivered through non-state development actors does not directly engage government authorities and goes to non-state actors for project implementation. Examples of what bypass looks like in practice include donor projects that directly fund international NGOs to implement the aid for them. Service delivery INGOs, like World Vision, Care, or Catholic Relief Services, among many others, typically have their headquarters in OECD donor countries but are well connected to local NGOs in developing countries, with whom they collaborate in the implementation of the aid. Donors can also directly fund local NGOs in the aid-receiving country but the proportion of direct delivery through local NGOs is low relative to aid delivered through INGOs.[3]

Donors can further channel bilateral aid through international organisations. The bilateral funding of IOs, also known as multi-bi aid, is different from the more conventional multilateral aid category. Unlike traditional multilateral aid that is given to IOs in the form of core contributions that enable IOs to spend the resources as they see

---

[3] For previous use of this definition of aid delivery tactics see Dietrich (2013, 2016).

fit,[4] multi-bi aid allows donors to earmark their contributions for specific purposes and countries.[5] Once funded by donors, IOs can choose to work directly with the public sector abroad. But as implementers of multi-bi aid, it is up to the IOs to hold the recipient government accountable and to ensure that the aid reaches the objectives as specified by the donor. Since the 1990s, bilateral financing of multilateral organisations has significantly increased and has begun to replace traditional multilateral financing as IO funding mechanism.[6]

To construct a measure of aid delivery I use data on official development assistance[7] drawn from the OECD's Credit Reporting System (CRS) bilateral aid activity database. The OECD has only recently begun to collect information on the 'channel of delivery'. Before 2005, the OECD reporting requirements did not ask for more granular information on how donors channel their aid by individual project.[8] Each individual project, including the amount of foreign aid provided, is coded as one of five possible aid channel categories. The categories include government-to-government aid delivery, which I identify as foreign aid that engages with the recipient government.[9] They also include bypass delivery, which includes aid delivered to multilaterals,[10] NGOs, public–private partnerships, and an 'other' non-state actor residual, which is empirically negligible. Among the non-state channels, the IO and NGO channels are by far the most common. Private sector or public–private partnership channels trail behind them in terms of usage. Although my conceptualisation of bypass aid includes many different non-state actors that each deserve more individual

---

[4] Studies of traditional multilateral aid allocation and effectiveness include Milner (2006); Girod (2008); Schneider and Tobin (2013).

[5] See Reinsberg et al. (2015).   [6] Dietrich et al. (2019b).

[7] Consistent with common practice in the literature on foreign aid, I exclude foreign aid flows that are concessional in nature and could be considered investment tools.

[8] The OECD's aid delivery coding does not include information on potential further steps in the delegation chain. That is, it does not provide data on other development actors that the principal aid delivery actor may bring into the aid delivery process. Future collection of these data would allow for interesting research questions to be answered concerning the chain of delegation of multiple development actors.

[9] According to discussions with the OECD DAC, this category includes a negligible proportion of tied aid that, as such, is not specifically identified in the reporting.

[10] International organisations such as the UN or the World Bank increasingly rely on bilateral aid as a source of financing. This has increased the number of projects that IOs implement directly on behalf of donor governments.

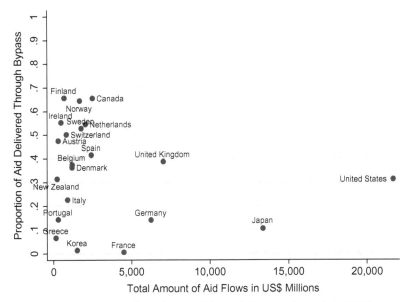

Figure 4.1 Proportion of aid delivered through bypass channels in 2010.
Source: Dietrich (2013)

scholarly attention as implementing actors, my research focuses on a donor's decision to directly engage with or bypass government authorities, leaving more individual attention for these actors for further research.

Consistent with my previous research on aid delivery, I operationalise a donor country's propensity to bypass the recipient government in straightforward manner: for each donor–recipient pair, I calculated the amount of aid that was delivered to the recipient country by non-state channels as a proportion of the donor's total annual commitment to that country.[11] To illustrate variation in the measure across donor governments, I plot, in Figure 4.1, the proportion of bypass aid that each donor country allocates (y-axis) over its total aid flows in 2010. Among OECD donors, Finland channels the greatest proportion of aid through bypass actors, nearly 70 per cent, followed by Canada, Norway, and Ireland. The United States outsources more than 30 per cent of its bilateral funds. At the low end of the bypass axis are France, Greece, and South Korea, which send

---

[11] Dietrich (2013, 2016); Dietrich and Murdie (2017).

less than 8 per cent of their aid through bypass channels. This cross-donor variation remains very similar throughout the temporal range of the empirical statistical tests, which ranges between 2005 and 2015.

In the statistical analyses that follow, I will log transform the bypass proportion. As Aitchison has shown, the advantage of log transforming proportional outcomes is that the outcome becomes effectively unconstrained, allowing for a straightforward estimation through OLS.[12] The coefficient of the log-transformed non-state share variable describes how the log ratio of non-state aid changes with respect to government-to-government aid. Importantly, the statistical analyses will also include a total aid per capita variable that serves to account for variation in overall magnitude of the aid. In the next section, I turn to a central concept in the book, the character of national structures.

4.3 Measuring Political Economy Type

My argument suggests that national structures constrain aid officials towards using particular aid delivery strategies while precluding others. In my theoretical framework, I make a broad distinction between two types of structures or political economies: I distinguish between national governance structures that are neoliberal in character and those that follow a traditional public sector logic.

As I have argued in previous chapters, neoliberal governance rulebooks incentivise aid officials towards bypass under conditions of poor recipient governance. Traditional public sector rulebooks, on the other hand, yield preferences for engagement with the government. Because rulebooks constrain aid officials of the same structure to hold a similar preference for one aid delivery tactic over the other, I expect delivery preferences to aggregate up and shape patterns of aid delivery at the country level.

Before I can test my argument across a large sample of twenty-three OECD DAC donor countries, however, I first need to operationalise political economy type. I need to measure whether the donors' national aid systems are on a neoliberal or a traditional public sector trajectory. My measurement strategy proceeds in several steps. First, I draw on pre-existing theoretical frameworks in the study of comparative political economy. Specifically, my donor typology builds on the binary

---

[12] Aitchison (1986).

political economy measure of the *Varieties of Capitalism* (*VoC*) literature.[13] *VoC* scholarship distinguishes countries or, better, market types by looking at how firms coordinate their activities. They emphasise market institutions as 'providing capacities for the exchange of information, monitoring, and the sanctioning of defections relevant to cooperative behavior among firms and other actors', including governments.[14] Variation therein has led to a typology that separates industrialised democracies into liberal market economies (LMEs) and coordinated market economies (CMEs). In LMEs, hierarchies and competitive market arrangements characterise how firms go about coordinating their activities. In CMEs, firms organise economic activity through institutionalised, non–market-based relationships that emerge from corporatist bargaining and/or include various forms of state intervention and regulation.

In my theory, I focus on state institutions that coordinate goods and service provision. On the one hand, there are political economies with neoliberal bureaucratic structures that coordinate goods and service delivery via competitive contracting. On the other hand, goods and service delivery is coordinated through more institutionalised arrangements, as is the case in political economies with traditional public sector structures. Consistent with the *VoC* measure of CMEs, I group Germany, France, Japan, South Korea, Germany, Austria, Netherlands, Switzerland, Italy, Belgium, and Luxembourg in a category that captures more statist and non–market-based coordination of goods and service delivery. In this category, I also include Spain, Portugal, and Greece, although they differ from other OECD countries insofar as they were recently recipients of EU assistance themselves. I then label this donor political economy type 'Traditional Public Sector'.[15]

Consistent with the *Varieties of Capitalism* coding, I group the following Anglo-American donor countries as being neoliberal political economies: United States, United Kingdom, Ireland, Australia, New Zealand, and Canada. In *LMEs*, governments organise economic activity and their relationships with firms largely through markets.

---

[13] For example, see Estevez-Abe et al. (2001); Hall and Soskice (2001); Franzese (2002); and Hall and Gingrich (2009).

[14] Hall and Soskice (2001), pp. 10–11.

[15] Any of the statistical results do not hinge on my decision to include Spain, Portugal, and Greece in the traditional public sector category. The results are similar on inclusion and exclusion of the three political economies.

Importantly, these political economies also structure their public sectors in a neoliberal image. To account for recent paradigmatic changes in public sector structures in Scandinavian political economies, I expand this category to include these countries. While, traditionally, Scandinavian economies have been described as neo-corporatist, economic crises in the 1990s brought about fundamental changes in public sector governance. In Chapters 2 and 3, I have explained this structural shift in more detail for Sweden. Other scholars have identified similar trends in other Scandinavian countries.[16] I thus include Scandinavian countries in the neoliberal category, with the label 'Neoliberal'. Throughout the statistical analyses that follow, I show, however, that results do not hinge on my decision to include Scandinavian countries in the neoliberal governance type category. Instead, I will present results of Anglo-Saxon and Scandinavian donors side by side, showing strong similarities in aid delivery patterns.

As a final step, I draw on one proximate expression of how political economic order occurs in politics in donor countries – a measure of 'domestic government outsourcing' of services used by the general government as per cent of GDP. This measure is continuous and captures the nature of bureaucratic structures across donor political economies. These data are from the OECD National Accounts Database and measure the degree to which governments use private contractors or the third sector to provide support services or perform back office functions.[17] These data are available for 2000, 2009, and annually from 2012 onwards. I construct an outsourcing average between 2000 and 2015 for domestic government outsourcing of goods and services used by general government as per cent of GDP. In Figure 4.2, I plot this average of government outsourcing across all donor governments. This measure varies considerably from 3.5 per cent in Japan to 11 per cent in Finland.[18] The outsourcing average in 2009 is only a 2 per cent increase from the average outsourcing in 2000, which implies that outsourcing does not change much over time.

---

[16] See Steinmo (2010); Gingrich (2011); and Cohen et al. (2012) for compelling accounts of this change.
[17] OECD National Accounts Statistics (2020).
[18] For robustness, I constructed an alternative proximate variable, government outsourcing of goods and services used by general government as per cent of government spending, and plot the distribution in Figure 4.A1 in the appendix.

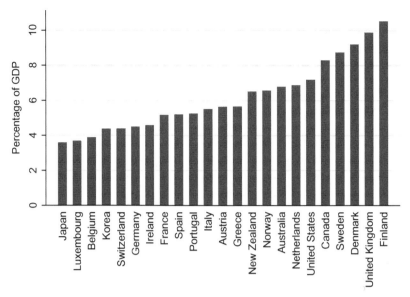

Figure 4.2 Domestic government outsourcing across individual donors. Calculated averages of expenditures on government outsourcing to non-state actors for goods and services used by the government as percentage of GDP, 2000–2015.
Source: OECD National Accounts Database (2018), and authors' calculation

Figure 4.2 demonstrates that Anglo-Saxon and Scandinavian political economies have higher levels of domestic outsourcing than the remaining OECD countries that are in my sample. This continuous measure lends empirical support for my typology insofar as the line-up of countries along the outsourcing continuum reflects how I have grouped countries into neoliberal and traditional public sector categories.

4.4 Measuring Risk in Aid Delivery

My argument predicts that purposeful aid officials from different national structures should promote different aid delivery tactics under condition of risk in aid–recipient countries. To test the argument, I need a measure of risk. As I have elaborated in previous chapters, a key source of risk in aid delivery is aid capture through a corrupt or weak recipient state. I defined aid capture broadly as resulting from the mismanagement of aid in the recipient country, either by intentional diversion through corrupt authorities or the waste of aid due to weak institutions and/or lack of absorptive capacity.

As my interviews across donor countries revealed, aid officials, when making decisions about aid delivery, seek out information about governance risks abroad and turn to in house or publicly available indicators that allow for comparisons across countries and over time. If recipient governance is of relatively high quality, donor officials expect a lower quality of aid capture. Low governance quality, on the other hand, signals higher risks of capture. The quality of recipient governance is, therefore, an important factor in aid delivery decisions.

To measure the quality of recipient governance, I draw on data from the World Bank's Governance Matters project.[19] I select this measure because aid officials most frequently referred to it. In more than half of my interviews with donor officials, respondents specifically mentioned World Bank governance data as informing their risk assessments. The Governance Matters project offers cross-country data for six governance dimensions: voice and accountability; regulatory quality; government effectiveness; rule of law; corruption control; and political stability and violence.

I construct the RECIPIENT GOVERNANCE variable by including corruption control, government effectiveness, regulatory quality, and rule of law as indicators and averaging across them for any given year. The governance variable ranges between -2.5 and $+2.5$, which I rescaled to 0 and 5, with higher values representing a higher quality of governance. Among aid-receiving countries, there is no country with a governance rating of 4 and higher. Subsequent graphical illustrations will provide a 0 to 4 range of the variable.

As illustrated by Figure 1.1 in Chapter 1, donor governments deliver foreign aid differently across recipient countries that vary in the quality of governance. There, we saw that France, Japan, or Germany do not bypass in Sudan and Sri Lanka to the same extent as the United States, the United Kingdom, and Sweden. These differences lend prima facie evidence to my claim that heterogeneity in foreign aid delivery results from national structures, from different orientations about the appropriate role of the state in public sector governance and goods and service delivery.

---

[19] Kaufman et al. (2011).

Figure 4.3 Delivery patterns for binary political economy division. Whisker plots show data range with 95 per cent confidence intervals. Black diamond symbol of whisker plot represents average bypass share in badly governed countries, while white diamond symbol shows bypass average in well-governed countries.

Source: OECD CRS database (2018)

Figure 4.3 presents further descriptive statistics that provide prima facie evidence that differences in aid delivery tactics exist across political economy types. The y-axes represent the mean share of bypass. This mean share is separated into aid recipients that have 'bad governance', depicting countries with governance scores of 1.5 and lower, and aid recipients that have 'good governance', or a governance score of 2.0 and higher. The whisker plots are useful for illustrating the change in bypass share across the two types of political economies when moving from environments of high probability of aid capture to low probability ones. The raw data indicate that, regardless of political economy type, donors are responsive to the probability of aid capture in the recipient country. Importantly, however, the degree to which countries bypass recipient governments varies by political economy type. The graph depicts differences between the traditional public sector and neoliberal donor countries, whereby neoliberal countries exhibit greater reliance on markets than their traditional public sector counterparts, which is indicated by the relatively steep drop in bypass shares as the quality of governance changes from bad to poor.

4.5 Other Covariates in the Statistical Analyses

Aside from the two main explanatory variables, my statistical model of donor bypass includes a number of other covariates. By controlling for these other covariates, I subject my hypothesis linking political economy type and foreign aid delivery to the hardest possible test. To inform my choice of covariates, I turn to the literature on foreign aid policy and select variables that have been shown to be systematically associated with foreign aid decision-making; or, that could be potential alternative explanations for variation in donor bypass or engagement. All time-varying right-hand side variables are lagged one year to reduce bias resulting from simultaneity. Although most of the covariates in my model appear in research on foreign aid, not all of them have an a priori unambiguous relationship with foreign aid delivery.

Political and Other Factors in the Recipient Country

In the first instance, I include a measure for recipient democracy in the model. I control for DEMOCRACY based on the understanding that donors may conceive of democratic institutions as political constraints that limit the ability of recipient governments and bureaucratic officials to capture aid flows.[20] DEMOCRACY is measured using the combined score of the Freedom House civil liberty and political rights indicators.[21] To make the scale of the measure more intuitive I invert DEMOCRACY so that '1' represents the lowest level of democracy, whereas '7' stands for the highest level of democracy. The Freedom House data are widely used among donor governments in their assessments of democracy. During interviews with donor officials across OECD donor countries, the Freedom House measure was an often mentioned source of information on political regimes.[22]

---

[20] Winters and Streitfeld (2018).   [21] Freedom House (2018).
[22] In robustness tests I use Polity2 as measure for democracy. The results are very similar.

I then control for NATURAL DISASTER DEATHS. I include this variable based on the understanding that a greater number of deaths caused by natural disasters in the aid recipient, as recorded by the EM-DAT database, may prompt donors to provide a larger share of the pie to non-state development actors that are specialised in post-disaster reconstruction efforts.[23] At the same time, the opposite might also be true: it may be that donors decrease the proportion of bypass aid in countries with a high death toll to ensure that the government has the capacity to respond to citizen calls for help.

Following a similarly ambiguous logic, I include an indicator of political stability, or low-scale CIVIL CONFLICT, in the model. On the one hand, political instability, by creating grievances in poor countries, may provide incentives for donors to deliver aid through the non-state or bypass channel to ensure that aid reaches people in need. Alternatively, it may also encourage donors to deliver the aid through the recipient government so that it might help stabilise the situation. The measure comes from the PRIO database.[24]

In the next step, I include DISTANCE to account for the geographical proximity between donor and aid-receiving countries. As distance between donors and aid-receiving countries grows, government-to-government relations between donor and recipient governments are expected to weaken, thus increasing donor propensity to channel aid through non-state development actors. The distance data are drawn from Bennett and Stam's Eugene software and are logged.[25]

Strategic Factors and Aid Characteristics

I include several covariates that capture donor strategic, non-developmental objectives in the aid recipient country. In nearly every study of foreign allocation, scholars include a measure that captures economic ties between donor and recipient country. Across most studies, this variable is a consistent predictor for aid levels: as economic ties become more intense, donor aid goes up. In the context of aid delivery, I expect TRADE INTENSITY, measured as the logged sum of imports and exports between the recipient and the OECD countries from the IMF-DOT database, to decrease the proportion of bypass aid.[26]

[23] EM-DAT (2018).   [24] Gleditsch et al. (2002).
[25] Bennett and Stam (2000).   [26] IMF (2018).

In a similar vein, I include FORMER COLONY status, as recorded by the CIA World Factbook. Through this variable, I seek to capture long-standing historical ties between donors and aid-receiving governments that are likely to bias aid delivery in favour of government-to-government aid. This variable is coded '1' if the donor–recipient dyad have a colonial history, and it is coded '0' if there is no colonial history for any given dyad.

The literature studying strategic factors suggests that donors use aid to buy votes. To control for the potential of vote-buying affecting variation in foreign aid delivery, I include a binary measure, SECURITY COUNCIL, which indicates whether the aid recipient is an elected member on the UN Security Council. As works by Kuziemko and Werker as well as Vreeland and Dreher show, donor governments use aid to buy votes from rotating members of the UN Security Council.[27] In the context of foreign aid delivery, we would expect vote-buying to decrease the share of bypass aid.

I incorporate a binary control for MAJOR POWER status to account for the fact that major donors, including the United States, United Kingdom, Japan, Germany, and France, are in dominant positions of influence in world politics.[28] As Hans Morgenthau and others have argued, global powers, more than minor powers, have many geostrategic goals that can be advanced through direct aid provision. When these goals are in conflict with developmental objectives, donors may be more likely to pursue realpolitik and opt for the government-to-government channel, even if their economic orientation, however institutionalised, would support bypass of recipient authorities.

Finally, I include a set of variables that describe the sectoral characteristics of the aid flows. I include a variable that measures TOTAL AID PER CAPITA to account for important variation in donor contributions across recipient countries. I further include a measure that captures DEMOCRACY AID and SOCIAL SECTOR AID individually. I would expect democracy aid to have a positive effect on bypass insofar as democracy aid may be more likely to be associated with civil society support. Traditionally, democracy aid has been studied in the context of democracy or good governance promotion where donors

---

[27] Kuziemko and Werker (2006); Vreeland and Dreher (2014) find that the United States, Japan, and Germany give more aid to Security Council members, but France and the United Kingdom do not.
[28] Dietrich and Murdie (2017).

seek to strengthen bottom-up accountability in the recipient country by directly financing civil society actors.[29] Importantly, good governance promotion through civil society is distinct from my argument that associates bypass with neoliberal thinking about a reduced role of the state in public services in favour of non-state actors. It is therefore imperative that I control for good governance efforts in the analyses. By including SOCIAL SECTOR AID, I control for the possibility that donors channel aid through non-state development actors because NGOs and IOs may be in a better position to deliver services. This is distinct from my argument that suggests that donors turn to non-state development actors because they want to decrease the probability of aid capture.

4.6 Methods of Analysis

To test the correlates of aid delivery, I fit a linear ordinary least square (OLS) model. To account for the proportional nature of the bypass share data,[30] I log-transform the dependent variable, as indicated previously. To account for heteroscedasticity across recipient countries, I calculate clustered standard errors on the recipient country. For purposes of robustness, I also calculated clustered standard errors on the donor and the donor–recipient dyad. The results from the statistical analyses remain unchanged.

I also investigate my data for potential bias from autocorrelation. Serial correlation bias arises in my case when there is a systematic relationship between my outcome variable, foreign aid delivery, and a lagged version of itself; or put differently, when the past share of bypass predicts the future bypass share. To investigate bias from serial correlation I apply the Wooldridge test for panel data.[31] The significance of the test-statistic indicates that autocorrelation may introduce bias in the estimates. I therefore include a lagged dependent variable in some of the model specifications.

---

[29] Goldsmith (2001); Finkel et al. (2007); Scott and Steele (2011); Bush (2016); Ziaja (2020).
[30] I provide a brief discussion of the statistical implications of using a proportional outcome measure, that is, compositional data analysis, in the chapter appendix.
[31] Wooldridge (2002), pp. 282–83.

4.7 Discussion of Results

I now turn to discuss the results of the statistical analyses. Table 4.1 presents my findings. The first two columns present OLS results for two specifications (Models 1 and 2) that do not include political economy variables. They include the RECIPIENT GOVERNANCE measure and other potentially confounding factors. Model 1 includes three-way fixed effects for donor, recipient, and year. This specification allows me to show the average effect of RECIPIENT GOVERNANCE prior to introducing the donor invariant political economy measures. Model 2 includes the lagged dependent variable but excludes fixed effects. The results show that donors, on average, condition aid delivery tactics on the quality of recipient governance. The coefficient of RECIPIENT GOVERNANCE is negative and statistically significant. This indicates that donors, on average, react to changes in governance. As governance improves, donors reduce the share of aid channelled through non-state development actors. As governance quality declines, donors increase the aid through bypass channels.

To test my main argument, I turn to results in Models 3–8. Initially, my discussion of the results focuses on the size and direction of the coefficients. Subsequently, I visualise the marginal effects by graphing the interaction. Models 3 and 4 present results using the binary division between neoliberal and traditional public sector categories. Model 3 includes recipient and year fixed effects. I treat the fixed effects specification as the main model in my analyses. Recipient-year fixed effects allow me to account for characteristics of recipients and time periods which are left unspecified by the model, and thus only estimate coefficients from variation of more comparable units. Model 4 corrects for serial correlation by including the lagged dependent variable.[32] The coefficient of RECIPIENT GOVERNANCE expresses the statistical association between governance and bypass for the omitted group of traditional public sector countries, which is negative as expected.

At the heart of the statistical results are the political economy variables and their respective interactions with recipient governance.

---

[32] The size of the sample decreases from Model 3 to Model 4 because of the inclusion of the lagged dependent variable.

Table 4.1. *Donor political economies and bypass, 2005–2015*

	1	2	3	4	5	6	7	8
Governance, Ec. Inst lagged	-1.808*** (0.611)	-0.422*** (0.143)	-1.140* (0.627)	-0.466*** (0.166)	-1.045 (0.631)	-0.443*** (0.166)	-0.663 (0.528)	-0.714** (0.296)
Neoliberal × Rec Gov			-0.783** (0.302)	-0.199 (0.136)			-0.602*** (0.219)	-0.376 (0.288)
Neoliberal			4.076*** (0.637)	1.585*** (0.283)			4.572*** (0.456)	2.980*** (0.575)
Anglo-Saxon × Rec Gov					-0.617** (0.289)	-0.130 (0.130)		
Anglo-Saxon					4.247*** (0.557)	1.630*** (0.250)		
Scandinavian × Rec Gov					-1.231** (0.492)	-0.372 (0.253)		
Scandinavian					4.063*** (1.071)	1.631* (0.537)		
Major Power			-2.208*** (0.169)	-0.948*** (0.100)	-2.401*** (0.172)	-1.040*** (0.102)	-3.157*** (0.206)	-4.029*** (0.191)
Freedom House, rescaled lagged	-0.140 (0.184)	-0.082* (0.046)	-0.156 (0.189)	-0.082* (0.048)	-0.155 (0.191)	-0.087* (0.049)	-0.061 (0.183)	0.101 (0.092)
Natural Disaster Deaths, lagged	0.027 (0.025)	0.103*** (0.017)	0.035 (0.026)	0.087*** (0.017)	0.035 (0.026)	0.090*** (0.017)	0.024 (0.023)	0.195*** (0.027)

139

Table 4.1. (*cont.*)

	1	2	3	4	5	6	7	8
Civil Conflict	0.261	0.330**	0.250	0.288*	0.243	0.290*	0.214	0.119
	(0.235)	(0.150)	(0.224)	(0.154)	(0.220)	(0.155)	(0.175)	(0.291)
Distance	-0.254	-0.266***	-1.568***	-0.255***	-1.726***	-0.290***	-1.261***	-0.720***
	(0.210)	(0.072)	(0.200)	(0.079)	(0.199)	(0.080)	(0.226)	(0.175)
Former Colony	0.393	-0.288*	-0.836***	-0.148	-0.953***	-0.206	-1.093***	1.670***
	(0.370)	(0.158)	(0.315)	(0.154)	(0.317)	(0.157)	(0.412)	(0.413)
Trade Intensity, lagged	-0.150*	-0.249***	-0.558***	-0.171***	-0.614***	-0.178***	-0.401***	-0.342***
	(0.064)	(0.021)	(0.058)	(0.022)	(0.061)	(0.023)	(0.063)	(0.044)
Security Council Rotating Membership	-0.216	0.166	-0.201	0.124	-0.207	0.131	-0.375*	0.280
	(0.166)	(0.160)	(0.181)	(0.162)	(0.180)	(0.162)	(0.162)	(0.314)
Total Aid, lagged	-0.061***	-0.078***	0.022	-0.023	0.034	-0.025		
	(0.020)	(0.023)	(0.022)	(0.026)	(0.022)	(0.026)		
Democracy Aid, lagged	-0.013*	0.007	0.007	-0.009	0.013	-0.006		
	(0.008)	(0.005)	(0.010)	(0.006)	(0.010)	(0.006)		
Social Sector Aid, lagged	-0.029**	-0.005	-0.021	0.008	-0.024*	0.007	0.032***	
	(0.011)	(0.009)	(0.014)	(0.009)	(0.014)	(0.009)	(0.010)	
Economic Sector Aid, lagged								0.038***
								(0.007)

Total Bypass Share, lagged		0.604***		0.585***		0.584***		
		(0.009)		(0.010)		(0.010)		
N	19120	17063	19120	17063	19120	17063	19211	19211
Year FEs	yes	no	yes	no	yes	no	yes	yes
Recipient FEs	yes	no	yes	no	yes	no	yes	yes
Donor FEs	yes	no	no	no	no	no	no	no
R2	0.378	0.428	0.202	0.436	0.205	0.436	0.190	0.119

Various model specifications. * p < .1, ** p < .05, *** p < .01

The interaction NEOLIBERAL × REC GOV offers a direct test of the empirical implication of my argument. This implication suggests that donors differ systematically in how they approach aid delivery under conditions of risk: compared to donors of traditional public sector economies, I expect donors with neoliberal governance structures to be more likely to condition their aid delivery tactics on changes in recipient governance.

Conforming with this empirical expectation, the coefficients of the interactions in Model 3 and Model 4 are negative. The negative direction of the coefficients suggests that compared to their traditional public sector counterparts, donors with neoliberal bureaucratic structures reduce the share of bypass aid as the quality of recipient governance improves. Or, expressed differently, only donors with neoliberal structures increase the share of bypass aid if the quality of recipient governance declines. The statistical significance of the interaction term in Model 3, the fixed effects specification, suggests that the differences are systematic across donor recipient observations in my sample. A glance at the positive and significant NEOLIBERAL constituent terms in Models 3 and 4 suggests that a move from a traditional public sector economy to one that is underwritten by neoliberal governance principles yields a significant increase in bypass when governance quality in the recipient country is 0.

In the next step, I plot the interaction and visually inspect how the statistical relationship between donor type and aid delivery unfolds across different levels of recipient governance. Figure 4.4 plots the interaction resulting from Model 3 in Table 4.1, which uses the binary political economy distinction as independent variable. The y-axis on the right side presents a histogram of the RECIPIENT GOVERNANCE variable that depicts the frequencies of observations occurring across the different values of the variable. It indicates that the majority of observations occur between the governance values 1 and 3. The y-axis on the left displays the share of bypass. As the coefficients of Table 4.1 indicate, the slope of NEOLIBERAL is consistently negative. I capture differences in statistical significance through 95 per cent confidence intervals, which I visualise through stars. The stars along the slope indicate that the effects of NEOLIBERAL are significantly different from traditional public sector donors. Overall, the results indicate that a change from the baseline category of traditional donors to the neoliberal

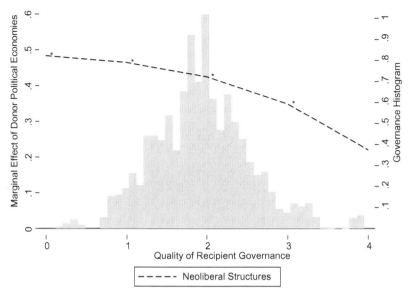

Figure 4.4 Marginal effects of political economy types across quality of recipient governance. Effects of binary political economy division estimated by Model 3. Stars signal statistical significance at the 0.05 from the traditional public sector donor category.

category yields a statistically significant increase in bypass share. For recipient countries that score a 1 on governance quality, for example, neoliberal donors increase bypass by 0.48 from the baseline traditional public sector type. In better-governed recipient countries that score a 3 on governance quality, the statistically significant increase associated with becoming a neoliberal political economy type is smaller at 0.36, relative to the baseline traditional public sector donor category.

These findings offer statistical confirmation of initial inspections of the raw data as presented in Figure 1.1. Bad governance, as is the case in Sudan and Sri Lanka, encourages the United States and the United Kingdom to bypass recipient authorities to a greater degree than Germany, France, or Japan. When governance quality is higher, as is the case in Tanzania, the same donors are willing to engage with the state. As I have argued in Chapter 2, this is because, on the one hand, a better governed recipient is a more trustworthy and capable development partner. Given how expensive it is to set up functioning parallel structures in recipient countries, engagement with the recipient government may turn out to be more efficient under the right circumstances, when the recipient government is expected to deliver on promises in aid implementation. On the other hand, every donor, regardless of economic orientation, recognises that there is a non-financial cost of not engaging with the government insofar as it limits policy dialogue with the recipient governments. Even the staunchest defender of markets is thus likely to opt for government engagement under favourable circumstances.

Models 5 and 6 in Table 4.1 present results for regressions that disaggregate the neoliberal political economy type into a more fine-grained typology that separates Anglo-Saxon from Scandinavian donor economies. As before, while Model 5, my main specification, includes recipient and year fixed effects, Model 6 includes the lagged dependent variable. The coefficients for ANGLO-SAXON and SCANDINAVIAN have positive and significant constituent terms. This indicates that moving from the omitted traditional public sector donor type to the neoliberal or Scandinavian type yields a significant increase in bypass when governance quality in the recipient country is 0.

The two neoliberal donor economies have negative interaction terms, which indicate steeper negative slopes, relative to the omitted traditional public sector donors. Significance tests of the political economy constituent terms reveal that neoliberal and Scandinavian donors do not differ significantly from one another in terms of their aid delivery tactics. This suggests that they exhibit similar degrees of responsiveness to changes in recipient governance.

As was the case in Model 4, which includes the lagged dependent variable, the interaction term results are in the expected negative direction but not statistically significant. Given the large and persistent effect of donor political economy alone on aid bypass decisions, it is arguably challenging to pick up the additional marginal effect of its interaction with donor governance. Across the board, however, these analyses offer strong evidence that, while neoliberal donors typically tend to make greater use of bypass aid, they also react more strongly to recipient governance than their traditional public sector counterparts.

One may be concerned that the results of Models 3–8 are sensitive to how I group countries into the political economy types. I address this potential criticism by using the jackknife resampling technique.

The basic idea behind the jackknife variance estimator in this application is that it systematically re-computes the statistic, dropping individual donor countries from the political economy type one at a time from the sample set. From this new set of replicates of the statistic, an estimate for the bias and an estimate for the variance of the statistic can be calculated. The changes are slight and negligible and increase my confidence in the specification of the models.

Finally, Models 7 and 8 probe the extent to which cross donor differences persist across different aid sectors. I divide foreign aid into two sectors, one consisting of social sector aid while the other incorporates aid projects that contribute to economic development.[33] I then re-estimate the main model with recipient and year fixed effects for social sector aid (Model 7) and economic sector aid (Model 8) separately, using the binary political economy measure. For both social sector and economic sector aid models, I find results consistent with my expectations: neoliberal donors give greater proportions of bypass aid, and they react more strongly to increases in recipient governance by further reducing the proportion of bypass aid. In the case of economic sector aid, the interaction term misses statistical significance at the aggregate level. In Figure 4.5. I visualize the interaction effects. A comparison of the two panels suggests that the slope associated with the economic aid sector may be slightly steeper than the slope of the social aid sector but that this difference is negligible. Instead, the interaction patterns are similar across sectors. This supports the claim that donors use the same decision-making model for all aid sectors.

The impact of national structures, revealed in the statistical analyses of foreign aid delivery, is marked: In poorly governed countries, a shift from a traditional public sector donor to one whose national aid system is organised by a neoliberal rulebook yields an increase in bypass under conditions of poor recipient governance, all else being

---

[33] My definition of social sector includes aid earmarked for education, health, population, water supply and sanitation, government, human rights, and other social infrastructure and services. Economic sector aid includes aid earmarked for transport and storage, energy generation and supply, banking and financial services, business and other services, agriculture, forestry, and fishing, industry, mineral resource and mining, construction, trade policy and regulation, tourism, as well as multi-sector/cross cutting aid. The corresponding sector-specific results are not sensitive to the exclusion of any categories subsumed under the social and economic sector.

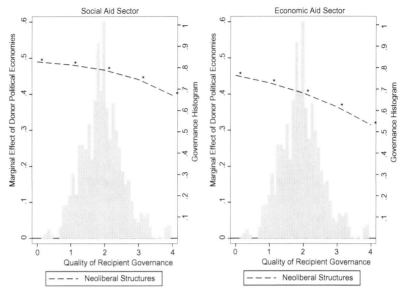

Figure 4.5 Marginal effects of political economy types across quality of recipient governance. Left panel: Effects of binary political economy division for social sector aid only, estimated by Model 7. Right panel: Effects of binary political economy division for economic sector aid only, estimated by Model 8. Stars signal statistical significance at the 0.05 from the traditional public sector donor category.

equal. Among the strategic covariates that I included in the model, some but not all exhibit a systematic effect on aid delivery. For example, the coefficient of TRADE INTENSITY is statistically significant and negative, as predicted, suggesting that higher levels of trade cooperation between donors and recipients make it less likely that donors employ bypass tactics under conditions of poor governance. Similarly, the coefficient of MAJOR POWER is statistically significant across most models, and its negative sign is in the predicted direction: as donor status changes from a minor to a major donor category, the share of bypass decreases. Contrary to expectations, the coefficient of FORMER COLONY has a negative sign in the main model specifications, which suggests that donors are more likely to employ bypass tactics when delivering aid to their own former colonies. Finally, the indicator SECURITY COUNCIL ROTATING MEMBER does not significantly correlate with aid delivery across any of the specifications, suggesting that vote-buying may not be a systematic concern when aid officials decide about aid delivery tactics.

Concerning the other covariates that describe affairs in the recipient country, results are mixed. Although the coefficient of DEMOCRACY behaves in the predicted direction, it is not significantly correlated with bypass. This may suggest that donors, on average, are not as responsive to the quality of government as they are to the quality of governance, all else being equal. As expected, NATURAL DISASTER DEATHS is positively and significantly correlated with bypass, suggesting that donors increase the share of aid delivered through non-state actors as the magnitude of the disaster increases, measured by number of deaths incurred during a natural disaster. The results for low-level CIVIL CONFLICT are insignificant across the models. Yet, the positive direction of the coefficient was anticipated. It suggests that donors, albeit not systematically, have a tendency to increase the amount of bypass during years of conflict. This finding surely merits further study and has implications for important research that investigates aid allocation during or after episodes of conflict.[34] The results associated with characteristics of aid, *Total Aid*, *Social Sector Aid*, and *Democracy Aid*, lack consistency across the model specifications.

To ensure robustness of the results, I estimated several additional models that differ in their specifications and whose results are available in Table 4.A1 in the Appendix. In Model 1, I present results from a stripped down specifications that includes a minimal set of control variables and the main fixed effects specification. In Model 2 and 3, I use only cross-sectional information and estimate between-effects models that average data across donor recipient dyads. The results remain very similar.

Finally, readers might be concerned about potential endogeneity. If bypass undermines or strengthens state institutions then the quality of governance is endogenous. However, the theory does not offer clear predictions for the direction in which the bias works. In interviews, more statist donor government officials suggested that bypass hurts recipient state institutions because it diverts resources away from the public sector and towards parallel structures that often lack alignment with public sector policy. Neoliberal government officials, on the other hand, believe that bypass creates incentives for recipient

---

[34] For example, see Flores and Nooruddin (2009, 2012).

governments to improve their governance quality as non-state actors compete with the recipient public sector for foreign aid. To address the concern statistically, I estimate a model that controls for INITIAL GOVERNANCE, which measures the value of governance during the first year of the estimation sample. By measuring governance at the earliest possible time, I minimise the effect of bypass on governance. What is more, recipient governance is a measure that changes slowly over time. Accounting for initial governance, the results do not change.[35]

4.8 Conclusion

The statistical evidence that I presented in this chapter reveals that national structures influence donor–recipient interactions in a systematic way. During the time-period 2005–2015, on a large sample of twenty-three OECD DAC donors, political economies that are on a neoliberal governance trajectory are systematically more likely to select bypass tactics when recipient countries are poorly governed than their traditional public sector counterparts. This finding is robust to different model specifications and robustness tests.

However, a quantitative test at the country level overlooks the more fine-grained institutional and processual evidence that can only be collected at the level at which the theory is specified, at the level of the aid official who works for a national aid organisation whose structures either take on neoliberal or traditional public sector character. In the next chapter, I evaluate originally collected data from closed- and open-ended surveys with aid officials across six donor countries. Apart from asking aid officials from different aid organisations to reveal their aid delivery preferences across recipients that vary in quality of governance, I collected data about institutional practices and goals of their organisations. By leveraging individual level data, I am able to produce further evidence that institutional constraints define the delivery choice set insofar as they enable and justify particular aid delivery tactics, while precluding others.

---

[35] The results for estimations that include *Initial Governance* in the estimations can be found in the Appendix, Table 4.A1, Model 4. The interaction effect of Model 4 is plotted in Figure 4.A2.

For example, my argument posits that political economy differences should be palpable when comparing administrative rules and practices. Aid officials who work in bureaucratic structures that are organised around neoliberal norms are incentivised to frequently measure and account for results. To accomplish this, the institutional rulebook prescribes aid officials to frequently monitor and report about the level of input, activity, output, or outcome of an aid initiative; and to evaluate success in the short run. Their peers in traditional public sector economies, on the other hand, do not operate under the same pressure for results.

In addition, my argument suggests that national structures also influence what objectives aid officials seek to accomplish with aid, or consequently, what they perceive as aid success. Because formal rules and practices are in place to help aid organisations reach their objectives, I expect neoliberal rulebooks to advance different objectives than rulebooks of traditional public sector donors. Neoliberal rulebooks, more than others, prioritise results that can be measured easily, and in the short run. I thus expect aid officials from the two political economy types to provide systematically different answers when asked about whether they preferred aid to provide short-term basic needs relief or long-term capacity building that is much more difficult to measure and requires more time to bear fruit. Depending on the ideological origins of the institutional rulebook, whether it is neoliberal or has a traditional public sector character, aid officials prioritise either results delivery or recipient capacity-building; and, consequently, are more likely to choose either bypass or engagement with the recipient government as the rational course of action.

These important additional implications cannot be tested at the country level. They require data collection and analysis at the micro-level. They also require me to shed light on what motivates and drives aid officials within their organisations, and to go beyond standard assumptions about what makes agents tick, including their preferences, knowledge, understanding, and expectations. I turn to an examination of micro-level evidence in the next chapter.

Appendix

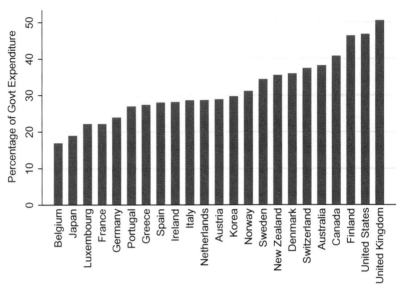

Figure 4.A1 Domestic government outsourcing across individual donors. Calculated averages of expenditures on government outsourcing to non-state actors for goods and services used by the government as percentage of government spending (excluding transfers) across donor countries, 2005–2015. Source: OECD National Accounts Database (2018), and author's calculation

Table 4.A1. *Donor political economies and bypass, 2005–2015*

	A1	A2	A3	A4
Governance, Ec. Inst	-1.587^{***}	-2.252^{***}	-1.300^{***}	-1.140^{*}
lagged	(0.571)	(0.234)	(0.308)	(0.627)
Neoliberal × Rec Gov	-0.937^{***}	-0.912^{**}	-0.376	-0.783^{**}
	(0.286)	(0.358)	(0.352)	(0.302)
Neoliberal	4.484^{***}	4.855^{***}	3.456^{***}	4.076^{***}
	(0.610)	(0.736)	(0.730)	(0.637)
Major			-2.833^{***}	-2.208^{***}
			(0.290)	(0.169)
Freedom House,			-0.137	-0.156
rescaled lagged			(0.094)	(0.189)
Natural Disaster			0.287^{***}	0.035
Deaths, lagged			(0.055)	(0.026)
Civil Conflict			0.498	0.250
			(0.406)	(0.224)
Distance			-0.930^{***}	-1.568^{***}
			(0.196)	(0.200)
Former Colony			-0.657	-0.836^{***}
			(0.521)	(0.315)
Trade Intensity, lagged			-0.519^{***}	-0.558^{***}
			(0.051)	(0.058)
Security Council			2.339^{**}	-0.201
			(0.937)	(0.181)
Democracy Aid, lagged			0.053^{***}	0.007
			(0.016)	(0.010)
Social Sector Aid,			-0.049^{**}	-0.021
lagged			(0.019)	(0.014)
Total Aid, lagged	-0.217^{***}	-0.308^{***}	-0.019	0.022
	(0.020)	(0.034)	(0.050)	(0.022)
Initial Governance				-3.539^{***}
				(0.924)
N	21136	21136	19120	19120
Aid dyads		2819	2611	
Year FEs	yes	no	no	yes
Recipient FEs	yes	no	no	yes
R2	0.147	0.15	0.247	0.202

Various model specifications. $^{*}p < .1$, $^{**}p < .05$, $^{***}p < .01$

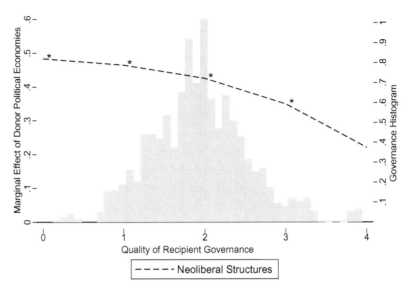

Figure 4.A2 Marginal effects of political economy types across quality of recipient governance. Effects of binary political economy division controlling for initial governance, Model A4, Table 4.A1. Stars signal statistical significance at the 0.05 from the traditional public sector donor category.

5 | Testing the Argument with Evidence from Aid Officials from the United States, United Kingdom, Sweden, Germany, France, and Japan

5.1 Introduction

Statistical analyses of country-level evidence in the previous chapter demonstrated a statistically robust and substantively strong association between national structures and foreign aid delivery. Through a series of statistical tests, I showed that donor governments of neoliberal governance structures promote significantly different aid delivery tactics than their counterparts from traditional public sector economies in the aid-receiving country. To further convince the reader about the utility of my theoretical framework, this chapter provides evidence on the empirical relevance of the micro-foundations of my argument.

To get at the origin of bypass or engagement with recipient governments, my theory places aid officials and their institutional constraints front and centre. My argument asserts that within their organisations aid officials, as purposive agents, seek to optimise their behaviour. They follow institutional rulebooks and thus take a particular course of action under conditions of poor recipient governance. Depending on the character of the rulebook, whether it is neoliberal or has a more traditional public sector character, aid officials are more likely to choose either bypass or engagement with the recipient government as the rational course of action. This suggests that past decisions to organise state institutions, including national aid organisations, make it difficult and costly to change aid delivery tactics, even when these policies are considered dysfunctional.

To establish the empirical relevance of my micro-theory, this chapter leverages results from quantitative and qualitative analyses of originally collected individual-level survey data of foreign aid officials across multiple OECD donor countries. Between 2013 and 2015, I interviewed sixty-five selected aid officials from six OECD DAC donor countries, the United States, United Kingdom, Sweden, Germany, Japan, and France. The broad scope of aid officials from different donor governments is unprecedented for original field research in the study of foreign aid decision-making. The interviews consisted, in the first part, of a closed-ended within-subject survey to collect quantitative data. As I will argue in more detail later, I believe that these data enable me to observe individual decisions of relevant decision-makers in a theoretically informed and controlled environment. They allow me to strengthen my causal claims linking governance orientations and foreign aid delivery at the individual level of the decision-maker. The second part consisted of an open-ended interview that asked aid officials follow up questions about their response in the closed-ended survey. These follow up questions were included to further probe the processual logic of my argument as well as the causal mechanism.

Several factors motivate my decision to conduct empirical tests at the level of the individual aid official across donor countries. First, it provides a direct test of the micro-foundations of my theoretical argument. While the evidence in the previous chapter indicates that my theorised preferences of aid officials aggregate up to the donor country and influence aid commitments and donor–recipient interactions in a profound way, a quantitative country-level study does not provide any evidence about the individual decision-maker, the aid official, who I posit assumes a central role in aid delivery decisions. According to my theory, it is the aid official who is responsible for the delivery of aid projects and programmes, who processes and evaluates information about recipient governance, and who engages with the recipient government or non-state development actors on the delivery of foreign aid. Only a direct test at the level of the aid official can reveal whether officials formulate their preferences in aid delivery consistent with my theoretical expectations and, most importantly, whether significant differences exist across aid officials from different political economies.

To evaluate whether information about deteriorating quality of recipient governance evokes systematically different reactions from donor officials of different political economies, I exposed all foreign aid officials to three recipient country scenarios that shared the same level of development but that varied only in how I described the quality of their recipient country governance, including a scenario with good governance, one with a corruption scandal, and one that conveyed the presence of weak state institutions. Immediately after the different scenarios, I asked officials to decide which aid delivery channel they perceived as 'best' to implement foreign aid in the aid-receiving country. Consistent with the main measures used in the cross-country analyses conducted in Chapter 4, I asked them about how much government-to-government aid they perceived as appropriate given governance conditions. I also asked them to rank delivery channels that included the government-to-government channel as well as other non-state actors that deliver foreign aid abroad, including international organisations, international and local NGOs, and private sector companies. This tests the micro-foundations of the argument.

Second, an empirical shift to the individual level enables me to test important empirical implications that are related to more fine-grained organisational aspects of the theory, such as, for example, intra-organisational rulebooks and administrative practices that incentivise agents to deliver aid in particular ways. My argument about political economy differences suggests that aid bureaucracies follow different rules, procedures, and standards depending on their type. In Chapter 2, I posit, for example, that aid officials from neoliberal aid organisations evaluate aid success under shorter time horizons than their counterparts in traditional public sector organisations. This practice incentivises aid officials to select aid projects and delivery channels that are successful in the short run, introducing systematic bias towards bypass channels under conditions of poor recipient governance. While Chapter 3 demonstrates how aid practices differ markedly across select donor countries, this chapter will substantiate my claim about systematic differences in practices with quantitative evidence and interview quotes, collected at the level of the aid official.

As I will show, I tested this empirical implication by asking aid officials specific questions about their evaluation practices. As expected, I find that the mean number of years that aid officials wait before they reflect on success of aid efforts is lower among officials from the United States, the United Kingdom, and Sweden than among officials from Germany, France, and Japan.[1] This suggests that the link

---

[1] To the careful reader it might come as a surprise that Japanese officials are part of this chapter's empirical analyses, while Japan is not a case that I used to illustrate the causal mechanism in Chapter 3. While I had initially planned on including Japan as a case, my lack of Japanese language skills made it difficult to comprehensively research and evaluate information about the Japanese aid system that is available mostly in Japanese. The interviews with Japanese aid officials were conducted in English.

between beliefs and foreign aid delivery decisions operates through the organisation of public sectors and, more specifically, national aid systems. These insights help me push back against claims that aid organisations share similar rules and practices, and we can thus assume them to structure donor–recipient interactions in similar ways.

Third, this chapter leverages individual responses by aid officials to support the important contention that aid success is at heart subjective, and endogenous to the organisation of the public sector. As purposeful agents, aid officials, across aid organisations, maximise goals of their organisations. If institutional rulebooks are set up to generate results in foreign aid delivery, officials will prioritise aid objectives that can be more easily measured. If rulebooks are set up to promote recipient capacity, then officials will prefer to use more aid towards this particular objective than the other.

The empirical evidence establishes that in the world of foreign aid there may not just be tensions between donors and recipient governments, but there are also tensions among donors in what aid should accomplish and how it should be given. These differences, I argue, find their origin in national structures and the material incentives that actors derive from this structure. These incentives, as I have argued in previous chapters, generate regular and stable tendencies to deliver aid more through bypass than through engagement with recipient governments in poorly governed countries. These tendencies, due to their material origin, are difficult to change, even when donor governments want to cooperate more with one another on how to promote development abroad. For years, scholars and practitioners have pushed for a more coordinated approach to poverty but donor coordination in the field remains lacklustre, as indicated by research.[2] My argument implies that national structures may be at the heart of donor cooperation problems and any significant and lasting change in delivery patterns would first require changes to national structures.

Finally, qualitative evidence from the open-ended interviews allowed me not only to evaluate the plausibility of my causal mechanism, institutional constraints. Insights from the open-ended part of the interview also enable me to assess an important claim of this book: that institutional constraints, and not ideas or ideology per se, guide

---

[2] Knack and Rahman (2007); Winters (2012); Nunnenkamp et al. (2013); Steinwand (2015).

aid officials in their decision-making. Time and time again, the interviews revealed that aid officials consider themselves first and foremost constrained by rules. Although different ideas about aid delivery float around and are debated among officials within organisations, existing rulebooks remain determinative, even when existing practices of aid delivery are considered dysfunctional. Such candid engagement by aid officials substantiates my claim that beliefs in governance approaches alone, though frequently debated among aid officials of the same organisation, do not incentivise aid officials to act in a systematic way. As I argued in Chapter 2, I expect beliefs only to be consequential when in line with the institutional rulebook.

By combining macro- and micro-level empirical analyses, I make a substantial contribution to a literature which has, thus far, limited their empirical strategies to either country-level or individual-level data but rarely both. In the next section, I turn to a more detailed description of survey design.

5.2 Foreign Aid Officials as Research Subjects: Scope and Methods of Recruitment

This section describes the scope of the survey and methods of recruitment. I collected a unique data set of current and former officials across six countries who have direct experience in foreign aid decision-making. The six countries are the United States, the United Kingdom, Sweden, Germany, France, and Japan, and I chose them for the following reasons: I sought to target large donor countries whose share of aid makes up a substantial share of the overall aid flows from OECD donor countries. Since 1990, these six donor countries never provided less than 70 per cent of overall aid flows from OECD DAC donor countries. Also, I exploit variation in my independent variable, governance orientations. The binary political economy typology as developed in Chapters 2 and 3 and operationalised for the first time in the context of cross-country analyses conducted in Chapter 4 categorises France, Germany, and Japan as traditional public sector economies. The United States, the United Kingdom, and Sweden, on the other hand, are categorised as economies that are on a neoliberal trajectory. Among these cases, Sweden, as described in Chapters 2 and 3, represents an interesting transition case, as it has recently undergone a transformation in political economy type from coordinated to market-oriented after extensive neoliberal reforms reorganised the public sector and the provision of goods and services.

Within the select donor countries, I accounted for the fact that decisions about foreign aid delivery are made by officials belonging to different ministries, aid agencies, and aid implementing agencies, although the degree of decentralisation in decision-making varies by donor country. For instance, more than twenty government or department units make decisions about foreign aid spending, although the lion's share of spending goes through the United States Agency of International Development (USAID), the State Department, the Treasury, and the Millennium Challenge Corporation. In Japan, the Ministry of Foreign Affairs is responsible for aid policy and the Japanese International Cooperation Agency is in charge of delivering aid through Japanese, international, or local partners. In the United Kingdom, on the other hand, the Department for International Development (DFID), at the time of writing this book, was the primary institution in charge of foreign aid. My sampling strategy sought to reflect the heterogeneity of foreign aid actors within donor countries by recruiting respondents from different government agencies when multiple agencies were tasked with foreign aid delivery.[3]

My recruitment efforts targeted current and former aid officials who have direct experience in foreign aid decision-making within their organisation. The aid officials in my sample had garnered this experience either at the middle or upper management levels of their organisation. At these levels, aid officials feel the direct pressure of contributing in the best way possible to their organisation's foreign aid objectives. At the same time, they interact with recipient authorities and other donor officials and are thus tightly clued into political, non-organisational incentives in foreign aid. My recruitment strategy of donor officials was non-random. It included different methods of recruitment. For example, I relied on recommendations by aid officials from inside the aid organisations with whom I had cultivated professional relationships over the years. In other cases, academic colleagues suggested contacts within aid organisations who then directed me to relevant officials. In some cases, I used organisational charts or direct

---

[3] Table 5.A1 in the appendix lists the number of interviews by donor country and agency.

calls to identify senior aid officials who were heading departments or ministry units. Finally, several interviews came about because aid officials with whom I conducted interviews encouraged me to contact relevant colleagues within their organisation.

As other scholars have pointed out, the direct study of elites, more broadly defined, can be difficult. For example, Hafner-Burton, Hughes, and Victor suggest that 'experienced elites are difficult to obtain as subjects because they are generally busy, wary of clinical poking, and skittish about revealing information about their decision-making processes and particular choices'.[4] In the process of collecting the individual-level data for this book, however, I found aid officials to be more interested and cooperative than previous papers had made me believe.[5] The overall response rate for the combined closed- and open-ended survey was 69 per cent. Compared to existing survey research that draws on elite subjects, this response rate is relatively high.

I believe that several factors facilitated recruitment. First, I spent a considerable amount of time trying to identify relevant people to contact and used existing connections to approach each particular contact. Second, once I had identified a contact, I invested time and resources into (often multiple) direct follow-ups or through their secretaries. In several cases, I needed to persuade busy aid officials to participate. For example, I made a case for why a comparative study of aid delivery tactics was of value for them; or how it might inform their own work. Third, I noted that aid officials appeared to be at greater ease when I talked or wrote to them about my own background as a development practitioner in Bosnia from 2002 to 2004. Though the recruitment was time and resource-intensive, an overall positive reception and interesting exchanges with aid officials motivated me to continue to try to, where applicable, further specify and test IR theories at the level of the individual decision-maker.

Over a period of twenty-eight months, I collected qualitative and quantitative data from my respondents. I did so primarily in person, either face-to-face or by telephone.[6] While the majority of interviews was conducted face-to-face, telephone interviews proved efficient, particularly if respondents agreed to be interviewed after I had already

---

[4] Hafner-Burton et al. (2013), p. 368.   [5] Dietrich et al. (2021).
[6] In a few instances, aid officials who needed to cancel a face to face or telephone interview filled in the quantitative survey online.

visited their headquarters; or, as was the case for my Japanese respondents, if the office was located in a more distant region. In general, telephone interviews provided aid officials with more flexibility as they could schedule the interview at short notice. Between the two main interview methods, I did not notice significant differences in length, although the average length of face-to-face interviews was, at fifty minutes, slightly longer than for the telephone interviews, which were around forty-five minutes.

In the process of setting up the interviews, many respondents asked for their names to remain confidential. However, a majority allowed me to attribute their response to their organization. Several respondents explicitly said that they could be more candid if they remain anonymous; that they could be more forthcoming about the challenges they face in decision-making and how their own views and beliefs may at times contrast with what the agency wants them to do.

Initially, I was concerned about not being able to provide greater transparency regarding my sources but, ultimately, the decision to trade off transparency for more detailed off-the-record information seemed justified. I wanted aid officials to be candid and unbiased when responding to my questions.[7]

5.3 Integrating Closed- and Open-Ended Survey Components: Design and Implementation

As suggested previously, my interviews with sixty-five aid officials included a structured survey component and an unstructured one where I asked aid officials open-ended questions. The purpose of the closed-ended structured survey was to test my theory of decision-making with quantitative evidence at the individual level. The open-ended interview component then asked a series of follow-up questions where I asked aid officials to say more about the process that guided their aid decision-making and its origins inside the organisation. On most occasions, aid officials in face-to-face or telephone interviews were eager to expand on the answers they had given during the closed-ended interview, either by putting decision-making into the context of

---

[7] See Dietrich et al. (2021) for guidance on how to design and implement survey experiments with elites.

their aid organisation or reflecting further on the importance of risk for foreign aid delivery, and the corresponding process of decision-making. Such reflections proved very valuable from a theoretical and empirical perspective. For example, I asked them why they selected the aid delivery channels that they chose in the closed-ended survey. Across the board, aid officials were keen to specify why and how they arrived at their decisions to bypass or engage.

My interviews further serve to push back against potential alternative explanations. To demonstrate the empirical usefulness of my argument, I need to show, for example, that aid officials from neoliberal aid organisations do not choose bypass under conditions of poor governance because they believe that, at any given moment where aid delivery decisions are made, it is a more appropriate approach. Although ideas matter insofar as they shape the rules and character of aid organisations, aid delivery decisions result, so I argue, because aid officials pursue material interests in the context of their institutions. My interviews revealed that aid officials felt constrained and limited in their ability to respond to high risk in aid-receiving countries, whereas at times they might have opted for a different tactic.

The focus of the closed-ended survey was to evaluate empirical support of my argument at the individual level and to see whether my institutional constraints mechanism received empirical support. To test my argument I employed a within-subject survey design,[8] which exposes each individual aid official to information about three different recipient countries that describe the state of the world in aid recipient countries. That is, I presented the aid officials with hypothetical scenarios about three countries (Country A, Country B, and Country C) that share the same development features and patterns but vary in how I describe the quality of governance. Country A has a relatively good governance environment, while Country B exhibits weak state institutions, and in Country C the recipient government is involved in a major corruption scandal.

Before I add further details about the survey's treatment conditions, I want to explain my choice of within-subject design for this particular survey. The alternative design would have been a between-subject design, where I would have randomly assigned aid officials to only

---

[8] See McDermott (2002) for a discussion of within and between-subject designs.

one governance condition. There are three advantages of within-subject designs. First, within-subject designs require fewer participants than between-subject designs. Because individual aid officials react to all three treatments, I get three data points per individual. For a between-subject design, I would have needed three times as many aid officials to get the same number of data points in my final sample. A significant increase in sample size would have required significantly more resources and time. What is more, at the early stages of the research design I was quite uncertain about how aid officials would react to invitations to participate in my research. After all, the basso continuo from previous research was that recruiting elites was a particularly difficult and time-consuming endeavour.[9] To reduce concerns over sufficient statistical power, I thus chose to implement a within-subject design.

Second, within-subject designs minimise random noise. Going into the survey, I worried about the error variance associated with individual differences among the aid officials across several donor countries. In a small-N, between-subject experimental set-up, it was very likely that, despite random assignment into the treatment conditions, remaining differences among aid officials would have created random noise that may have made it less likely to uncover significant differences between the conditions. Potential factors that contribute to these individual differences even after randomisation include, for example, aid officials' own history, their background knowledge, and survey-taking context. These differences could affect their responses, in spite of random assignment to any one of the treatment conditions.

Third, I believe that the within-subject design approximates the process of decision-making across donor countries. As my interviews with aid officials revealed, aid officials not only look at individual recipient countries in isolation but they make risk assessments across all of their aid-receiving countries, and they consider the ensemble of aid recipients when making individual aid delivery decisions. In many instances, aid officials, when learning about the different country scenarios, volunteered comparisons with actual countries. Country A, whose description in the survey I will present later, for example,

---

[9] Hafner-Burton et al. (2013).

was frequently referred to as a good performer in the donor officials' portfolios.

While I believe that within-subject design is the optimal choice for this particular study, it is important to identify its limitations. Because within-subject designs expose respondents to multiple treatments, it is possible that responding to the first treatment, regardless of treatment substance, will influence the aid officials' choices of aid delivery tactic in the second and third scenario. Carryover effects would thus act as confounders for the responses to subsequent treatments.[10] One type of carryover effect is a fatigue effect, where aid officials might get tired or bored responding to the treatment and therefore might perform differently in the latter treatment conditions than they do in the first. Being exposed to Country A first might also change how aid officials perceive or interpret their decision task in the subsequent country scenarios B and C. Or, aid officials might become more practiced at responding to the country descriptions.

I believe that neither of these potential carryover effects is likely to manifest itself in the survey. I minimise any lasting concerns over potential fatigue effects by limiting the number of scenarios to three. I also minimise concerns over practice effects by using accessible language to describe the scenarios and employ straightforward measures to capture aid delivery choices. Overall, the survey design approximates real world decision-making insofar as aid officials think about risk and aid allocation by comparing countries on how they score on quality of governance. While this is certainly not the only dimension, it is one that evokes systematically different reactions across political economy type. The hypothetical nature of the treatments allows me to isolate the quality of governance dimension in a way that using real world recipient country examples does not. By using specific country examples in the vignettes, the individual aid official might consider other confounders, including historical, economic, or geostrategic concerns, as consequential for aid decision-making. This would pose important challenges for estimating treatment effects through a cross-national individual-level survey.

Survey Treatments. The within-subject survey component consists of three hypothetical recipient country scenarios that vary only in how

---

[10] Charness et al. (2012).

they described the quality of governance in the aid-receiving country. My argument predicts that changes in the quality of recipient governance cause changes in aid delivery tactics, but that the degree to which these tactics change depends on political economy differences, or the micro-institutional environment in which the aid official operates.

All respondents begin their evaluation with Country A. I decided to anchor respondents because I was concerned that aid officials from different countries may differ in how they respond to the information presented in the treatments. A failure to account for this potential heterogeneity might result in (incorrect) findings that mask treatment effects. By starting each survey with Country A, I ensured that aid officials across different countries were anchored around a common reference point as they make their evaluations and decisions about foreign aid delivery channels.

I constructed Country A as a proxy for what development practitioners call a 'good performer'. A good performer exhibits relatively low levels of corruption and relatively high levels of indigenous capacity; and thus poses relatively little threat to government-to-government aid delivery in developing countries. In such an environment, aid officials should opt for government-to-government when determining the relative effectiveness of the recipient government and other channels in implementing the foreign aid project. The Country A scenario reads as follows,

Imagine that your country allocates bilateral aid for development in Country A, which is an average low-income country. The country's economic growth has been modest, yet consistently positive. More children are enrolled in schools and infant mortality has declined. However, poverty remains widespread. Corruption is relatively low and state capacity is relatively strong.

The large majority of all the aid officials, on learning about Country A, reacted to the vignette by describing Country A as a 'good performer', or 'more trustworthy partner', or 'less risky', without receiving a prompt. These reactions not only served as a valuable 'manipulation check' insofar as my hypothetical country description triggered the kinds of associations that I had hoped to encourage but they also suggest that the anchoring vignette is equivalent across all respondents and perceived as representing the same absolute position on the aid recipient spectrum. The downside of anchoring respondents on Country A is that the results need to be interpreted with the particular question order in mind: that is, my inference is valid for contexts in which aid officials evaluate poorly governed countries after having received and reacted to information about a well-governed country. Though all officials received Country A as their first scenario, the subsequent order of the hypothetical scenarios of Country B and C was random to ensure that the responses would not be biased as a result of a specific question order (of either B followed by C or C followed by B). In terms of content, the descriptions of Country B and C are identical to Country A, except for the description of the country's governance characteristics. Country B captures a country that has weak state institutions.[11]

Imagine that your country allocates bilateral aid for development in Country B, which is an average low-income country. The country's economic growth has been modest, yet consistently positive. More children are enrolled in schools and infant mortality has declined. However, poverty remains widespread. Most people agree that Country B lacks state/absorptive capacity. The state institutions are weak and the national government is not capable of doing a good job in managing the country's economic and social resources in a way that improves the conditions for the average people. There is not much evidence of large-scale corruption, however.

Country C differs from Country B only in the type of governance problem that I present. While Country B suffers from capacity problems but is relatively free from large-scale corruption, Country C exhibits a major problem with corruption insofar as high-level officials were embroiled in a corruption scandal of a very high magnitude.

[11] Existing studies that have theorised about the consequences of risk associated with aid capture by government suggest that risk of aid capture increases in more corrupt recipient countries. In my argument, as I suggested in Chapter 2, I broaden the definition of risk thereof by including weak state institutions. Information about weak state institutions should signal risk insofar as indigenous institutions cannot assure that donor funds will be used for their intended purposes. I thus expect donor officials to respond to information about corruption and weak state institutions in the same way. Although corruption and weak state institutions often overlap and are correlated, I build in two separate scenarios where one highlights problems in corruption (Country C), while the other highlights problems of state capacity (Country B). They serve as robustness checks for my thesis.

Compared to Country B, however, the country does not lack state capacity and can promote indigenous development.

Imagine that your country allocates bilateral aid for development in Country C, which is an average low-income country. The country's economic growth has been modest, yet consistently positive. More children are enrolled in schools and infant mortality has declined. However, poverty remains widespread. The country's state institutions exhibit indigenous development capacity. Recently, however, an independent international audit revealed that senior government officials were involved in a large-scale corruption scandal whereby government funds of more than US$ 50 million were used to pay foreign and local companies for services that were never delivered.

Outcomes. Subsequent to presenting each country scenario, I asked respondents to answer questions about their aid delivery preferences in their capacity as aid officials. My argument posits that aid decision-makers react to changes in the quality of governance in the recipient country and that aid officials from different political economies differ in the degree to which they use bypass tactics under conditions of bad governance in the aid-receiving country. The first question asked respondents to rank-order five aid delivery channels, including the recipient government, international organisations, international NGOs, local NGOs, and private sector actors. The scale ranges from 5 'works best for my country' to 1 'works worst for my country'. I focus on the rank-order associated with aid delivered through the recipient government. The second question asked respondents to determine the amount of government-to-government aid out of overall aid flows to the country, with answer categories including 'none', 'some', 'quite a bit', 'a large amount', and 'all'. Both of these outcome questions, particularly the second one, closely mimic the cross-country analysis undertaken in Chapter 4. Consistent with the cross-country results from Chapter 4 I would expect heterogeneity in governance orientation to explain different reactions by donor officials to the same information about a deteriorating quality of governance.

Finally, my survey seeks to test empirical implications of the theory that pertain to the modes of governance that shape how aid officials assess the effectiveness of foreign aid. My argument posits that, on average, donor officials from countries whose bureaucracies rely on competitive benchmarking practices for determining the relative effectiveness of the recipient government in aid implementation are under pressure to evaluate more frequently than donor officials from coordinated market economies. They are also under more pressure to evaluate the effectiveness of foreign aid in the short run, rather than focusing on the long-run effects on aid. To measure this difference, the survey asks officials to identify the appropriate time horizon for the evaluation of foreign aid success, measured in number of years. I expect respondents from France, Japan, and Germany to indicate preferences for longer time horizons than their counterparts from the United States and Sweden.

To further shed light on the effect of neoliberal governance on aid officials' preferences for short- versus long-term development goals, I asked aid officials to consider the trade-offs between short-run (emergency) and long-run (state-building) aid goals and asked them to state how much of the overall aid should be directed at long-run state-building, compared to short-run goals. The answer categories included 'none', 'some', 'quite a bit', 'a large amount', and 'all'. Consistent with the previous question, I would expect respondents from France, Japan, and Germany to exhibit a preference for aid directed at long-run capacity building, and respondents from the United States, the United Kingdom, and Sweden to be more favourably inclined towards short-term assistance.

As a follow-up to this question, I asked officials whether they perceived differences in views for prioritising either short- or long-term development goals across OECD donor governments, offering a binary 'yes' or 'no' answer option. Turning next to perceived consequences associated with different national orientations about the role of the state in goods and service delivery, I asked aid officials to indicate the extent to which they thought these differences would hamper donor coordination in developing countries, with answer categories including 'not at all', 'occasionally', 'frequently', and 'always'. Although a systematic analysis of the ramifications of differing aid delivery preferences on donor coordination is beyond the scope of this study and should be investigated in future research, the last two questions help shed light on officials' awareness of existing differences in governance orientations and whether they perceive them as fundamental enough to impede international cooperation in foreign aid.

5.4 Closed-Ended Survey of Foreign Aid Officials: Results

I draw my inferences about the way in which information about the quality of governance in aid-recipient countries affects aid officials' views by looking for differential responses across my aid delivery measures between aid officials from different political economies when the quality of governance deteriorates. My argument predicts that changes in delivery tactics when moving from Country A to Country B or from Country A to Country C differ significantly by national orientation. I expect officials from the United States, the United Kingdom, and Sweden, on average, to change towards greater levels of bypass than their counterparts from France, Japan, and Germany; and I expect these differences to be statistically significant.

First, I evaluate changes in aid delivery preferences using simple differences across the country scenarios. As described previously, aid officials were asked to rank five different aid delivery channels from best to worst in response to information about a country with good governance (Country A), a country with weak state institutions (Country B), and a country with high-level corruption (Country C). My argument predicts that officials who operate in aid bureaucracies that are organised around neoliberal norms are more likely to resort to bypass tactics in countries with poor governance than their counterparts who work in aid bureaucracies that are not organised around market norms, but whose institutions embody more statist or neo-corporatist principles.

Figure 5.1 shows the averages in rank-order by country groupings across the three different country scenarios. The figure visualises the distribution of rank-order responses between aid officials from different political economy types through whisker plots that include a 95th confidence interval. These raw data lend prima facie support for my argument. On average, aid officials across both types of political economies felt that government-to-government aid was the preferred channel of delivery for well-governed countries. It is worth noting that although respondents from France, Japan, and Germany exhibit a slightly higher mean than their counterparts from the United States, United Kingdom, and Sweden, the difference is not statistically significant. I further note that among respondents from France, Japan, and Germany, few respondents deviate from ranking government first after

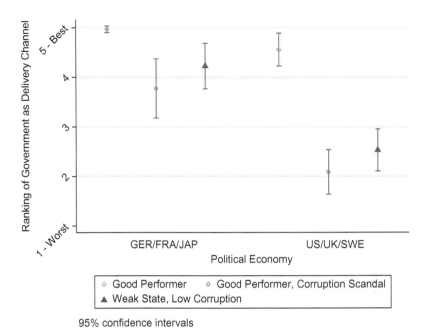

Figure 5.1 Point estimates and 95% confidence intervals for 'no bypass/yes government engagement' aid delivery rank-order. By donor political economy across governance scenarios. Country A: Good Performer, Country B: Weak State Institutions, Low Corruption, Country C: Good Performer, Corruption Scandal.

Source: Survey data of senior aid officials from Germany, France, and Japan (left side of the graph), United States, United Kingdom, and Sweden (right side of the graph)

learning about good governance in Country A. For the other donor type, we observe more variability in ranking government first when learning about Country A, as indicated by the plot's longer whiskers. This variability is driven by US respondents who are slightly less likely to rank the government first in a good governance environment. However, this difference is not statistically significant with respect to aid officials from the United Kingdom or Sweden.

Marked differences arise, however, when we move from the well-governed Country A to the two poorly governed country scenarios. After receiving information about poor governance, officials across political economy types no longer respond in similar ways, as predicted by my argument. In contrast, responses from aid officials differ significantly. While, on average, aid officials from both political economies moved away from government-to-government aid as their preferred channel, US, UK, and Swedish respondents did so to a higher degree, with statistically significant differences in means in the case of Country B and C. This suggests that poor governance, regardless of whether it is operationalised as a corruption scandal or weak state institutions, encourages aid officials from donor countries whose aid bureaucracy is organised around neoliberal principles to bypass more. Again, this finding provides prima facie evidence in support of my claims.

When asking aid officials about their preferences regarding the proportion of government-to-government aid going to developing countries the results are similar and consistent with my expectations: on average, all donor officials preferred the share of government-to-government aid to be higher in the well-governed country scenario. Officials from France, Japan, and Germany had a higher mean than officials from the United States, the United Kingdom, and Sweden; and the differences between the two different political economy types are not statistically significant. As respondents move from well to poorly governed scenarios, however, the differences are pronounced *and* statistically significant. Again, this result is consistent with the results from the observational data analysis. Figure 5.2 presents point estimates for the government-to-government share outcome measure, as well as the associated confidence intervals for changes in quality of governance across aid officials from different political economies.

Moving beyond a descriptive assessment of the raw data, I now subject the data to statistical tests. I estimate the difference in differences (DiD) to measure the effect of deteriorating governance within subjects, while accounting for expected differences across groups. My argument predicts that the change in delivery tactics induced by Country B and Country C scenarios differs significantly across officials from different political economies. I expect officials from the United States, the United Kingdom, and Sweden, on average, to change towards greater bypass than their counterparts from France, Japan, and Germany.

The results from the DiD estimations confirm my thesis and are consistent with the country-level data analysis presented in Chapter 4. Table 5.1 shows the DiD estimates. The upper half of Table 5.1 represents the results of the estimates explaining the rank-order measure, NO BYPASS-RANKING, as in government-to-government aid. The estimated difference between officials from the two types

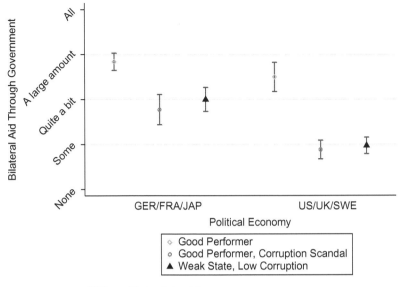

95% confidence intervals

Figure 5.2 Point estimates and 95% confidence intervals for 'no bypass/yes government-to-government' share of all bilateral aid by donor political economy across governance scenarios. Country A: Good Performer, Country B: Weak State Institutions, Low Corruption, Country C: Good Performer, Corruption Scandal.
Source: Survey data of senior aid officials from Germany, France, and Japan (left side of the graph), United States, United Kingdom, and Sweden (right side of the graph)

of political economies who indicated their preferred rankings of the delivery channels as they move from Country A to Country B is [−1.29] and statistically significant at the 0.01 level. Moving from Country A to Country C yields a statistically significant estimated difference of [−1.28] at the 0.01 level. This substantiates my claim that officials from the United States, United Kingdom, and Sweden are significantly more likely to prefer bypass channels and tactics in poorly governed environments than their counterparts in more statist donor countries.

The results for NO BYPASS-PROPORTION, as in government-to-government proportion, are presented in the lower half of Table 5.1. Again, the differences in response as respondents move from Country A to Country B or C are statistically different across officials from the

Table 5.1. *Difference-in-difference estimates of aid delivery ranking by donor political economy*

	Country A to B Diff in Diff	Country A to C Diff in Diff
No Bypass-Ranking	−1.287***	−1.277***
Std. Error	0.29	0.36
R-square	0.47	0.49
No Bypass- Proportion	−0.691***	−0.553**
Std. Error	0.19	0.21
R square	0.52	0.50

Difference-in-difference estimates of aid delivery ranking by donor political economy. p < 0.05, p < 0.01. Standard errors clustered at the level of the individual official. In the top half of the table, respondents evaluate Country A (Good Performer), followed by Country C (Corruption Scandal). In the lower half of the table, respondents evaluate Country A (Good Performer), followed by Country B (Weak State Institutions). The 'No Bypass-Ranking' is based on rank-order of aid delivery preferences with '5' indicating recipient government is first choice. 'No Bypass-Proportion' is based on proportional measure for aid delivery preferences with '5' indicating all aid should go through the recipient government.
Source: Survey Data of Senior Aid Officials from France, Germany, Japan, United States, United Kingdom, and Sweden.

two types of political economies. The estimated difference between officials from the two types of political economies who, this time, indicated their preferred bypass proportions as they move from Country A to Country B is [−0.69] and statistically significant at the 0.01 level. Moving from Country A to Country C yields a statistically significant estimated difference of [−0.55] at the 0.05 level. This suggests that officials of any background prefer to lower the government-to-government portion of bilateral aid in poorly governed countries but that, importantly, the US, UK, and Swedish respondents did so to a higher degree, with statistically significant differences in means.

To ensure that the results were not driven by respondents from a particular country, I performed an important robustness check. That is, I re-estimated the DiD models, taking out respondents from one of the six countries at a time. Across all models and samples, the sign and statistical significance of the coefficient did not change in meaningful ways, suggesting that the effect for either political economy type is not driven by a particular country that is included in that type.

Overall, the results from the survey experiment substantiate my theoretical claims advanced in Chapter 2. Across the different experimental scenarios, aid officials respond to information about the quality of recipient governance. What matters most is that the officials' reaction to the information varies by political economy type. When moving from Country A (the good performer) to Country C (corruption scandal) or B (weak state institutions), the modal response for officials with a neoliberal orientation in service delivery was to substantially reduce the proportion of aid delivered through the public sector. When asked to respond to governance changes by ranking the delivery channels for recipient countries that had either experienced a corruption scandal or who had weak state institutions, the modal response for 'best' channel changed from the government (in the good performer) to the international organisation, a non-state channel of aid delivery.

Institutional Constraints: Probing the Causal Mechanism

Why do we see this differential response in delivery tactics across officials? My argument posits that the organisation of aid organisations shapes how officials approach the delivery of foreign aid abroad. In this section, I probe two individual-level empirical implications that emerge from my argument: First, bureaucratic organisation and processes influence the way in which officials go about evaluating the effectiveness of development assistance. They enable and justify particular aid delivery tactics, while precluding others. In Chapter 3, I elucidated the link between organisational practices and aid delivery. Here I want to document that political economies have systematically different evaluation practices.

My argument posits that in donor countries where aid organisations are organised around market norms, officials face relentless pressure to report on and measure the success of aid projects. These pressures are embedded in reporting practices that prescribe the need to engage in frequent reporting on whether foreign aid is delivered according to plan. In this particular institutional context, aid officials adopt relatively short time horizons for evaluating aid success. In contrast, aid officials from donor organisations where reporting practices do not

Table 5.2. *Simple differences*

	N	Mean	Standard error	Difference	t-stat	p-value
Time horizon (GER/FRA/JPN)	31	6.35	0.43			
Time horizon (US/UK/SWE)	32	4.59	0.37	1.76	3.09	0.001
State-building effort (GER/FRA/JPN)	31	3.74	0.92			
State-building (US/UK/SWE)	32	3.09	0.11	0.65	4.42	0.001

Respondents indicate preferences for time horizon with which they evaluate aid success and how much they prioritise state-building efforts.

follow the same neoliberal logic are under less pressure to report on the success of aid in the short run and should have less restrictive time horizons in evaluation. The empirical implication of this argument suggests that aid officials from neoliberal structures should report shorter time horizons than their counterparts in traditional public sector structures.

I subject this theoretical prediction to a quantitative empirical test in the closed-ended survey, where I ask all aid officials to indicate, considering their experience as an aid official in their country, after how many years foreign aid should be evaluated for its success. Aid officials could answer anything from one to ten years, in one year intervals, as well as a final answer that suggested 'ten or more years'. If my prediction is borne out empirically, I expect to see that aid officials from the United States, the United Kingdom, and Sweden select shorter time horizons than their counterparts from France, Germany, and Japan, on average.

Table 5.2 presents the results of simple differences in responses of the aid officials. Consistent with my expectations, the time horizons that aid officials selected in their answers differ significantly across the two different political economies; and they differ in the expected direction: time horizons are shorter for aid officials from neoliberally organised aid organisations. For officials from the United States, the United Kingdom, and Sweden the mean number of years after which aid needed to be evaluated for its success is 4.56 years, while their counterparts in France, Japan, and Germany exhibit a mean of 6.27 years. The difference of 1.71 years is statistically significant at the 0.01 level. This evidence corroborates the plausibility of my causal mechanism insofar as I show that differences in reporting practices exist across aid organisations, and that these practices influence how aid officials think about evaluating aid and the time horizons attached to evaluation.

In the next step, I test another empirical implication of my argument. I have argued that the foreign aid priorities of aid officials are endogenous to political economy type. If national structures are set up to maximise accountability through results that are achievable in the short run, aid officials are going to want to pursue aid projects that can deliver on the measurement front. On the other hand, if national structures reaffirm the importance of the state in public sector governance, I expect aid officials to be more likely to focus less on projects that deliver results in the short run, but, instead, prioritise capacity-building efforts. If we find statistically significant differences in preferences between these two aid objectives I can interpret the evidence to be in support of my contention that aid success is, at heart, subjective and has its origin in national structures.

I measured what aid objectives officials prioritise by asking respondents to consider the following trade-offs between short-run (basic needs) and long-run (state-building) aid goals: 'Aid experts disagree over whether to prioritize short- or long-term development goals. For instance, aid that provides sick people with life-saving drugs does not directly contribute to strengthening indigenous health care systems and to making health care systems sustainable.' Immediately following this, I asked respondents to consider their experience as an official of their government to indicate how much of the overall aid their government directs at state-building. The answer categories included 'none', 'some', 'quite a bit', 'a large amount', and 'all'. A value of 5 indicates that 'all' aid should be directed towards capacity building. Again, I expect political economy differences to shape aid officials' responses about what aid objectives they prioritise. If my argument is correct, I expect respondents from the United States, the United Kingdom, and Sweden to be less likely to prioritise state-building efforts than their counter-parts in France, Japan, and Germany.

The second row of Table 5.2 presents the results of simple differences in responses of the aid officials. The patterns conform with my theoretical expectations insofar as there are marked differences across political economy type in how much aid officials propose to put towards state-building efforts in developing countries. As expected, aid officials from the United States, the United Kingdom, and Sweden are, on average, less supportive of state-building measures than their counterparts from France, Japan, and Germany. On a scale from 1 to 5, where 5 indicates that 'all' aid should be directed towards capacity building, respondents who work in organisations that are organised around neoliberal principles produce an average of 3, while their counterparts from traditional public sector economies exhibit a higher mean of 3.76. The 0.76 difference is statistically significant at the 0.01 level.

These results buttress my claim that aid officials' priorities are endogenous to political economy type. If institutional rulebooks are set up to generate results in foreign aid delivery, purposeful aid officials will prioritise aid objectives that can be more easily measured. If rule-books are set up to promote government-to-government aid and recipient capacity, then officials will prefer to use aid more towards achieving this particular objective than the other.

In a subsequent closed-ended question, I sought to get a better sense of whether aid officials, after indicating a preference for more short-term aid or long-term capacity-building efforts, perceived that OECD donors differed markedly in this regard, and by extension in their aid objectives. Specifically, I asked respondents whether they perceived there to be differences across donors in whether they prioritised short-term results or capacity-building efforts in their aid giving. The left panel of Figure 5.3 presents the results. About 80 per cent of aid officials responded to this question by answering 'yes'. I interpret this evidence to support my contention that in the world of foreign aid, there are not just tensions between donors and recipient governments about aid priorities, as William Easterly and Angus Deaton and many others suggest. There are also marked differences in aid priorities among donors that, as per my argument, find their origin in national rules of the game and that direct aid officials either towards bypass or

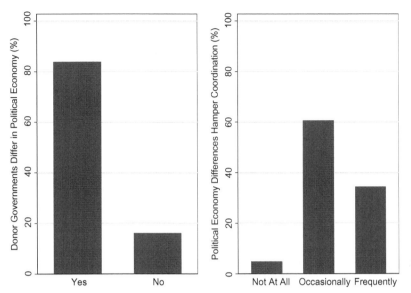

Figure 5.3 Simple distribution of aid officials' responses. Left panel question asked to indicate whether political economy differences were perceived to be pronounced. Right panel asked to indicate whether political economy differences between donor countries hamper donor coordination.

engagement with the recipient government in the world's poorest countries.

Do aid officials perceive these differences in aid priorities to hamper coordination efforts among donors? In a final question I asked aid officials to indicate the extent to which they thought these differences would hamper donor coordination in developing countries, with answer categories including 'not at all', 'occasionally', 'frequently', and 'always'. Although a systematic analysis of the ramifications of differing aid delivery preferences on donor coordination is beyond the scope of this study, the answer to this question will shed some light on the question of whether aid officials perceive these differences to be sufficiently fundamental to impede coordination among bilateral donors in international development. As the response distribution in the right panel of Figure 5.3 indicates, about 60 per cent suggested that they perceived different aid priorities among donors to 'occasionally' impede donor coordination, while about 35 per cent answered 'frequently'. Less than

5 per cent indicated that national priorities did not have a negative effect on cooperation among donors. These results suggest that aid officials are not only aware of different development priorities and approaches but that these differences may act as an impediment to donor cooperation in international development. I interpret these results to suggest that aid officials are aware of respective tension among donors. I return to a more in-depth discussion of the implications of my argument on donor coordination in Chapter 7.

5.5 More Evidence from Open-Ended Interviews with Foreign Aid Officials

My argument asserts that regardless of political economy type, aid officials are compelled by their institutional rulebooks to maximise a particular objective with foreign aid, and to do so through a particular course of action under conditions of poor recipient governance. Depending on the ideological origins of the institutional rulebook, whether it is neoliberal or has a traditional public sector character, aid officials prioritise either results-delivery or recipient capacity-building; and, consequently, are more likely to choose either bypass or engagement with the recipient government as a course of action.

As I elaborated in earlier chapters, my theory characterises the world of aid officials as one of risk and rational expectations. In this world, I assume that aid officials, regardless of political economy type, agree on what constitutes risk in foreign aid; and that they select aid delivery tactics that help overcome this risk and enable them to promote the aid objectives of their organisation. What course of action they take, however, is, as per my argument, endogenous to national structures and the varying objectives donor governments seek to pursue with aid.

The open-ended interview gave me the space to probe this contention. I wanted to see whether these assumptions were empirically relevant: whether risk in aid-recipient countries mattered for aid delivery and whether recipient governance was a key proxy for risk in the real world. Across the large majority of interviews, aid officials demonstrated comfortable certainty about how international development works, and what obstacles or risks they needed to address. Aid officials listed governance quality, or, more specifically, aid capture through corrupt recipient authorities or fragile state institutions, as a major obstacle, or source of risk, that impedes aid implementation. To receive information on governance conditions in aid-receiving countries, aid officials turn to in-house or publicly available governance information on a regular basis. This information provides them with important information about risks of aid implementation abroad.

The open-ended interviews also revealed more information about the kinds of governance data that officials in donor governments use when assessing risk of aid capture abroad. While each donor government draws on internal information on governance reported from donor field offices or embassies in recipient countries, aid officials also make use of publicly available governance data sets as a source of information on governance quality. The most frequently mentioned set of publicly available indicators was that of the World Bank. This finding not only corroborates the theorised importance of governance quality in donor decision-making but it also lends support to using the World Bank governance as a specific measure of governance when assessing the statistical association between recipient governance and foreign aid delivery in Chapter 4.

Aside from asking questions that serve to substantiate essential assumptions that are part of my theoretical framework, I used the open-ended questions to probe the institutional constraints mechanism. I did so by asking aid officials to briefly elaborate on their aid delivery choices through simple 'why?' questions: I asked aid officials to share the reason(s) why they selected the outcome they did; why they indicated more or less support for government-to-government aid or why they ranked the channels the way they did. Across the board, the proposed institutional constraints mechanism received substantial confirmation. As predicted by my theory, respondents from the United States, United Kingdom, and Sweden, in their role as aid officials, worried principally about results risk, and justified bypass as an organisational prescription if the quality of recipient governance is low.

Consider this remark from a former DFID official,

For DFID the demand side has moved into the background. DFID has shifted its priorities to vaccinating children and sending them to school. The national government complexities have increasingly moved into the background. This is not naïve development thinking but, rather, ministers have been calling DFID to become better at demonstrating results. The Independent Commission for Aid Impact (ICAI) is snapping at DFIDs heel, and have to some extent reinforced the accounting identity that DFID shows results for every Pound that the British tax payer spent, or what they are getting for the pound. Today, any bidding for overseas assistance would have to specify the results it expects to deliver given resources. Like, for this money, I [the bidder, added by author] can put one million children in school, I can vaccinate this many people, I can increase the rate of growth by this much. As you can see, these are spectacular chains of attribution between what the money buys and does, and they make it more likely that non-state actors deliver the aid, especially when the state lacks the capacity.[12]

When asked to explain their aid delivery decision in poorly governed countries, several Swedish respondents pointed to the presence of value conflicts within Swedish aid. A senior Sida official who had been working on Swedish aid for decades offered the following perspective during the open-ended interview.

Although we have our rules and processes of managing aid, I think that the government, even if it is corrupt, remains an important partner and we need to work with them more, like we used to in the 1980s and 1990s. My official role today requires me to work around the state more often than I would like. We tend to abandon governments too quickly as soon as there are signs of corruption or similar problems. But we need to work with governments to make it function better. We cannot do that if we focus on NGOs or IOs for service delivery. The recipient government remains an important actor in development cooperation.[13]

This quote illustrates that when neoliberal institutional rulebooks were imposed in Sweden, 'old' doctrines about the importance of the state no longer found their expression in the rules of the game and thus lacked teeth to incentivise more government-to-government action. What used to be conventional action now invites friction insofar as institutional prescriptions for delivery point in substantially different directions. The quote further illustrates an important point that carries over across aid officials in the United States and the United Kingdom. It suggests that aid officials are keenly aware of the negative conse-quences of setting up parallel structures in poor countries. Across numerous interviews, aid officials directly criticised their own practices of trying to quantify, measure, and guarantee results in the short run; or more broadly, of being subjected to what Muller has called the

---

[12] Author interview with former DFID official, London, 24 June 2014.
[13] Author interview with Sida official, Stockholm, 1 November 2013.

'tyranny of metrics'.[14] In the end, however, respondents felt, as the two quotes illustrate, that institutional constraints dictate interests, more than any alternative idea ever could – unless, of course, this idea conforms to the rules. Examples of more incremental, system-conforming changes were frequently noted in the interviews. USAID officials referred to USAID Forward as one initiative that allowed aid officials to be more open to local solutions on a small scale, but that, in the end, the initiative was only possible because it was accompanied by enhanced measures that would control risks of aid capture. Several Swedish officials talked about incremental internal efforts to better respond to recipient country needs and input. For example, they discussed efforts to revise results and performance frameworks so that they place less emphasis on formal and quantitative monitoring at all levels.[15] In more recent years, Sida's staff training materials even warn against the risk of relying too much on quantitative indicators in some contexts, encouraging their staff to use 'learning-based methods' and to work with their partners to build monitoring systems that are relevant to context.[16] In spite of these incremental changes, both US and Swedish aid systems fit onto the neoliberal trajectory during my study's time frame, as I have documented in Chapter 3. The evidence from the interviews suggests that alternative ideas can indeed be incorporated, as long as they do not require aid officials to go against the principles or objectives stipulated by their organisation.

In a similar fashion, I expect aid officials from traditional public sector economies to be constrained by their institutional rulebook. As per my theory, however, the direction of the constraint would enable and justify government-to-government tactics. As per the statistical analyses, aid officials from Germany, France, and Japan were indeed significantly more likely to rank the recipient government as 'best' delivery channel when learning about poor governance conditions in the aid-recipient country. They were also significantly less likely to advocate a reduction in government-to-government aid under the same conditions.

In the interviews, the large majority of aid officials from Germany, France, and Japan talked about being constrained and answered my 'why' question with answers linked to institutional obligations. As a

<hr>

[14] Muller (2018). [15] OECD DAC (2017).
[16] Sida 2016c, cited in OECD DAC (2017).

German official explained his reaction to the poor governance scenario in the survey,

We are required to use local systems, to work with the public sector in developing countries, as much as possible. We are similar to our French counterparts for wanting to work with the recipient government. The Kreditanstalt für Wiederaufbau (KfW) is much like the Agence Française du Développement (AFD) in this regard. They have due diligence procedures in place. For the procurement of goods, the Gesellschaft für Internationale Zusammenarbeit (GIZ), our implementing partner, controls the process more heavily when local systems are not fit to ensure that the process is not corrupted. The GIZ sends experts and training staff that assist and monitor the local governments so that the implementation of the project works as desired. The role of the government is very important here because it sets the objectives the projects, and is involved in the process of implementation.[17]

In the same context, another German aid official claims,

Sometimes when our partner countries fail to cooperate it might be better to stop working together and ask our civil society to step in. We have made very small adjustments in this regard but our budget processes and institutional rules just do not allow us to make big changes in how we do development cooperation.[18]

The latter quotes are representative of responses from aid officials in a traditional public sector economy, where the institutional rulebook reproduces interests and action that reaffirms the role of the state in public sector governance. This rulebook enables and justifies government-to-government aid when recipient governance is low. To prevent aid capture, as illustrated in the last quote, government-to-government delivery contains more hands-on provisions that serve to monitor the implementation process and ensure that recipient authorities follow through with the aid contract. Throughout the interviews with aid officials from traditional public sector economies, respondents indicated that government-to-government delivery was a rational tactic, although alternative ideas were contemplated and discussed inside the aid organisations. As one French aid official noted during the author interview, 'Even if we wanted to, and, trust me, sometimes we feel that

---

[17] Author interview with senior German official, Paris, 17 July 2013.
[18] Author interview with senior German official, Bonn, 16 July 2013.

working with a corrupt partner is not a sensible choice, we work with our partners because this is how we do things. It may appear rigid from the outside but it is reality.'[19]

Again, aid officials' critical reflection of their own practices suggests that they are very much aware of the problems associated with aid delivery through government structures, especially when these structures are corrupt or weak. The qualitative evidence thus reveals that, across political economy types, decisions about how to promote aid abroad are systematically influenced by institutional rules and practices. What is more, the open-ended interviews further revealed differences in aid priorities. Unlike their counterparts in the United States, the United Kingdom, and Sweden, who ranked measurable results on the top of their priority list, aid officials from Germany, France, and Japan did not spend much time talking about results. Rather they stressed that continued engagement with authorities was necessary and was to be prioritised for building up much needed capacity abroad. At the same time, aid officials displayed a keen understanding of the difficulties that come with their own, rule-induced preferences for government-to-government. They stressed how resource-intensive government monitoring can be and how, at times, the maintenance of donor–recipient government relations can be difficult under conditions of poor recipient governance. As elsewhere, alternative ideas are discussed to solve the obstacle course in aid implementation but, in the end, only conforming beliefs prevail.

The empirical insight that, above all else, constraints determine aid officials' course of action in aid delivery pushes back against claims that normative beliefs per se, which aid decision-makers may hold at any given moment, produce stable preferences for donor–recipient interactions.[20,21] The qualitative interview material also supports the contention that the world of aid officials is, in fact, characterised by risk. I find that the average aid official, independent of political economy type, thinks about risks in aid implementation and considers aid capture through recipient governments a key obstacle to their

---

[19] Author interview with former senior German aid official, Bonn, 12 August 2014.

[20] Van der Veen (2011).

[21] Other scholars who have argued that norms, identities, or social interpretations create interests that explain patterns in world politics include Abdelal (2001); Parsons (2003); Herrera (2005); Jabko (2006); Vreeland (2008).

development efforts. I find that aid officials resort to institutional rules and practices as a guide for action. Under conditions of poor governance, aid officials from different political economies resort to dissimilar strategies because their rules prescribe a particular course of action. This insight deviates from the view that the world of decision-makers is characterised by uncertainty and that, under conditions of uncertainty, beliefs or identities guide policy-makers and directly inform decisions.[22]

An additional point worth noting is that, throughout the open-ended interviews, the large majority of aid officials with whom I spoke revealed that they were passionate about their development mandate. Many spoke about their desires to help promote prosperity abroad and to make foreign aid more effective. In many of the interviews, however, respondents, regardless of political economy type, then went on to suggest that bureaucratic organisation, with its rules and business as usual practices, can stifle intrinsic motivation, especially when rules and practices were associated with pathologies and unintended outcomes.[23] For example, one Swedish official pointed to 'measurement frenzy' in Swedish aid as demotivating insofar as

spending most of my time on trying to measure highly complex development outcomes through simple indicators that are also expected to work across wildly different countries makes it really hard not to get cynical or withdraw. But if I ignore management strategy then I jeopardize my own career.[24]

Similarly, a German official indicated that being constrained by rules and practices can dampen enthusiasm

In a world like foreign aid where there is so much innovation and opportunities for forming new partnerships with different types of non-state actors, it can be frustrating not to be able to take advantage of it and to have to stick to the partnerships to whom our organization is committed. Overall, I wished we had more flexibility when it comes to aid delivery. I think it would speed up development abroad.[25]

---

[22] Nelson (2017).
[23] For research that studies the effect of organisational rules on employees' motivation see Giauque et al. (2012); Giauque et al. (2013).
[24] Author interview with senior Sida official, Stockholm, 20 June 2013.
[25] Author interview with former senior German aid official, Bonn, 12 August 2014.

I interpret these anecdotal insights to corroborate my institutional constraints mechanism but I also read them as suggestive evidence that contrasts with Williamson's depiction of bureaucratic agents as 'self-interest seeking with guile'.[26] Instead, many officials displayed a real passion for their mandate. It may thus be that the same institutional rules and practices that were set up to incentivise aid officials to work towards the organisation's mandate may stifle aid officials' passion and motivation to respond to today's development challenges. It remains for further research to examine the extent to which and under what conditions institutional rulebooks stifle aid officials' motivation.

5.6 Conclusion

Overall, this chapter provides substantial quantitative and qualitative evidence in support of my theoretical framework. Through individual-level analyses, I showed that the micro-foundations of my theory are borne out empirically: aid officials of different political economy types make systematically different choices about foreign aid delivery tactics, and they do so in the expected direction. I find that aid officials from governance systems that are on a neoliberal trajectory are systematically more likely to promote bypass in poorly governed countries than their counterparts from traditional public sector economies. These micro-level findings dovetail with results from macro-level analyses in the previous chapter, corroborating the empirical usefulness of my theoretical framework.

The findings of this chapter also support the more fine-grained organisational aspects of the theory. While Chapter 3 elucidated how variation in aid evaluation practices yields markedly different aid delivery decisions, this chapter confirms that rules incentivise aid officials to evaluate the success of aid in varied ways. I also show that aid priorities of aid officials differ: while respondents from neoliberal structures prioritise results in the short run, their counterparts from traditional public sector economies are more interested in promoting capacity-building activities. More broadly, the data presented in this chapter confirm that my theoretical framework that characterises the world of aid officials as one of risk and rational expectations corresponds with reality.

---

[26] Williamson (1985).

Importantly, I can also substantiate the empirical plausibility of the institutional constraints mechanism insofar as the open-ended interviews revealed that aid officials consider themselves constrained by rules. Or, put differently and in opposition to Blyth,[27] I find that national aid organisations do come with an instruction sheet that guides aid officials along a materialist obstacle course. Everyone is incentivised to promote their organisations' goals and minimise risk, but what these goals are and how aid officials go about doing that has ideological origins, which are rooted in governance beliefs that gave rise to institutional structures and practices decades ago but that continue to shape aid delivery today.

Finally, the chapter sheds more light on the divisions that, as I have argued, exist inside the donor community in terms of priorities and approaches to international development. The findings of this chapter also indicate that donors differ not only in aid priorities and aid delivery tactics but, as I suggested in Chapter 2, that they may also be at variance when it comes down to supporting agreed principles or best practices in the context of international aid forums. For example, I expect donor governments whose structures are of neoliberal character to more strongly support and focus on effective aid management principles that enable them to 'be seen to do the right thing', while I predict that their counterparts will be more likely to support the principle of government ownership that is designed to strengthen recipient capacity towards reaching common development goals. I will return to this issue in Chapter 7 when discussing the implications of my research for policy.

In the last empirical chapter of this book, Chapter 6, I now turn to examining the role of public opinion as a potential alternative explanation for the observed heterogeneity in aid delivery tactics across donor governments. One might argue that aid officials decide to bypass or engage with recipient governments in poorly governed countries because these tactics are broadly supported at home. If this is true, we would expect to find publics of neoliberal governance systems to be more bypass-oriented or punitive than publics in traditional public sector economies with regard to corrupt or weak countries. The next chapter is devoted to exploring this potential alternative explanation on the basis of public opinion data in the United States and Germany.

---

[27] Blyth (2003).

Appendix

Table 5.A1. *Number of interviews by donor country and agency*

No. of Respondents	Agency	Country
4	State Department	US
5	USAID	US
2	MCC	US
1	Treasury	US
1	Office of Budget and Management	US
7	Department for International Development	UK
6	Ministry of Foreign Affairs	Sweden
8	Sida	Sweden
6	Ministry of Foreign Affairs	France
4	French Agency for Development	France
3	Ministry of Finance	France
9	Ministry of Development Cooperation	Germany
4	Kreditanstalt fuer Wiederaufbau (KfW)	Germany
3	Ministry for Foreign Affairs	Japan
2	Japanese International Cooperation Agency	Japan

6 | Examining Public Opinion as an Alternative Explanation

Evidence from Survey Experiments with Voters in the United States and Germany

6.1 Introduction

In this book, I locate the origin of bypass or government-to-government tactics inside aid organisations. It is my principal claim that aid organisations, like other state organisations, are at heart ideological institutions that are underwritten by particular conceptions about the appropriate blend of roles between the state and the market, or the 'kind' of state involvement in public sector governance. These conceptions, though locked in by institutional rules and practices many decades ago at different times in different donor countries, continue to shape donor decisions about aid delivery. They affect how aid officials negotiate and interact with recipient countries, and they influence the goals that aid officials prioritise in foreign aid, and how regimes think and measure aid success.

In previous chapters, I have established that, empirically, the character of the institutional environment, my hypothesised explanation, varies markedly in organisation across donor governments. In Chapter 3, I show that, today, aid systems in the United States, the United Kingdom, and Sweden are on a decidedly neoliberal trajectory, as their aid systems exhibit pervasive neoliberal footprints. Aid structures in France and Germany, on the other hand, despite some limited reform efforts continue to be on a public sector trajectory that reaffirms a more traditional role of the state in public sector governance. This insight pushes back against claims suggesting that the institutional environments are similar across donor countries, that aid organisations share the same objectives with aid.[1]

---

[1] For example, Honig (2018) assumes that donor aid organisations are broadly similar in their organisation and predicts that aid officials across aid organisations will converge on similar delivery policy under similar conditions.

Importantly, I then elucidated how substantive differences in the institutional environment produce different aid objectives as well as a set of constraints that incentivise aid officials to work in different directions when they decide how to deliver aid abroad. The reason why we observe more bypass under conditions of poor recipient country governance in the United States than Germany is because, in the 1970s and 1980s, powerful political actors seized politically opportune moments to coalesce around and promote neoliberal doctrine as the best solution for solving challenges associated with globalisation. The structural reforms that ensued also reorganised the US aid system into one that prioritises bypass.

In Chapter 5, I leveraged evidence to push back against claims in the literature suggesting that what donor officials think at any given moment is the more appropriate aid delivery tactic influences aid delivery decisions. I have argued and documented that aid officials may hold different views about the appropriate aid delivery tactic, and these may be in tension with rulebooks. In the end, however, views are inconsequential unless they conform with or are embedded in the organisational structures and practices that motivate and incentivise action. For alternative ideas to become consequential, they need to be preceded or accompanied by new rules of the game that guide the behaviour of aid officials in a new direction.

In this chapter, I will pay attention to another alternative explanation. Some might argue that the reason why we see regular and stable patterns of more bypass in the United States than in Germany under poor recipient governance is because the US public is more punitive than the German public and acts as a constraining force on aid delivery decisions. Scholars of democratic politics have long debated the role of public opinion in constraining policy choices of elected officials.[2] Classical accounts of representative democracy suggest that publics constrain decision-making among elected officials. Citizens can apply pressure if they feel that governments make policy choices that have gone too far outside what is broadly popular among voters. Governments who fear pressure or, at worst, electoral sanctions thus promote policy that receives broad support.[3]

---

[2] Downs (1957); Przeworski et al. (1999).
[3] E.g. Loewen and Rubenson (2011).

As I have pointed out in Chapter 1, a considerable number of scholars have investigated the link between public opinion and foreign aid.[4] One set of explanations links foreign aid spending to citizens' moral views.[5] Other studies have linked public support for aid to self-interest that is determined by how the economy does and how much people have to spare in their pockets.[6] Yet, studies show that these individual attitudes do not always aggregate up in expected ways; and that, for example, the links between individual or domestic solidarity and foreign aid budgets is not self-evident and mitigated by other factors.[7] Nor can we necessarily expect the hypothesised link between public opinion and foreign aid decision-making to be robust. Foreign aid is primarily formulated out of public view and is not considered a salient issue for voters at the ballot box. So, even if voters had a clear position on how to spend aid, it is not clear that this position would be consequential for how people cast their vote in elections.[8]

Alternatively, scholars have argued that public opinion reflects attitudes or preferences of elites,[9] especially in areas like foreign policy[10] or foreign aid, where citizens know very little about international development in general, and wildly overestimate how much donor governments actually contribute to overseas development.[11] In foreign aid, it may thus be that citizens take cues sent by political actors to form their views about foreign aid and whether or through what delivery channel they support it. In this chapter, I do not try to determine whether public views on foreign aid delivery result from opinion leadership or whether they are views that constrain aid officials from the bottom-up. Nor do I develop and test a theory about why and how public opinion shapes foreign aid delivery. I merely focus on ruling out a competing explanation, which suggests that aid officials and donor publics have similar positions on foreign aid

---

[4] Others have examined the role of public opinion in foreign policy more broadly, including, for example, Fearon (1994); Foyle (1999); Chapman (2011); Milner and Tingley (2015).
[5] Lumsdaine (1993); Noel and Therien (1995).   [6] Heinrich et al. (2016).
[7] Prather (2014).   [8] Dietrich et al. (2020).
[9] Kinder and Sanders (1990); Zaller (1992); Lupia (1994); Tesler (2015).
[10] Berinsky (2007); Kertzer and Zeitzoff (2017).   [11] Scotto et al. (2017).

delivery.[12] If aid officials are, for example, beholden to or constrained by their donor publics we would expect there to be congruence between what aid officials and publics advocate as the most suitable delivery channel. To investigate this alternative empirical implication, I collected original survey data from ordinary citizens that measures citizen attitudes towards aid delivery tactics. Specifically, I embedded a survey experiment in two nationally representative surveys fielded in the fall of 2016 in the United States and Germany, who represent two different political economy types. I also draw from evidence collected over the course of the many author interviews I conducted for this book.

The quantitative and qualitative evidence reveals that the reactions of the two donor publics do not mirror the heterogeneous aid delivery patterns observed at the level of the aid official, or at the cross-country level. When presented with information about poor recipient governance, the US and German publics are similarly punitive insofar as they opt to abandon the state. If anything, the German public is more punitive than the US public. These results work against the alternative public opinion mechanism, which would expect aid officials to promote aid delivery decisions that are broadly supported at home. Furthermore, a tentative comparison between the aid official and donor public samples within country suggests that donor publics, compared to aid officials, are, on average, less favourably disposed towards government-to-government aid in general. To understand differences across aid officials and members of the donor public, it is important to recognise that these two samples, or groups of populations, represent different worlds. Aid officials work for aid organisations. My argument expects aid officials, in the first instance, to be purposive actors that engage in optimising behaviour. They profit from following institutional rulebooks that are set up to advance the mandate of the organisation. What is more, for aid officials international development is a central, but not necessarily exclusive, objective. As government representatives, aid officials need to juggle different objectives in interactions with recipient authorities. In my theory, I suggest that donor governments incur non-financial costs when they

---

[12] To date, there is no cross-country data set that records public sentiment towards foreign aid, or, more specifically, towards aid delivery practices, which I could have included as co-variate in my quantitative analyses in Chapter 4.

do not engage with state structures, given that aid relations, or foreign policy more broadly, is constructed around donor–recipient interactions. I thus expect aid officials, even from neoliberal aid organisations, to want to avoid these non-monetary costs and maintain government-to-government aid, when it is possible.

Unlike aid officials, voters are effectively unconstrained. They do not work for aid organisations. They are not beholden to institutional rulebooks that prescribe a certain type of donor–recipient interaction, while precluding another. They are not required to reflect on broader foreign policy objectives, nor do they interact with recipient authorities. As scholarship of domestic sources of foreign aid support has demonstrated, individuals make decisions based on their own moral beliefs and economic situation. In the context of this chapter, I thus expect citizen attitudes on foreign aid to be unconstrained and similar across donor publics, regardless of political economy type. When voters are asked to react to information about bypass, they can be punitive without the constraints imposed by foreign policy mandates, or organisational structures and practices.

Overall, I interpret these empirical insights to suggest that donor publics do not constrain aid officials to opt for either bypass or engage. If anything, they corroborate the theorised institutional constraints mechanism of this book. In political economies that organise aid delivery on the basis of neoliberal rulebooks, aid officials are constrained towards bypass under conditions of poor governance, making delivery decisions more in line with what the public wants. This is different from the view that the public constrains aid officials to behave consistently with their views. This interpretation dovetails with research on the politics of bureaucratic reform. In this literature, Suleiman and others have shown that correlations between public opinion and neoliberal policies, such as the outsourcing of goods and service delivery, may be tenuous at best.[13] Instead, scholars have shown that attitudes of citizens across OECD countries remain an ambiguous mix of support and denial of government involvement, and depend on particular measures for government support.[14]

---

[13] Suleiman (2003).   [14] Dalton (2013).

Finally, this chapter's results contribute to a burgeoning study of an elite–public gap in international relations.[15] My findings corroborate studies that show that elites differ from ordinary citizens in the policies that they support. While scholars have explained these differences on the basis of actor-level characteristics, including, for example, personality traits,[16] experience, or domain-specific knowledge, I point to the importance of the institutional environment or the context in which elites and ordinary citizens operate and whose attributes shape their decision-making. I find that the institutional context constrains elites to adopt particular policies, while members of the public are effectively unconstrained and are free to articulate their views. In Germany, which represents a traditional public sector economy, the elite–public gap is relatively large insofar as aid officials maintain government-to-government relations when recipient governance is poor, even when their public has a preference for bypass. In the United States, the size of the gap is somewhat narrower but still sizable.

In the next section, I describe how I collected the public opinion data that I will use to make the comparisons. I do so by comparing aid officials' preferences about aid delivery to ordinary citizen attitudes towards bypass or engagement with aid recipient governments.

6.2 Research Design of Survey Experiment on Donor Publics in the United States and Germany

I embed a survey experiment in two nationwide surveys in the United States and Germany. Specifically, the experiment was embedded in the Aid Attitudes Tracker (AAT) Survey,[17] which examines public attitudes and behaviours towards development, poverty, and foreign aid.[18] The surveys that include the survey experiment were administered online by YouGov in 2016. The questions analysed in this survey appeared towards the end of the AAT survey, which means that respondents had already been confronted with and answered questions about development, poverty, and foreign aid. In the United States, 6,143 responded to the survey.

---

[15] McDermott (2011); Kertzer and Tingley (2018); Kertzer (2020).
[16] Hafner-Burton et al. (2013).
[17] The AAT project examines public attitudes and behaviours towards development, global poverty, and overseas aid.
[18] Clarke et al. (2017).

The German sample counts 6,131 respondents. The experimental conditions and the survey outcomes closely mimic the survey that I used to collect individual-level data from aid officials across select donor countries, for which I presented results in the previous chapter.

Treatments

At the beginning of the aid delivery module, people were asked to imagine that their country governments were about to give foreign aid to a hypothetical Country A. 'Please imagine that your government plans to give overseas aid to help the poor in "Country A".' Subsequently, people were randomly assigned into one of five treatment conditions.

In the *control* condition, people were given basic, neutral information about Country A's development status, 'Country A is poor but has improved health and education provision for its citizens over the last five years.' The remaining four experimental conditions offered that same basic information but *added* further information about the quality of governance in the aid-receiving country. The first governance treatment captures a relatively positive governance situation in a developing country context (*Good Governance Treatment*). In addition to basic developmental information, the treatment said, 'According to international experts the country has relatively low levels of corruption and relatively strong development institutions.'

The second governance treatment captures a situation where government officials were involved in a corruption scandal (*Government Corruption*). In addition to basic developmental information, the treatment said, 'Recently, international news reported that high-level government officials were involved in a corruption scandal.'

The third governance treatment captures an environment where state institutions are weak and unable to promote indigenous development (*Weak Institutions Treatment*). In addition to basic developmental information, the treatment said, 'Most people agree that the recipient country's institutions are currently too weak to promote development further.' Finally, I included a fourth governance treatment that was not part of the survey with aid officials but that is meant to capture a situation where the government of Country A presents a governance challenge by engaging in anti-democratic behaviour against its opposition party (*Political Violence Treatment*). In addition to the basic developmental information, the treatment stated, 'Recently, international news reported that the government was attacking members of the opposition party to discourage them from challenging them in the upcoming elections.' I included *Political Violence* as an additional treatment for three reasons. First, due to the large sample sizes I had sufficient statistical power to detect treatment differences across the governance conditions when such difference actually existed. Second, I plan on using a more fine-grained conceptualisation of governance quality to understand correlates of public support for foreign aid delivery in a separate research project. And third, in the context of this book, I consider it another robustness check as I examine donor publics' reactions to poor governance in recipient countries. Table 6.1 summarises the treatment components and experimental groups.

The remainder of the survey included questions that allow me to measure respondent preferences for aid delivery. As in the survey with aid officials reported in the previous chapter, I use two questions to get at aid delivery attitudes. One outcome question asks respondents to indicate how much of the foreign aid that their government was about to give to Country A should be channelled through Country A's government. The second outcome measure asks respondents to rank-order four possible delivery channels, the recipient government, international organisations, not-for-profit organisations, and for-profit companies. As I mentioned earlier in this chapter, the ranking measure for donor publics did not distinguish between local and international NGOs as separate channels. I did this because I did not want to confuse respondents who might not immediately recognise the differences between the two types of NGOs. Finally, I include a question that asks respondents to select one out of several reasons that captures why, previously, they had rank-ordered channels the way they did. I included this question to further probe voters' motivation for selecting aid delivery responses.

Before I turn to the analyses, I investigate whether random assignment to any of the experimental conditions produced balanced treatment groups in terms of demographic characteristics. That is, I want to rule out that any individual-level characteristic of the respondent was systematically linked to the respondent's assignment into either the control or any of the treatment groups. To do this I implement balance checks for available demographic information on

Table 6.1. *Summary of experimental conditions*

Experimental group	Treatment components				
	Basic developmental information about Country A	Relatively low corruption, strong institutions in Country A	Government corruption in Country A	Weak state institutions in Country A	Political violence against opposition in Country A
Control	X				
Good Governance	X	X			
Government Corruption	X		X		
Weak Institutions	X			X	
Political Violence	X				X

"X" indicates that the conditions are included in the respective treatments.

age, gender, income, and education.[19] Across both samples, the experimental groups are well-balanced with some minor imbalance on the gender variable in the US sample.[20]

6.3 Results of Public Opinion Survey Experiment

I now turn to reporting the results from the survey experiments in the United States and Germany. I present the results for my two main post-treatment outcome measures in turn. In the first step, I will report on the measure that asked respondents to indicate how much aid the recipient government should receive in Country A, with possible answers including 'None of it', 'Some of it', 'Quite a bit of it', 'A lot of it', 'All of it', as well as 'Don't know'. In the second step, I will report results on how respondents ranked aid delivery channels in terms of their suitability given what they had learned about Country A via the treatment conditions.

The Effects of Good and Bad Governance on Amount of Aid Channelled through the Government

Figure 6.1 presents the simple distribution of responses for the first, proportional outcome measure. This figure excludes respondents who selected 'Don't know' as an option, which I recorded to be at 23 per cent in the German sample and 30 per cent in the US sample.[21] Among the respondents who placed themselves on the government-to-government answer scale, I note two initial patterns. First, the German public has a greater baseline acceptance of government-to-government aid than US respondents, as the answer distribution in the control condition indicates. While more than 70 per cent of Germans opt for government-to-government levels of 'Quite a bit of it' and more, only 25 per cent of US respondents selected the same answers. Second,

---

[19] Because this survey experiment was embedded in a survey conducted by other researchers, I was only authorised to use demographic variables in my analyses.

[20] Tables 6.A1a–6.A1d in the appendix show that the control and treatment groups are balanced on standard demographic variables.

[21] A further analysis of the systematic factors that increases the likelihood of a 'Don't Know' suggests that women, younger respondents, the less educated, people with lower incomes, and those who are more socially engaged are more likely to select that option.

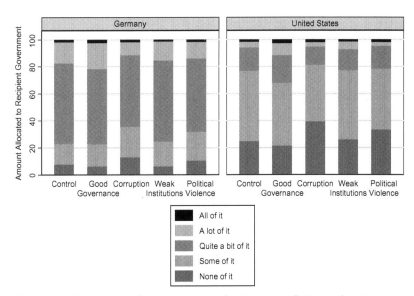

Figure 6.1 Distribution of responses across the German and US samples. Outcome variable: amount of aid delivered through the recipient government channel.

I note that regardless of the baseline differences, the distribution of responses indicates more opposition to government-to-government aid as the quality of recipient governance decreases.

In the next step, I estimate difference-in-means tests, whereby, for each test, I compare responses of the control group with responses from any of the four treatment groups. In Table 6.2, I report the results from these tests on the first outcome variable that captures recipient government involvement in foreign aid delivery. In the first column of Table 6.2, I show results from the US sample. In the second column, I present the results from the German sample. When comparing answers from US respondents in the control condition, who receive no information about governance quality, with respondents in the *Good Governance* condition, who learn about a state with good governance, I find that people, on average, want to channel more aid through the recipient government. Specifically, the *Good Governance* treatment causes a 0.15 point increase on the 5-point scale. Among German respondents, the treatment only increased demand for government aid delivery by 0.07 points. Importantly, however, I note that baseline attitudes about levels of government-to-government aid delivery vary between the two countries, with the control group in the

Table 6.2. *Response to question about aid delivery through government*

Experimental conditions	United States	Germany
Control	2.06	2.88
	(0.03)	(0.03)
	N = 825	N = 983
Good Governance	2.25	2.95
Difference	(0.03)	(0.03)
p-value for H_0	N = 908	N = 905
	−0.19	−0.07
	(0.03)	(0.04)
	0.000	0.089
Government Corruption	1.87	2.65
Difference	(0.03)	(0.03)
p-value for H_0	N = 871	N = 926
	0.19	0.24
	(0.04)	(0.04)
	0.000	0.000
Weak Institutions	2.06	2.86
Difference	(0.03)	(0.03)
p-value for H_0	N = 849	N = 935
	0.003	0.03
	(0.04)	(0.04)
	0.946	0.491
Political Violence	1.95	2.73
Difference	(0.03)	(0.03)
p-value for H_0	N = 869	N = 982
	0.11	0.15
	(0.04)	(0.04)
	0.010	0.000

Cells represent mean responses in each treatment group with standard errors in parentheses. The p-values are based on t-tests of H0: no difference in means between control and various treatment groups.

United States at 2.06 on a 5-point scale, and Germany at 2.88 on a 5-point scale. The results are similar when estimating regression-based tests, for which I present the results in the appendix, Table 6.A2.

Looking back at the response distribution of the two donor samples in Figure 6.1 as well as cross-tabulations of treatments and the outcome variable in appendix Tables 6.A3a and 6.A3b, I note that for the

German sample the modal answer is 'Quite a bit', with over half of respondents in that category, followed by 'Some of it', which was selected by 19 per cent of the respondents. Most of the movement that explains the positive effect of the *Good Governance* treatment in the German sample came from respondents who otherwise would have said 'None of It' and 'Quite a bit of It'. The distribution for the United States is different from the Germany sample, with 'Some of it' accounting for nearly half of respondents, followed by 'None of it', which was selected by 29 per cent in the US sample. This leaves only 20 per cent of respondents to populate the other categories. In the United States most of the movement that explains the positive and statistically significant effect of the *Good Governance* treatment came from respondents who otherwise would have said 'None of it' and 'Some of it', with several respondents rewarding good governance with positive changes across more than just the next highest category.

Next, I want to see whether information about corruption or weak state institutions in the aid-receiving country causes people to change their views on channelling foreign aid through the recipient government. When comparing answers from respondents in the control condition with respondents in the *Government Corruption* condition, I find that information about government corruption encourages people to channel less aid through the recipient government. Importantly, this finding holds across both samples and is thus empirical evidence against the public opinion mechanism.

In the US sample, I note that the *Government Corruption* treatment decreases willingness to channel the aid through the government by one fifth of a point on a 5-point scale. If I look back at Figure 6.1, or consult the respondent distributions across control conditions in Tables 6.A3a–6.A3b in the appendix, I note, again, that the US sample records nearly 80 per cent of respondents in the 'None of it' and 'Some of it' categories, leaving only one quarter of the US sample to populate the other categories. Most of the movement in the US sample that explains the negative and statistically significant treatment effect came from respondents who would have otherwise answered 'Some of it'.

As pointed out earlier, the German respondents, in comparison, are relatively less concentrated in the lower answer categories, with nearly 10 per cent of respondents in the 'None of it' category and 73 per cent selecting the answer categories 'Quite a bit', 'A lot of it', and 'All of it'. In comparison to the US sample, this distribution is wider across the answer categories and gives respondents greater ability to be punitive in response to the *Government Corruption* treatment. Indeed, we observe a decrease government-to-government aid by a quarter of a point on a 5-point scale, which is statistically significant. The movement in the German sample that explains the negative treatment came from people who would have otherwise chosen 'A lot of it', 'Quite a bit', and 'Some of it'. This suggests that German respondents, although they have greater baseline tolerance for government-to-government aid as measured in the control condition, are just as if not more punitive than the US public when it comes to decreasing government-to-government aid when recipient governance quality is low.

I now turn to examine whether publics react to information about weak state institutions. As in the survey with aid officials, I use the weak state treatment as a robustness check, as another proxy for bad governance. In the literature on foreign aid, weak state institutions not only lead to problems for indigenous development efforts but they also put aid transfers between donor and recipient countries at risk. For example, an aid programme aimed at helping deliver government-directed vaccine campaigns could stall or fail altogether if the state does not provide enough facilities to store the vaccines, or if there is insufficient local medical staff to deliver the vaccines. Alternatively, foreign aid could simply go to waste because of bureaucratic inefficiencies, such as lack of professional accounting expertise.

Table 6.2 presents the results for the *Weak Institutions* treatment when given to donor publics in the United States and Germany. Across the country samples, information about weak institutions in the recipient country does not seem to encourage people to change their positions on aid delivery. As the fourth row of Table 6.2 indicates, the treatment evokes a negligible and statistically insignificant decrease on a 5-point scale in both samples. One possible explanation may be that the treatment may be too weak to encourage people to change the amount that they want to see channelled through the recipient government. The *Weak Institutions* treatment may have been too ambiguous or people did not understand the implications of weak state institutions on foreign aid implementation. But, when presented with different aid delivery channels as is the case with the second outcome measure that asks people to rank the different aid delivery channels, as I will show in the second set of results, the treatment may be sufficiently strong to encourage people to opt for a different delivery actor.

Finally, the last row of Table 6.2 presents results for the *Political Violence* treatment, which provides people with information about aggressive, anti-democratic behaviour by the recipient government before asking them to determine the amount of foreign aid that should be channelled through the government. When comparing responses in the control condition with responses in the *Political Violence* condition across the two donor publics, I see a statistically significant decrease in government-to-government aid in both the US and German samples. In the US sample, the treatment yielded a 0.11 decrease on a 5-point scale. Among German respondents, information about political violence led to a 0.15 decrease on the same scale. This suggests that both publics are punitive. Compared to the two publics' reactions to government corruption, German and US reactions to political violence are less forceful in terms of effect size than what I had observed under the *Government Corruption* treatment.

In addition to the difference in means tests, I estimate regression models that include available individual-level covariates, including age, gender, education, and income as well as population weights.[22] I then estimate predictive margins of aid delivered through the recipient government for each treatment group. In Figure 6.2, I plot the predictive margins, including 95 per cent confidence intervals across all experimental conditions for the US and German donor public. Notably, the results are almost identical in terms of magnitude and statistical significance to the difference-in-means tests. This first set of results suggests that donor publics behave in very similar ways in response to governance changes in recipient countries. If anything, the German public is slightly more punitive than the US public.

The Effects of Good and Bad Governance on Ranking the Government Channel First

I now turn to reporting findings from analysis of the second outcome measure, which captures the proportion of respondents ranking the

---

[22] Table 6.A2a in the appendix presents results from regression models that include population weights. The full sample models also include country indicators and interactions between country indicators and treatment conditions to test for differences across the three samples. The results are almost identical in terms of magnitude and statistical significance to the difference-in-means tests.

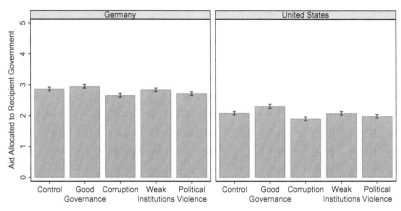

Figure 6.2 Predictive margins for government-to-government aid across experimental conditions for German and US samples. Whisker plots represent 95 per cent confidence intervals.

recipient government as the most effective channel of delivery. The dependent variable is coded '1' when a respondent ranked the government first (as most effective) and '0' if otherwise (or any other of the three remaining channels including international organisations, NGOs, and for-profit development actors). Based on the findings in the previous section, I expect information about good governance to increase the proportion of people who rank government first. On the other hand, I would expect negative governance information to decrease the proportion of people who rank government first.

As in the previous section, I present the raw distribution of ranking responses across the two samples. Figure 6.3 plots the proportion of first-rankings across the four delivery channels in the German and US samples. The results on ranking the recipient government first mirror the results from the first outcome measure. Across the two donor samples, there are baseline differences in how likely respondents are to rank the government first. German respondents in the control condition are more likely to rank the recipient government first than US respondents in the same condition. Nearly 40 per cent of Germans rank the recipient government first, while only 25 per cent of US citizens do so. The implication of this baseline difference across the two political economy types, or donor countries, is that, relative to US respondents, German respondents can react to bad governance information more because distribution of their answers has more variability

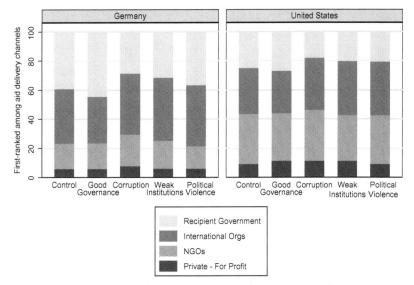

Figure 6.3 Distribution of responses across the German and US samples. Outcome variable: first-ranked aid delivery channel.

and room to move away from the recipient government. Simultaneously, because a sizable portion of German respondents has a pro-recipient government attitude as a baseline, fewer Germans can actually reward the government channel in response to good governance information by ranking the government first.

Importantly, we continue to see very similar patterns across the two donor publics in how their citizens respond to information about poor recipient governance. Both publics turn away from the recipient government when learning about bad governance. To corroborate the pattern in the raw data, I estimate a difference-in-means test and present the results in Table 6.3. Across both samples, the *Good Governance* treatment increases the proportion of respondents that rank the government first. In the US sample, the increase is not statistically significant. In the German sample, the *Good Governance* treatment increases the proportion of first-ranked recipient governments by 4 per cent.

As expected, the *Government Corruption* treatment has a sizable negative effect in both samples. US and German respondents react to recipient corruption by being less likely to rank government first. Among US citizens, the corruption treatment decreases the proportion of respondents ranking government first by 0.07. In the German

Table 6.3. *Response to question about aid delivery ranking*

Experimental conditions	United States	Germany
Control	0.25	0.39
	(0.01)	(0.01)
	N = 1,202	N = 1,268
Good Governance	0.27	0.44
Difference	(0.03)	(0.01)
p-value for H_0	N = 1,253	N = 1,149
	0.02	0.05
	(0.02)	(0.02)
	0.255	0.001
Government Corruption	0.18	0.29
Difference	(0.01)	(0.01)
p-value for H_0	N = 1,201	N = 1,221
	−0.07	−0.10
	(0.01)	(0.02)
	0.000	0.000
Weak Institutions	0.20	0.32
Difference	(0.01)	(0.01)
p-value for H_0	N = 1,207	N = 1,214
	−0.05	−0.08
	(0.02)	(0.02)
	0.007	0.000
Political Violence	0.21	0.37
Difference	(0.01)	(0.01)
p-value for H_0	N = 1,280	N = 1,279
	−0.04	−0.02
	(0.02)	(0.02)
	0.010	0.175

Outcome measured as proportion of respondents who ranked government first. Cells represent mean responses in each treatment group with standard errors in parentheses. The p-values are based on t-tests of H_0: no difference in means between control and various treatment groups.

sample, as before, the decrease is more pronounced at 0.10. The *Weak Institutions* treatment also has a negative effect, though not as big as we observe with the *Government Corruption* treatment. Being told about a country's inability to promote development on its own decreases the proportion of US respondents ranking the government channel as first by 0.05 and the German respondents 0.08. Unlike for the first outcome measure, which captured levels of aid delivered through the government-to-government channel, the publics' responses to the *Weak Institutions* treatment are statistically significantly different from the control group and in the expected direction.[23] The last treatment, *Political Violence*, has a negative and statistically significant effect across the various samples. In the US sample, the treatment decreased the proportion by 0.04 and the effect is statistically significant. In the German sample, the treatment decreased the proportion by 0.02 and the effect is not statistically significant at conventional levels.

Again, I estimate regression models in addition to the difference-in-means tests. These models include available individual-level covariates, including age, gender, education, and income as well as population weights.[24] As before, the results are nearly identical to the findings reported in Table 6.3.[25] I also estimate predictive margins of the delivery channel ranking for each treatment group. In Figure 6.4, I plot these predictive margins, including 95 per cent confidence intervals across all experimental conditions for the US and German donor publics. This first set of results suggests that donor publics behave in very similar ways in reaction to governance changes in recipient countries. Compared to the US public, the German public is more punitive, as evidenced by a significant reduction in government-first rankings under conditions of corruption and weak state institutions.

The quantitative evidence thus far reveals that the reactions of the two donor publics do not mirror the heterogeneous aid delivery patterns observed at the level of the aid official or at the cross-country level. When presented with information about poor recipient governance, the US and German publics are similarly punitive insofar

---

[23] The smaller effect size might still support my previous conclusion that the *Weak Institutions* treatment may have been too ambiguous or that more people did not understand the implications of weak state institutions on foreign aid implementation.

[24] Table 6.A2b in the appendix presents results from regression models that include population weights. The full sample models also include country indicators and interactions between country indicators and treatment conditions to test for differences across the three samples. The results are almost identical in terms of magnitude and statistical significance to the difference-in-means tests.

[25] In Tables 6.A4a and 6.A4b in the appendix I present the specific movement in variables for the ranking outcome variable.

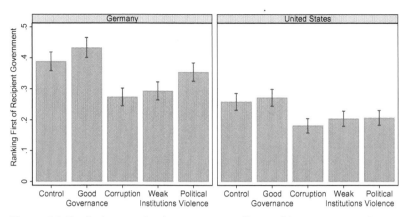

Figure 6.4 Predictive margins for government-first ranking across experimental conditions for German and US samples. Whisker plots represent 95 per cent confidence intervals.

as they opt to abandon the state. If anything, the German public is more punitive than the US public. These results do not support the alternative public opinion explanation, which hypothesises that the responses between aid officials and donor publics are congruent because aid officials promote aid delivery decisions that are broadly supported at home.

A tentative within-country comparison of the reactions of aid officials and their donor publics allows me to document another empirical implication of my argument. Because US and German aid publics are not discernably different from one another, I expect the magnitude of difference between what citizens want and what aid officials prefer in foreign aid delivery to differ by political economy type. On the one hand, I found that the two donor publics are similarly punitive under conditions of poor governance. On the other hand, results from Chapters 4 and 5 document that the German government and aid officials are more likely to engage with the recipient government than the US government under similar conditions. This suggests that a within-country comparison of the two samples across the two donor countries yields more convergence between publics and aid officials in the United States and more divergence between the same groups in Germany, especially when asked about aid delivery in poorly governed countries.

Furthermore, I want to use cautious direct comparisons to further examine the empirical implications of the fact that the two samples represent two different worlds, as suggested earlier in this chapter. As I had suggested earlier on, aid officials work for aid organisations and represent their governments. As purposive actors, aid officials are motivated to advance the mandate of their organisation. Voters, on the other hand, are effectively unconstrained. They do not work for aid organisations nor are they beholden to institutional rulebooks. Their role as private citizens does not require them to reflect on broader foreign policy objectives or interactions with recipient authorities. As I pointed out in Chapter 2, scholarship of domestic sources of foreign aid support has demonstrated that individuals make decisions based on their own moral beliefs and economic situation. In the context of this chapter, I have already shown empirically that citizen attitudes about foreign aid are similar across different donor political economy types. In direct comparison with aid officials, I expect publics, on average, to be less likely than aid officials to embrace government-to-government aid, and to be more punitive when they learn about poor recipient governance.

Before I proceed any further to investigate this difference in magnitude between the two political economy types, I want to stress that any direct comparison must be made with caution because the survey designs differ in important respects. First, the survey designs differ in the mechanism of treatment assignment: while the survey of aid officials relies on a within-subject design that assigns each respondent to all treatment conditions, the donor public survey is constructed on a between-subject design, whereby I randomly assign respondents into one treatment condition only. Second, the outcome measure used to rank aid delivery channels in the aid officials survey asks respondents to rank five aid delivery channels, the recipient government, international organisations, local NGOs, international NGOs, and private sector actors. To avoid potential confusion among members of donor publics about differences between local and international NGOs, I collapsed these two actors into a single NGO category. Third, unlike the aid officials survey, the members of donor publics survey, due to space constraints, only focused on the key treatments and main outcome measures and did not include the post-treatment questions nor the open-ended questions that I asked in the aid officials survey. Finally, the sample sizes differ dramatically. Importantly, however, these differences in survey designs are the same across the United States and Germany.

My cautious comparison of citizens and aid officials thus only focuses on rough patterns within the United States and Germany. First, I look at sample differences in reactions to good and bad governance regarding the two outcome measures. In Figure 6.5a, I present descriptive evidence for the hypothesised difference between the two samples within donor countries. In Germany and in the United States, information about good recipient governance encourages aid officials to channel more aid through the recipient government than voters would. In Figure 6.5b, I note a similar pattern for the ranking measure. In Germany and the United States, the good governance treatment makes it more likely that aid officials rank the government channel first than voters. I interpret this evidence, although it is descriptive and tentative, to corroborate my claim that aid officials are not constrained by what citizens think is best for aid delivery.

I then look at cross-sample reactions to information about poor recipient governance. As predicted, here I expect the magnitude of differences between the public and aid officials to be starkest in Germany, where institutional rulebooks make it more likely that aid officials embrace government-to-government aid than in the United States, where the rulebooks prescribe more punitive bypass behaviour. Figures 6.6a and 6.6b present prima facie support for this claim. When asked about how much aid they would channel to the recipient government under conditions of poor governance, German aid officials diverged more from their public than US officials.

Figure 6.6a shows that while nearly 20 percent of the German aid officials wanted to deliver either 'A large amount' or 'All' through the recipient government, just over ten per cent of the German public selected these two options. In the United States, the distribution shows considerably more overlap in responses between aid officials and the public. The distribution of the ranking responses shows a similar pattern in Figure 6.6b. In Germany, more than half of the aid officials ranked the recipient government first, while 28 per cent of the public selected that option. In the United States, the difference between aid officials and voters is less pronounced with 7 per cent of aid officials and 18 per cent of voters ranking government first. Although the results of the direct comparison must be interpreted with caution, they provide further empirical support for my contention that publics do not constrain aid officials in their decisions about aid delivery.

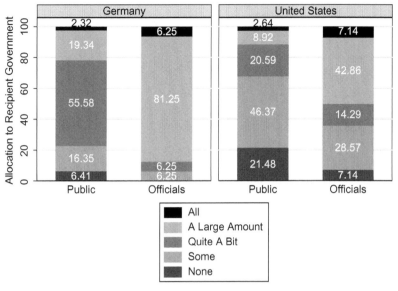

Figure 6.5a Aid to recipient government – good governance

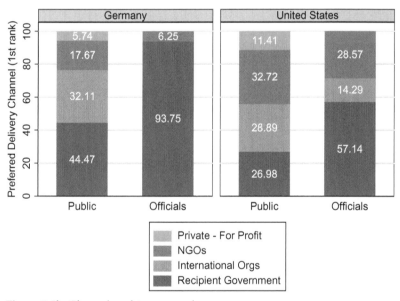

Figure 6.5b Channel rankings – good governance

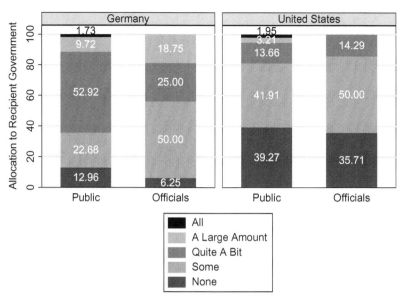

Figure 6.6a Aid to recipient government – bad governance

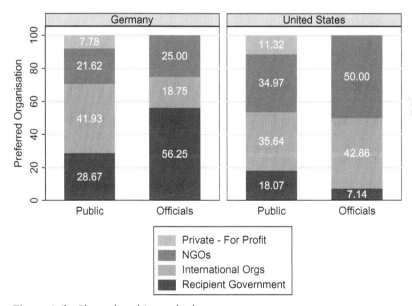

Figure 6.6b Channel rankings – bad governance

6.4 Conclusion

In this chapter, I have paid attention to an alternative argument, which suggests that donor publics might constrain aid officials to deliver foreign aid in ways that are consistent with the heterogeneous pattern delineated in previous chapters. As classical accounts of representative democracy have suggested, publics can constrain decision-making if they feel that governments make policy choices that have gone too far outside what is broadly popular among voters. Governments who fear pressure or, at worst, electoral sanctions thus promote policy that receives broad support. In the context of foreign aid delivery, the public opinion mechanism implies that aid officials and publics hold similar attitudes on delivery mechanisms; and that the aid delivery patterns that we observe at the country level receive broad support among donor publics. To investigate this possibility, I analysed originally collected public opinion data from the United States and Germany in 2016. I also leveraged my interview data with aid officials from the United States and Germany to learn more about how they perceived the role of the public when making decisions about bypass or engagement with recipient governments.

The results revealed that across both political economies, as represented by the United States and Germany, voters sanctioned poor recipient governance by promoting bypass: when respondents learned about bad governance conditions in the aid-receiving country, they decreased their support for government-to-government aid delivery, and were less likely to rank the government channel as the most effective delivery channel. In Germany, the difference between what the public said it wanted and what aid officials preferred was more pronounced than what we observed in the United States. While I consider this empirical test tentative, I interpret the empirical evidence to suggest that the link between national structures and delivery may not be driven by what citizens believe is the best approach to promoting development abroad. Instead, as my theoretical argument suggests, the link is driven by institutional rulebooks since their adoption has shaped the decisions of aid officials to bypass or engage with recipient authorities in foreign aid.

That said, the results of the public opinion data show that public opinion can mirror some of the observed political economy differences insofar as donor publics across political economy types vary in their baseline attitudes towards the state, as noted in cross-country comparisons of voters who were in the control group. There, I noted that German citizens were more favourable towards government-to-government aid than their counterparts in the United States. Although more research is needed to explain this particular pattern in the data, it is plausible that institutions, whose ideological rulebooks have been around and determinative for decades if not centuries, have also influenced, at least to some extent, public attitudes about the role of states and markets in governance.[26] As Blyth has argued in *Great Transformations*, powerful political and social actors, including politicians, business, and labour, not only coalesced around and promoted neoliberal reforms in the United States. They also engaged in collective action and, largely supported by the media, promoted a neoliberal discourse, to build new institutions and persuade the public of the new reform agenda.[27] In the context of the United States or other neoliberal political economies, studies suggest that neoliberal narratives that blame the state for societal ills may have contributed to making social groups less accepting of the state in general, and government-to-government aid in particular.[28]

Finally, the results in this chapter suggest that for aid delivery patterns to markedly change within donor countries, public opinion is unlikely to make a difference. Instead, donors require new institutional rulebooks that, when championed by influential political actors during opportune political moments, replace existing rules and structures. To scholars of representative democracy this finding may be disconcerting.[29] After all, I find that in traditional public sector donor countries such as Germany, aid officials are quite removed from how citizens want to promote aid. To others, the promotion of institutional forms that bring aid officials closer to what is broadly supported by the public may be detrimental for aid objectives that prioritise more long-term capacity-building, which may simply not be in the purview of ordinary citizens.

What is more, as public opinion research in foreign aid has demonstrated, citizen attitudes about foreign aid are diffuse, at best. As research in the area of trade has found, knowledge deficits among publics about the distributional implications of trade may help explain why a country's trade policy looks so different from the trade

---

[26] Research on elite persuasion and public opinion has argued that government elites can shape public opinion by emphasising how their policy decisions are in line with citizens' beliefs or by arguing that they will accomplish shared goals (e.g. Kinder and Sanders (1990); Tesler (2015)). Or, the public defers to policy decisions because they lack information or expertise on particular issues (e.g. Fox and Shotts (2009)).
[27] Blyth (2002).   [28] Harvey (2007).
[29] Ezrow and Hellwig (2014); Hays (2009).

preferences of the voting population.[30] In foreign aid, knowledge deficits may even be exacerbated because the beneficiaries of aid live in distant places, far removed from the donor public's eye. Aid officials, on the other hand, pursue their aid organisation's mandate, which, for better or worse, can be at odds with what the public wants.

Appendix

6.A1 Balance Checks (Control vs. Various Treatments)

Table 6.A1a. *Balance checks for control vs. good governance treatment*

Country	Variable	Control group mean (SE)	Treatment group mean (SE)	Difference (SE)	p-value for H_0: no difference
Germany	Age	49.25 (0.43)	49.30 (0.46)	−0.05 (0.63)	0.94
	Gender (Female = 2, Male = 1)	1.50 (0.01)	1.52 (0.01)	−0.03 (0.02)	0.18
	Education (5-point scale)	3.26 (0.02)	3.25 (0.02)	0.01 (0.02)	0.67
	Income (5-point scale)	2.30 (0.03)	2.24 (0.03)	0.06 (0.05)	0.23
United States	Age	49.23 (0.48)	49.00 (0.47)	0.23 (0.67)	0.73
	Gender (Female = 2, Male = 1)	1.55 (0.01)	1.54 (0.01)	0.01 (0.2)	0.82
	Education (5-point scale)	3.31 (0.02)	3.37 (0.02)	−0.06 (0.02)	0.09
	Income (5-point scale)	2.84 (0.04)	2.81 (0.04)	0.03 (0.05)	0.63

---

[30] Gusinger (2017).

Table 6.A1b. *Balance checks for control vs. government corruption treatment*

Country	Variable	Control group mean (SE)	Treatment group mean (SE)	Difference (SE)	p-value for H_0: no difference
Germany	Age	49.25 (0.43)	48.11 (0.43)	1.14 (0.61)	0.06
	Gender (Female = 2, Male = 1)	1.50 (0.01)	1.53 (0.01)	−0.03 (0.02)	0.22
	Education (5-point scale)	3.26 (0.02)	3.26 (0.02)	−0.001 (0.03)	0.96
	Income (5-point scale)	2.30 (0.03)	2.25 (0.03)	0.05 (0.05)	0.32
United States	Age	49.23 (0.48)	49.73 (0.47)	0.50 (0.67)	0.45
	Gender (Female = 2, Male = 1)	1.55 (0.01)	1.57 (0.01)	−0.02 (0.2)	0.26
	Education (5-point scale)	3.31 (0.02)	3.27 (0.02)	0.04 (0.03)	0.23
	Income (5-point scale)	2.84 (0.04)	2.79 (0.04)	0.05 (0.05)	0.39

Table 6.A1c. *Balance checks for control vs. weak institutions treatment*

Country	Variable	Control group mean (SE)	Treatment group mean (SE)	Difference (SE)	p-value for H$_0$: no difference
Germany	Age	49.25 (0.43)	48.96 (0.44)	0.29 (0.62)	0.63
	Gender (Female = 2, Male = 1)	1.50 (0.01)	1.51 (0.01)	−0.01 (0.02)	0.56
	Education (5-point scale)	3.26 (0.02)	3.26 (0.02)	0.005 (0.03)	0.86
	Income (5-point scale)	2.30 (0.03)	2.25 (0.03)	0.05 (0.05)	0.34
United States	Age	49.23 (0.48)	49.91 (0.47)	−0.69 (0.67)	0.30
	Gender (Female = 2, Male = 1)	1.55 (0.01)	1.51 (0.01)	0.03 (0.02)	0.12
	Education (5-point scale)	3.31 (0.02)	3.37 (0.02)	−0.05 (0.03)	0.11
	Income (5-point scale)	2.84 (0.04)	2.85 (0.04)	−0.01 (0.05)	0.81

Table 6.A1d. *Balance checks for control vs. political violence treatment*

Country	Variable	Control group mean (SE)	Treatment group mean (SE)	Difference (SE)	p-value for H_0: no difference
Germany	Age	49.25 (0.43)	48.92 (0.43)	0.33 (0.61)	0.58
	Gender (Female = 2, Male = 1)	1.50 (0.01)	1.52 (0.01)	−0.03 (0.02)	0.30
	Education (5-point scale)	3.26 (0.02)	3.22 (0.02)	0.04 (0.03)	0.14
	Income (5-point scale)	2.30 (0.03)	2.26 (0.03)	0.04 (0.05)	0.43
United States	Age	49.23 (0.48)	48.81 (0.47)	0.41 (0.67)	0.54
	Gender (Female = 2, Male = 1)	1.55 (0.01)	1.55 (0.01)	0.005 (0.02)	0.78
	Education (5-point scale)	3.31 (0.02)	3.32 (0.02)	−0.01 (0.03)	0.92
	Income (5-point scale)	2.84 (0.04)	2.83 (0.04)	0.01 (0.05)	0.94

6.A2 Regression-Based Analyses

Regression-Based Tests. Here I look for treatment effects in regression models that include country indicators for the combined sample. Across all models, I include sample weights that account for socio-demographic characteristics of our respondents (gender, age, education, newspaper readership). The regression models return coefficients of similar magnitude and levels of statistical significance to the difference-in-means tests reported in the main text.

Table 6.A2a. *Regression-based analyses for government aid*

	United States	Germany
Good Governance	0.152**	0.057
	(0.06)	(0.04)
High Corruption	−0.193**	−0.234**
	(0.06)	(0.04)
Weak Institutions	0.013	−0.029
	(0.04)	(0.04)
Political Violence	−0.135*	−0.153**
	(0.06)	(0.04)
N	4,322	4,731

Coefficient and robust standard error from OLS regression models including sample weights. For the combined sample, I also include country sample indicators. ** $p <$ 0.01, * $p < 0.05$, ^ $p < 0.1$.

Table 6.A2b. *Regression-based analyses for ranking government first*

	OLS	
	United States	Germany
Good Governance	0.028	0.054**
	(0.02)	(0.02)
High Corruption	−0.045*	−0.100**
	(0.02)	(0.02)
Weak Institutions	0.020	−0.076**
	(0.02)	(0.02)
Political Violence	−0.025	−0.020
	(0.02)	(0.02)
N	6,143	6,131

Coefficient and robust standard error from OLS regression models including sample weights. For the combined sample, I also include country sample indicators. Logit results are identical in terms of coefficient direction and statistical significance. ** $p < 0.01$, * $p < 0.05$, ^ $p < 0.1$.

6.A3 Specific Movement in Outcome Variables

Cross-Tabs of Aid-through-Gov't Variable and Treatments. Number of respondents and proportion of cases in each cell. χ^2 test of independence between rows and columns, for each of four pairs of control and treatment condition.

Table 6.A3a. *Cross-tabulations of treatments and government aid: German respondents*

	Control	Good governance	Government corruption	Weak institutions	Political violence	Total
None of it	77	58	120	59	103	419
	(0.08)	(0.06)	(0.13)	(0.06)	(0.10)	(0.09)
Some of it	149	148	210	171	209	887
	(0.15)	(0.16)	(0.23)	(0.19)	(0.21)	(0.19)
Quite a bit of it	586	503	490	561	533	2,673
	(0.60)	(0.56)	(0.53)	(0.60)	(0.54)	(0.57)
A lot of it	154	175	90	132	121	672
	(0.16)	(0.19)	(0.10)	(0.14)	(0.12)	(0.14)
All of it	17	21	16	12	16	82
	(0.01)	(0.02)	(0.02)	(0.01)	(0.02)	(0.02)
Total	983	905	926	935	982	4,731
Pearson χ^2		7.56	43.47	5.80	20.31	
(p-value)		(0.11)	(0.000)	(0.22)	(0.000)	

Table 6.A3b. *Cross-tabulations of treatments and government aid: US respondents*

	Control	Good governance	Government corruption	Weak institutions	Political violence	Total
None of it	204	195	342	220	289	1,250
	(0.25)	(0.21)	(0.40)	(0.26)	(0.33)	(0.29)
Some of it	429	421	365	435	391	2,041
	(0.52)	(0.46)	(0.42)	(0.51)	(0.45)	(0.47)
Quite a bit of it	144	187	119	133	148	731
	(0.17)	(0.21)	(0.14)	(0.16)	(0.17)	(0.17)
A lot of it	35	81	28	48	25	217
	(0.04)	(0.09)	(0.03)	(0.06)	(0.03)	(0.05)
All of it	13	24	17	13	16	83
	(0.02)	(0.03)	(0.02)	(0.02)	(0.02)	(0.02)
Total	825	908	871	849	869	4,322
Pearson χ^2		23.45	42.51	2.77	17.32	
(p-value)		(0.000)	(0.000)	(0.57)	(0.002)	

6.A4 Specific Movement in Outcome Variables

Table 6.A4a. *Cross-tabulations of treatments and ranking variable: German respondents*

	Control	Good governance	Government corruption	Weak institutions	Political violence	Total
0	770 (0.20)	638 (0.16)	871 (0.13)	831 (0.21)	810 (0.20)	3,920
Ranked First	498 (0.23)	511 (0.23)	350 (0.16)	383 (0.17)	469 (0.20)	2,211
Total	1,268	1,149	1,221	1,214	1,279	6,131
Pearson χ^2 (p-value)		6.70 (0.01)	31.17 (0.000)	16.17 (0.000)	1.83 (0.18)	

Number of respondents and proportion of cases in each cell. χ^2 test of independence between rows and columns, for each of four pairs of control and treatment condition.

Table 6.A4b. *Cross-tabulations of treatments and ranking variable: US respondents*

	Control	Good governance	Government corruption	Weak institutions	Political violence	Total
0	902 (0.19)	915 (0.19)	984 (0.21)	961 (0.20)	1,016 (0.21)	4,778
Ranked First	300 (0.22)	338 (0.25)	217 (0.16)	246 (0.18)	264 (0.19)	1,365
Total	1,202	1,149	1,201	1,207	1,279	6,143
Pearson χ^2 (p-value)		1.30 (0.26)	16.89 (0.000)	7.20 (0.01)	6.63 (0.01)	

Number of respondents and proportion of cases in each cell. χ^2 test of independence between rows and columns, for each of four pairs of control and treatment condition.

7 | Implications for Aid Effectiveness, Public Policy, and Future Research

7.1 Introduction

How can donors deliver foreign aid so that it mitigates institutional failure, avoids aid capture, and promotes efficacy? This question is especially relevant for countries such as Sri Lanka, Afghanistan, or Haiti, which have pressing and far-reaching needs, yet experience governance deficiencies that pose severe risks to effective aid implementation. One common approach is to bypass the recipient government and outsource the delivery of foreign aid to non-state actors. However, as I have shown, bypass tactics are contested among donor countries. Marked differences exist in the degree to which donor governments pursue bypass tactics in aid delivery. While donor governments such as the United States and the United Kingdom systematically resort to employing bypass tactics in poor governance environments, others, such as Germany or France, make more limited use of it. The latter are more likely to pursue a contrasting approach that engages with the recipient government to organise and distribute its assistance, while including hands-on mechanisms of control and oversight.

These contrasting aid delivery tactics under similar international economic and recipient country conditions represent the central puzzle that motivated the writing of this book. As I point out in Chapter 1, research on foreign aid has largely focused on explaining aid levels and has only recently turned more attention to aid delivery mechanisms. By shedding light on why donors deliver aid the way they do, and why some bypass more than others, I contribute to long-standing questions about the origins of donor motivations. Further, I engage with debates about foreign aid effectiveness by clarifying why and how donors pursue different goals in development. For public policy, my argument implies that that lasting and robust changes in aid delivery tactics necessitate institutional reforms that alter the incentive structures inside aid organisations and motivate aid officials to change towards a different tactic.

7.2 National Structures and Foreign Aid Delivery

The purpose of this book has been to develop and test a theory that provides answers as to why and under what conditions donor governments decide to bypass recipient authorities or engage with them; and why marked differences exist across donors in how they deliver aid in poorly governed countries. The explanation that I develop in Chapters 2 and 3 of this book is founded on empirically and theoretically informed views about aid officials and national aid systems. As I have argued and shown throughout, national structures, my independent variable, assumes a central and systematic role in explaining variation across donors and across time.

Aid organisations, like other state organisations, function on the basis of *institutional rulebooks* that prescribe how aid officials deal with risk in aid implementation at any given time. These rulebooks, as North reminds us, are 'humanly devised constraints that structure political, economic and social interactions', or *rules of the game*.[1] They prescribe whether aid officials bypass or engage with the recipient government when the quality of recipient governance is low.

But aid organisations and their rulebooks reflect and promote ideological positions. The rules of the game that structure interactions were created at different times, in different countries during critical junctures by political actors who held particular beliefs about what they considered an appropriate model of governance. These beliefs, as per my argument, correspond with different blends of roles between the state and the market in public sector governance. Throughout the book, I distinguish between traditional public sector and neoliberal beliefs that, once fixed and locked in through institutional rulebooks, become constraints on state action by justifying particular aid delivery tactics, while precluding others. More broadly, my findings suggest that the varied beliefs that underwrite aid organisations and their rules also create different priorities among donors in what the development

---

[1] North (1991), p. 97.

assistance should accomplish; whether donors prioritise results in the short term or recipient capacity-building.

In my theory and empirical tests, I thus locate the *origin* of bypass or government-to-government tactics *within* aid organisations. Importantly, my argument does not suggest that donors with neoliberal aid agencies never engage in capacity-building efforts. Nor am I saying that, for example, Germany or France never fund basic needs projects like vaccination campaigns implemented by non-state actors. Indeed, donors of all stripes combine short- and long-term approaches. But my argument suggests donors have tendencies to do more of one than the other. Moreover, I do not argue that foreign aid is never influenced by non-developmental strategic concerns. There are examples that support this possibility, to which I pointed in Chapter 1 of this book. Yet, a systematic account of donor–recipient interactions today as well as over time requires a more prominent place for the role played by national structures in international development.

In Chapter 3, I elucidated the institutional constraints mechanism. In this chapter, I established that all aid officials, regardless of political economy type, are motivated to help developing countries prosper. However, I make the case that how aid officials go about doing so, i.e. whether they choose to bypass or engage recipient authorities, depends on the character of the institution and the rules that incentivise aid officials to deliver aid in opposite directions. I show how neoliberal rulebooks in USAID, DFID, and Sida enable and justify bypass tactics, while aid organisations in Germany and France encourage more government-to-government engagement under similar international economic and recipient country conditions. I provide a historical perspective to illustrate how today's rules reproduce governance beliefs that were locked in during the time in which the institution was created many decades ago and that continue to shape aid delivery decisions today.

My empirical strategy promotes testing at different levels of analysis. The varied data that I collected and the methods that I employed to test my theoretical framework present a significant contribution to the study of foreign aid. In Chapter 4, I evaluated my theory at the country level across twenty-three OECD donors and their respective aid recipients from 2005 to 2015. Drawing on my earlier work that studies the determinants of aid delivery, I use an originally constructed bypass measure as my dependent variable.[2] The quantitative tests produced robust support for my theory, which predicts that donor countries of different political economy types diverge in their aid delivery under similar international economic and poor recipient country conditions.

In Chapter 5, I tested the micro-foundations of my argument on an original survey data set of sixty-five aid officials across six donor countries, the United States, the United Kingdom, Sweden, Germany, France, and Japan. Similar to the findings of the time-series cross country analyses, I found robust evidence for systematic differences in aid delivery preferences, with aid officials from the United States, the United Kingdom, and Sweden being significantly more likely to resort to bypass tactics under conditions of poor governance than their counterparts from Germany, France, and Japan. What is more, the individual-level data further substantiated the hypothesised institutional constraints mechanism as empirically useful insofar as additional empirical implications of my argument that linked national aid structures to different aid priorities and evaluation tactics received empirical support.

In the last empirical chapter, Chapter 6, I used originally collected, nationally representative public opinion data from the United States and Germany to rule out an important alternative explanation to my argument, namely that aid officials are constrained by their publics insofar as decisions to bypass or engage with the recipient government come about because these policies are broadly supported at home. The results indicate that the observed variation in aid delivery across donor countries does not appear to result from public opinion. Instead, I find that in both the United States and Germany publics are punitive when they learn about poor recipient governance, advocating bypass under similar international economic and recipient country conditions.

7.3 Implications for Aid Effectiveness and Public Policy

My findings carry a number of implications for aid effectiveness and public policy. First, my argument posits that the core mission or mandate of the aid organisation is not objectively defined. Rather it is subjective insofar as it reflects the ideological context in which it was created and is therefore endogenous to the organisation of the donor

---

[2] Dietrich (2013, 2016).

political economy. This insight informs our understanding of aid effectiveness because it establishes a link between political economies and the different priorities that donors pursue with foreign aid. Donor governments that have a preference for bypassing recipient authorities in countries with poor governance may achieve greater success in providing immediate relief to the poor through quickly implementable health interventions than their counterparts who place greater emphasis on state engagement. However, as I have noted throughout the book, the creation of parallel structures in recipient countries to deliver aid can hamper or even undermine donor efforts to build up a state capable of managing its own development – an objective that ranks high for donor governments who prefer a tactic of greater engagement with the government in the developing country.

Importantly, my book does not try to measure the effectiveness of bypass or government engagement directly. Nor do I wish to make a normative claim about which I believe is better suited to promote prosperity in countries with a poor governance record. Instead, I approach the question of aid effectiveness by claiming that aid success is in the eyes of the beholder, and endogenous to national structures: aid officials that follow neoliberal rulebooks are more likely than their traditional public sector peers to consider short-term results a success in foreign aid. In other words, *aid success means different things to aid officials from different political economies.* Any effort to evaluate which of the two regimes is better on the basis of single metrics is thus missing the point. We need to think more carefully about the different aid priorities of donors, how they measure aid success, and then come up with separate metrics and effectiveness tests that reflect more accurately the heterogeneity among donors as well as changes within donor countries over time.

Second, I put forward the insight that how aid officials from OECD countries structure donor–recipient interactions is explained, in part, by past decisions to organise state institutions. This suggests that aid officials only have a limited ability to adjust foreign aid delivery tactics. Although it is easy to find critics who bemoan the status-quo orientation of aid organisations,[3] my book argues that even if aid officials inside organisations knew how to optimise aid delivery following whatever tactic they or the market of ideas considers most promising

---

[3] E.g. Easterly (2002); Gulrajani (2011).

at any given time, institutional constraints would incentivise aid officials to stick to the rulebooks. They would ensure that, today, aid officials in the United States and United Kingdom structure donor–recipient interactions in ways that correspond with what neoliberal reformers around Thatcher and Reagan believed was the appropriate response to dealing with societal challenges many decades ago, as they seized on opportune moments to lock in their beliefs by radically transforming the public sectors. In Germany or France, aid officials act in similarly path-dependent ways but the bias of donor–recipient interaction points in the opposite direction: aid officials promote government-to-government delivery because the institutions are set up to guarantee a more prominent role of the state in public sector governance. In the end, it is rules and their ideological content, not ideas or beliefs per se, that create robust and lasting preferences that govern decisions and behaviour of aid officials, and by extension, donor–recipient interactions.

The findings of my book suggest that institutional constraints bias the aid system towards the status quo, making innovation and change difficult. Established rules and practices, regardless of their character, make it costly for aid officials to go against them and deliver aid in opposite ways. Aid delivery patterns thus remain sticky, even when the practice is considered outdated or dysfunctional or the evidence is stacked up against a particular tactic. Even as the landscape and demands of developing countries are changing, institutional rulebooks prevent donors from responding flexibly and variedly. Even if an alternative practice or policy were demonstrably better, the organisational incentives would work against a robust adoption by hampering their set up and implementation. Citing Schumpeter in Chapter 1, I suggested that ideas or beliefs may hold the seed of creative destruction, but for alternative beliefs to bring about lasting and robust changes in aid delivery practices, aid systems and their institutions require fundamental reform and rule changes. Or, they require governments to expend significant political capital to persuade aid officials to pursue aid delivery tactics that require them to ignore material incentives and go against their standard practices.

Yet, my book does not imply that alternative beliefs never matter. Indeed, I do not want to suggest that aid officials should not be optimistic about change. Many observers rightfully consider international development to be one of the most innovative sectors.

Recent proposals to solve global development challenges include ideas as varied as social investments, challenge prizes, trust funds, or cash-on-delivery, among many others. But wishful thinking is not helpful and might be counterproductive insofar as it can lead to frustration and discouragement down the road. As Hailey Swedlund points out in *Development Dance*, plenty of innovative ideas about aid delivery have made their way through aid bureaucracies across donor countries like 'fads and fashion' but only few of these ideas ever stick.[4]

My theory implies that institutional rulebooks act as gate-keepers for new ideas. They allow innovation to flourish as long as innovative ideas conform to or are compatible with the constituting rules, which define the repertoire of legitimate and stable action. Discontinuity between new ideas and institutions can lead to friction within the organisation. It may even induce small-scale change. In Chapter 5, I leveraged qualitative evidence from interviews with aid officials to support this contention. I documented, for example, that within the Swedish aid bureaucracy, recent internal efforts to make aid delivery more context-driven led to minor structural changes, such as, for example, reduced dependence on corporate results and performance frameworks.[5] However, the efforts did not lead to a reformulation of incentives for aid officials during the time frame of this study, thus falling short of large-scale political change. As long as careers turn on achieving yesterday's goals, the overall system remains on a neoliberal trajectory, as I document in Chapter 3.

My argument further implies that marked differences in institutional rulebooks and aid priorities, across countries and over time, should have implications for the development of an international development agenda. Over the past three decades, the international donor community has come together at regular intervals to discuss how to improve the effectiveness of international development efforts. After all, many of the world's poorest countries had not visibly improved in spite of decades' worth of development assistance during the Cold War. The United States and the United Kingdom, alongside leading international development actors such as the IMF and the World Bank, spearheaded neoliberal efforts in international development by advocating for foreign aid to became more accountability- and results-oriented. By bringing private sector thinking to international development efforts, it was

---

[4] Swedlund (2017).   [5] OECD DAC (2017).

argued, donors could restore trust in foreign aid and international development efforts more broadly.[6]

The International Development Goals (IDGs), a precursor to the Millennium Development Goals (MDGs), was an early effort to improve accountability and produce tangible and measurable results for development efforts. Set out via the OECD DAC's report 'Shaping the 21st Century: The Role of Development Cooperation',[7] the IDGs were the first global framework that proposed precise, quantitative development targets in the areas of poverty, nutrition, water, gender, and health.[8] These targets were set, in part, to assess the performance of donors. In parallel to the DAC's 'Shaping the 21st Century', the United Nations promoted international development as one of four main themes for the Millennium Assembly held in New York in September 2000.[9] The assembly produced the Millennium Declaration, which, in turn, served as a foundation for the MDGs that were adopted in 2001. The MDGs expanded on and ultimately replaced the IDGs.[10] The MDGs set the stage for the development of a more accounting-based approach to promoting international development, one that is founded on a structured global framework of goals, targets, and indicators. These targets would help steer, communicate, and justify donor policies and programmes in the areas of poverty reduction.[11]

With the adoption of the Monterrey Consensus in 2002, donor governments and international development actors directly linked aid policy to the Millennium Development Goals (MDGs) and thus reaffirmed their commitment to monitoring, measuring, and assessing donor development efforts in developing countries. This commitment, as David Hulme has noted, was underpinned by "results-based thinking".[12] By setting time-bound targets to measure progress in reducing poverty, hunger, and mortality, donor governments were now in a better position to steer their own development efforts and demand improved performance and use of economic resources from aid-receiving governments.[13] In practice, donor agencies could now

---

[6] Mawdsley et al. (2014).   [7] OECD (1996).   [8] Hulme (2007).
[9] Manning (2009).   [10] Hulme (2007).   [11] Hulme (2007).
[12] Hulme (2007), p. 11.
[13] Find information about goals and measures at mdgs.un.org/unsd/mdg/default.aspx.

directly link expenditures to development by reporting on targets including, for example, on how many water taps were installed and how many more people had received access to safe water. In 2005, donor governments united behind the Paris Declaration, which provided an "action-oriented roadmap" to improve foreign aid and its effects on development around five central pillars: recipient country ownership, alignment, harmonisation, mutual accountability, and managing for results.[14] If donors were to act in accordance with these principles, aid would be more effective. Not all of these principles turned out to be compatible, however. The strengthening of recipient country ownership prioritises long-term capacity-building while managing for results prioritises results in the short run. This dissonance between principles produced different interpretations regarding their importance for aid effectiveness. At the subsequent aid effectiveness conference in Accra in 2008 results became more central, as expressed in post-conference notes prepared to guide donor governments towards more effective aid strategies,

Achieving development results – and openly accounting for them – must be at the heart of all we do. More than ever, citizens and taxpayers of all countries expect to see tangible results of development efforts. We will be accountable to each other and to our respective parliaments and governing bodies for these outcomes.[15]

In Busan and thereafter demands for improving managerial practices in foreign aid continued to expand on conference agendas. Today, results-orientation has become a sine-qua non in discussions around foreign aid effectiveness.

What is more, key international development actors such as the OECD DAC promote results-orientation and management practices via platforms and forums that discuss and prescribe how to effectively manage for results in foreign aid.[16] These forums offer online resources, peer learning products on effective results frameworks for development cooperation, as well as guidelines and data for results-based decision-making. Through its Public Management Service 'PUMA', for example, the OECD channels expertise and guidelines on how to effectively implement managerial practices in the public

---

[14] OECD (2005).   [15] OECD (2008).   [16] OECD (2019).

sector. Over the years, the OECD's Development Coordination Directorate has used its agenda-setting role to ensure that a results-based approach to foreign aid receives traction in foreign aid effectiveness forums, starting out in Monterrey in 2002 and Paris in 2005. In Accra in 2008 and Busan 2011, results-orientation moved centre stage, often relegating discussions about country ownership to the sidelines. Although the results-oriented approach to foreign aid has gained traction over the years, not all donor governments have gravitated to this kind of development agenda. Instead, as this book argues, political economy differences bring about markedly different responses to this agenda insofar as results-orientation has received pushback from critics who claimed that the agenda's focus on demonstrating results and performance came at the expense of much needed system expenditures in recipient countries, for which it is more difficult to demonstrate results. The focus on accountability, or 'being seen to do the right thing', openly conflicts with other objectives of foreign aid, such as, for example, the strengthening of recipient government ownership or promoting development in the long run.[17]

More broadly, my book suggests that we should expect political economy differences to shape debates in global development forums that seek to unite donors behind aid effectiveness principles as varied as effective aid management, on the one hand, and recipient government ownership over the development process, on the other hand. This book makes predictions about which aid effectiveness principle donor governments are more likely to support, depending on their national structures. My research also suggests that, unless donors converge on a similar political economy type, the debate over aid delivery tactics will continue unabated in the future.

At the time of writing this final chapter of the book, the spread of COVID-19 preoccupies the world. As donor governments ramp up efforts to contain and prevent the spread of the virus in developing countries, it is likely that these very same kinds of trade offs will come into focus. The United States, for example, has announced more than US \$1.5 billion in emergency health, humanitarian, economic, and development assistance specifically aimed at helping governments, international organisations, and NGOs fight the pandemic.[18] These funds

---

[17] McGillivray and Pham (2017).   [18] United States Department of State (2020).

are expected to save millions of lives by improving, for example, rapid disease response capacity. The funds should further contribute to strengthening public information campaigns, disease surveillance, and laboratory capacities, as well as health care facilities in more than 120 countries.[19] In many respects, the way in which the US government has framed its response to COVID-19 is reminiscent of how it has tackled other (infectious) diseases. In Chapter 2, I used the President's Emergency Plan for AIDS Relief (PEPFAR) to illustrate a typical US response to health crises in developing countries – a programme that often sets up parallel structures to deliver treatments and prevention measures directly to the people. However, such targeted efforts can undermine the development of broader health care structures in recipient countries that provide important services to local populations.[20] This book suggests that donors might vary in how they respond to the virus; that, depending on their domestic structures they will position themselves differently: I expect neoliberal donors to focus more on the delivery of vaccines, ventilators, or face masks, among other targeted interventions, that are easy to quantify and promise to fight the pandemic in the short term. I expect traditional public sector donors to make a greater investment in a country's health care structures in order to build up its capacity in the long run.

The argument advanced in this book has implications for researchers and practitioners alike who seek to understand donor coordination. As a practice, the OECD DAC has encouraged more donor coordination for many years, pointing to high transaction costs for donors and the burden on developing countries that deal with many donors at the same time.[21] However, as studies have noted, little progress has been made in this respect.[22] Some say that donor coordination is difficult because it impedes donors from pursuing their national objectives through aid.[23] Others point to bureaucratic tensions between headquarters and field offices that impede the harmonisation of donor activities on the ground.[24] The findings of my book suggest that

---

[19] United States Department of State (2020).   [20] Pritchett et al. (2010).
[21] OECD (2006).
[22] See the following examples of scholarly research that discusses and investigates the effects of donor fragmentation on aid effectiveness: Acharya et al. (2006); Bigsten (2006); Knack and Rahman (2007); Frot and Santiso (2009); Aldasoro et al. (2010); Leiderer (2015).
[23] Steinwand (2015).   [24] de Renzio et al. (2005).

different aid priorities and delivery practices could systematically influence donor coordination patterns.

I have shown that institutional constraints make it difficult for donor officials to develop robust coordination efforts with peers in countries that do not share the same aid priorities and who deliver aid in different ways. For example, national structures may act as obstacles for aid officials in the United States attempting to coordinate robust capacity-building efforts with their German counterparts in countries where they would normally deliver aid through non-state actors. At the same time, French aid officials may lack the authorisation to coordinate closely with their UK counterparts on funding a parallel structure that installs water taps in regions where access to water is low. In both scenarios, national structures, or rules of the game, might push aid officials from different political economies in different directions, rendering joint aid initiatives more challenging. In my own interviews with aid officials I found that a large majority of them viewed national structures as at least somewhat constraining for donor coordination efforts, as demonstrated in Chapter 5.

Conversely, I would expect donor coordination to be more successful among countries of similar political economy type. Anecdotal evidence suggests that donors consider like-mindedness, or shared beliefs, a possible factor that facilitates coordination and joint assistant strategies in foreign aid. For example, USAID's former administrator Ravj Shah claimed during a 2011 conference titled 'MDG Countdown 2011: Celebrating Successes and Innovations' that like-mindedness between USAID and DFID enabled joint progress towards the MDGs. In his remarks, Shah noted that like-mindedness between the two countries 'helps us work together ever more efficiently and effectively', and that he saw USAID's work as 'very consistent with what Andrew Mitchell (then head of DFID, *author added*) is doing in the UK and other European countries'.[25] My argument suggests that as donors reorganise their public sectors around the same vision of development and similar rules and practices, organisational differences become muted and no longer impede donor coordination. Furthermore, as recipient countries become better governed and converge on high levels of governance quality, I also expect donor coordination to become easier, as, under good governance conditions, my argument predicts

[25] *The Guardian* (2011).

donor convergence on government-to-government delivery, regardless of political economy type.

Finally, my findings have implications for an emerging literature on global governance indicators. This literature investigates the efficacy of social indicators for global governance. Scholars ask whether quantifiable indicators, or standards of performance, effectively pressure governments, who want to avoid being at the bottom of a performance scale, to change their ways. Kelly and Simmons, for example, show that the United States effectively employs performance indicators to pressure illiberal regimes to change behaviour.[26] Another study shows that the United States successfully employs transparency indicators to pressure their recipient countries into becoming more transparent.[27] Together these studies suggest that domestic structures can be successfully projected outward to influence world politics. To date, however, studies on the influence of social indicators have largely focused on the United States or international organisations like the World Bank who are central promoters of global benchmarking efforts across numerous policy and issue areas.[28] Too much of a focus on the United States may thus overlook marked differences across countries in use of and reactions to global performance indicators.

My book suggests that OECD countries may diverge in whether and how they use benchmarking practices, and how they go about addressing risk. As the cross-country comparison of aid structures in Chapter 3 reveals, some aid systems today are set up to do economic management while others are not. At a minimum, the global proliferation of performance indicators implies that traditional public sector donors may feel pressured to make greater use of these tools. Indeed, over the course of the many open-ended interviews I conducted with aid officials, some respondents from Germany and France indicated that, at times, they felt pressured to employ performance indicators more often and robustly so in their aid organisations.

This suggests that, although national structures continue to produce competing conceptions of what makes foreign aid a success, the proliferation of neoliberal governance principles may lead traditional sector donors to ultimately converge on a neoliberal vision of international development. This surely makes an interesting topic for future research.

---

[26] Kelly and Simmons (2014).   [27] Honig and Weaver (2019).
[28] Kelly and Simmons (2014); Doshi et al. (2019); Kelly and Simmons (2019).

7.4 Implications for Future Research

My book presents an original political economy lens through which one can understand the role of beliefs and institutions in foreign aid. Ideology matters for aid delivery because, at different times in different countries, beliefs about the appropriate role of the state in public sector governance were mobilised to create new rules and practices which reproduce the character of national organisations in which foreign aid officials operate. Donor countries that embrace neoliberal doctrine rules and practices incentivise aid officials to select bypass tactics when the quality of governance is low. This preference is stable and reinforced by the tugs and pulls of non-state actors that stand to benefit from aid.

Looking beyond foreign aid, variation in domestic structures may help explain policy directions and variation therein across countries in other areas of foreign policy. For instance, OECD countries have, over the past 40 years, increased their outsourcing of military tasks to private contracting firms.[29] Yet, marked variation exists in the degree to which these countries have turned to private contracting to assume service provision in security-related areas as varied as logistics, communications, and electronic systems, as well as direct engagement on the battlefield. While the share of contractors is relatively high in the United States and the United Kingdom, France and Germany engage contractors to a lesser degree, leaving national security provision in the domain of state forces.[30] My book proposes a useful framework through which scholars can study this variation. It points to the importance of national structures in shaping decisions about how to provide domestic and international security. Similarly, a political economy lens, or a focus on state bureaucracies, might advance our knowledge of countries' migration policies or their behaviour in international forums that seek to structure global migration. There, too, we observe marked differences across countries in how the management, detention, prevention, and control of migration flows are handled, exhibiting marked variation in outsourcing to private actors.[31] Again, a political economy lens that focuses on how migration is governed or how migration-related services are delivered promises to

[29] Kinsey (2006).   [30] Petersohn (2008); McDonald (2013).
[31] Menz (2011).

shed light on what goals states seek to accomplish and how political economy beliefs shape interactions with other states about global migration policies.

Another potential area of future research might be to account for existing heterogeneity among the non-state actors that implement donor bypass tactics. Throughout the book, my definition of bypass actors has included actors as varied as international and local NGOs, international organisations, public–private partnerships, and development contractors. In the analyses, I collapsed aid that donors channel through these actors into my central bypass measure. In the future, scholars could theorise the variation among not-for-profit, for-profit actors, and international organisations and develop a more nuanced argument that explains the conditions under which donor governments channel aid through any of these three actor types. Relatedly, it would be interesting to further study how the different types of donors, through their different ways of managing aid, shape the incentives and behaviours of non-state actors in development. During a handful of my interviews, aid officials indicated that aid implementers perceived the variety of management practices as cumbersome insofar as they require them to develop different monitoring and reporting formulas that satisfy the organisational contexts of donor governments. If non-state actors receive funding from multiple donors, the burden resulting from catering to different practices might take important resources away from actually doing important ground work and adversely affect development. Or, donors might favour larger and more capable NGOs that are more able to comply with management standards and thus affect the civil society landscape in recipient countries.

Finally, this study may encourage scholars to study the effectiveness of bypass versus government-to-government aid. Throughout the book, I have argued that the way that aid officials look at the success of their aid projects and programmes is endogenous to the spirit of the institutional rulebook of national aid organisations: while aid officials whose work is organised by neoliberal principles prioritise cost-effectiveness and direct delivery to the poor, their counterparts in more statist organisational environments are more likely to prioritise capacity-building and government ownership. This suggests that aid success means different things to aid officials from different political economies. It also suggests that restricting aid effectiveness studies and comparisons across donors to one single metric misses the point. Instead, scholars need to identify suitable metrics that correspond with the goals of neoliberal and traditional public sector regimes as well as the time frames by which they expect their assistance to influence development in recipient countries. For example, donor assessments of a vaccine campaign are feasible in the short run. Capacity-building efforts, on the other hand, require more extended time frames with more intermediate metrics. Consider, for example, foreign aid that aims to build institutional capacity to enable a recipient government to effectively address climate change, including, for example, the building up of technical capacity to implement climate mitigation and adaptation actions at the local as well as the subnational and national levels; or, to design appropriate structures and coordination mechanisms that ensure consistency of strategy across the different levels. These capacity-oriented interventions require processes to play out that take time and that require the support of local authorities and relevant economic actors. Compared to bypass interventions such aid projects thus require longer time-frames to play out successfully.[32] For any scholar that evaluates donor delivery tactics or foreign aid more broadly, it is central to tackle the issue of time frames head on and specify them properly in their empirical models. Given that both bypass and government engagement tactics have been employed in similar settings, especially in more fragile contexts that require long-term engagement, it will be important to evaluate how the success and failure or the unintended consequences of both tactics become manifest over longer time frames and how each contributes towards promoting well-being abroad.

---

[32] Riddell (2007); Easterly and Williamson (2011); Krasner and Weinstein (2014); Chorev (2020); Kaplan (2021); Steele and Shapiro (2017).

Bibliography

Abdelal, Rawi E. 2001. *National Purpose in the World Economy: Post-Soviet States in Comparative Perspective*. Ithaca, NY: Cornell University Press.

Acharya, Arnab, Anna T. Fuzzo de Lima, and Mick Moore. 2006. 'Proliferation and Fragmentation: Transactions Costs and the Value of Aid.' *Journal of Development Studies* 42(1): 1–21.

Acheson, Dean G. 1959. 'Homage to General Marshall.' *The Reporter* 25.

Adhikari, Bimal. 2019. 'Power Politics and Foreign Aid Delivery Tactics.' *Social Science Quarterly* 100: 1523–39.

Ahmed, Faisal Z. 2012. 'The Perils of Unearned Foreign Income: Aid, Remittances, and Government Survival.' *American Political Science Review* 106(1): 146–65.

Aitchison, John. 1986. The statistical analysis of compositional data: Monographs on statistics and applied probability: Chapman & Hall Ltd.

Aldasoro, Inaki, Peter Nunnenkamp, and Rainer Thiele. 2010. 'Less aid proliferation and more donor coordination? The Wide Gap between Words and Deeds.' *Journal of International Development* 22: 920–40. https://doi.org/10.1002/jid.1645.

Alesina, Alberto and Beatrice Weder. 2002. 'Do Corrupt Governments Receive Less Foreign Aid?' *The American Economic Review* 92(4): 1126–37.

Alesina, Alberto and David Dollar. 2000. 'Who Gives Foreign Aid to Whom and Why?' *Journal of Economic Growth* 5(1): 33–63.

Allen, Susan H. and Michael E. Flynn. 2018. 'Donor Government Ideology and Aid Bypass.' *Foreign Policy Analysis* 14(4) : 449–68.

Amable, Bruno. 2017. *Structural Crisis and Institutional Change in Modern Capitalism: French Capitalism in Transition*. 1st edition. Oxford; New York: Oxford University Press.

Amann, Edmund and Werner Baer. 2005. 'From the Developmental to the Regulatory State: The Transformation of the Government's Impact on the Brazilian Economy.' *The Quarterly Review of Economics and Finance* 45(2): 421–31.

American Society for Quality. 2020. 'What Is Benchmarking? Technical & Competitive Benchmarking Process | ASQ.'

Annen, Kurt and Stephen F. Knack. 2019. *Better Policies from Policy-Selective Aid?* Washington, DC: The World Bank.

Arel-Bundock, Vincent, James Atkinson, and Rachel A. Potter. 2015. 'The Limits of Foreign Aid Diplomacy: How Bureaucratic Design Shapes Aid Distribution.' *International Studies Quarterly* 59(3): 544–56.

Ashoff, Guido. 2004. 'Donor Coordination: A Basic Requirement for More Efficient and Effective Development Cooperation.' German Development Institute/Deutsches Institut für Entwicklungspolitik. Briefing Paper 7/2004.

2009. Institutional Reform Needs of Germany's Bilateral Development Cooperation. Deutsches Institut für Entwicklungspolitik.

Asian Development Bank. 2009. *Technical Annex on Integrated Water Resources Management (IWRM)*. Manila: Asian Development Bank. Project Number: TA 4848.

Autesserre, Séverine. 2014. *Peaceland: Conflict Resolution and the Everyday Politics of International Intervention.* Cambridge: Cambridge University Press.

Baccaro, Lucio and Chris Howell. 2017. *Trajectories of Neoliberal Transformation.* Cambridge: Cambridge University Press.

Bach, Tobias and Werner Jann. 2010. 'Animals in the Administrative Zoo: Organizational Change and Administrative Autonomy in German.' *International Review of Administrative Sciences* 76(3): 443–68.

Bader, Julia and Jörg Faust. 2014. 'Foreign Aid, Democratization, and Autocratic Survival.' *International Studies Review* 16(4): 575–95.

Baldwin, David A. 1985. *Economic Statecraft*. Princeton, NJ: Princeton University Press.

Baldwin, Kate and Matthew S. Winters. 2020. 'How Do Different Forms of Foreign Aid Affect Government Legitimacy? Evidence from an Informational Experiment in Uganda.' *Studies in Comparative International Development* 55(2): 160–83.

Balogun, Paul. 2005. 'Evaluating Progress towards Harmonisation.' *Working Paper*: 15.

Bandyopadhyay, Subhayu and Howard J. Wall. 2007. 'The Determinants of Aid in the Post-Cold War Era.' *Federal Reserve Bank of St. Louis Review* 89(6): 533–47.

Barder, Owen. 2005. 'Reforming Development Assistance: Lessons from the UK Experience.' Working Paper 70, Washington, DC: Center for Global Development.

Barnett, Michael N. and Liv Coleman. 2005. 'Designing Police: Interpol and the Study of Change in International Organizations.' *International Studies Quarterly* 49(4): 593–619.

Barnett, Michael N. and Martha Finnemore. 2004. *Rules for the World: International Organizations in Global Politics.* Reprint edition. Ithaca, NY: Cornell University Press.

Barr, Abigail M., Marcel Fafchamps, and Trudy Owens. 2005. 'The Governance of Non-Governmental Organizations in Uganda.' *World Development* 33(4): 657–79.

Bates, Reid A. 2001. 'Public Sector Training Participation: An Empirical Investigation.' *International Journal of Training and Development* 5(2): 136–52.

Batley, Richard and George Larbi. 2004. *The Changing Role of Government: The Reform of Public Services in Developing Countries.* London: Palgrave Macmillan.

Bauer, Péter T. 1976. *Dissent on Development.* Cambridge, MA: Harvard University Press.

Bauhr, Monika, Nicholas Charron, and Naghmeh Nasiritousi. 2013. 'Does Corruption Cause Aid Fatigue? Public Opinion and the Aid-Corruption Paradox.' *International Studies Quarterly* 57(3): 568–79.

Bayer, Patrick, Christopher Marcoux, and Johannes Urpelainen. 2015. 'When International Organizations Bargain: Evidence from the Global Environment Facility.' *Journal of Conflict Resolution* 59(6): 1074–1100.

Bayram, A. Burcu. 2017. 'Aiding Strangers: Generalized Trust and the Moral Basis of Public Support for Foreign Development Aid.' *Foreign Policy Analysis* 13(1): 133–53.

Bayram, A. Burcu and Marcus Holmes. 2020. 'Feeling Their Pain: Affective Empathy and Public Preferences for Foreign Development Aid.' *European Journal of International Relations* 26(3): 820–50.

Bearce, David H. and Daniel C. Tirone. 2010. 'Foreign Aid Effectiveness and the Strategic Goals of Donor Governments.' *The Journal of Politics* 72(3): 837–51.

Bearce, David H., Steven E. Finkel, Anibal S. Pérez-Liñán, Juan Rodríguez-Zepeda, and Lena Surzhko-Harned. 2013. 'Has the New Aid for Trade Agenda been Export Effective? Evidence on the Impact of US AfT Allocations 1999–2008.' *International Studies Quarterly* 57(1): 163–70.

Behrman, Greg M. 2008. *The Most Noble Adventure: The Marshall Plan and How America Helped Rebuild Europe.* Reprint edition. New York: Free Press.

Belfrage, Claes A. and Markus Kallifatides. 2018. 'Financialisation and the New Swedish Model.' *Cambridge Journal of Economics* 42(4): 875–900.

Bennett, D. Scott and Allan C. Stam. 2000. 'A Universal Test of an Expected Utility Theory of War.' *International Studies Quarterly* 44(3): 451–80.

Benz, Arthur. 1995. 'Institutional Change in Intergovernmental Relations: The Dynamics of Multi-Level Structures.' In *European Yearbook of*

Comparative Government and Public Administration, eds. Joachim Jens Hesse and Theo A. J. Toonen Toonen. Baden-Baden/Boulder, CO: Nomos/Westview Press, 551–76.

2016. Paper presented at ECPR 2016 General Conference in Prague, Panel 340: 'Federalism and Varieties of Parliamentary Democracy – Canada and Germany Compared.' 19.

Benz, Arthur and Klaus H. Goetz. 1996. 'The German Public Sector: National Priorities and the International Reform Agenda.' In *A New German Public Sector? Reform, Adaptation and Stability*, eds. Arthur Benz and K. Gotz. Aldershot, Dartmouth: Routledge, 1–26.

Berinsky, Adam J. 2007. 'Assuming the Costs of War: Events, Elites, and American Public Support for Military Conflict.' *Journal of Politics* 69(4): 975–97.

Bermeo, Sarah Blodgett. 2011. 'Foreign Aid and Regime Change: A Role for Donor Intent.' *World Development* 39(11):2021–31.

2018. *Targeted Development: Industrialized Country Strategy in a Globalizing World*. New York: Oxford University Press.

Berrios, Ruben. 2000. *Contracting for Development: The Role of For-Profit Contractors in U.S. Foreign Development Assistance*. Illustrated Edition. Westport, CT: Praeger.

Bertelli, Anthony M. 2012. *The Political Economy of Public Sector Governance*. 1st edition. Cambridge: Cambridge University Press.

Berthélemy, Jean-Claude and Ariane Tichit. 2004. 'Bilateral Donors' Aid Allocation Decisions: A Three-Dimensional Panel Analysis.' *International Review of Economics & Finance* 13(3): 253–74.

Bezes, Philippe and Gilles Jeannot. 2011. 'The Development and Current Features of the French Civil Service System.' In *Civil Service Systems in Western Europe*, ed. Frits Van der Meer. Cheltenham: Edward Elgar, 185–2015.

2013. *Public Sector Reform in France: Views and Experiences from Senior Executives*. Coordination for Cohesion in the Public Sector of the Future (COCOPS).

Bigsten, Arne. 2006. Donor Coordination and the Uses of Aid. Department of Economics, Goteborg University.

Billing, Annika, Maja Forslind, and Karin Metell Cueva, 2012. *Swedish Development Cooperation in the Private Sector: The Role of Business in Poverty Alleviation and the Role of Donors in Promoting Private Sector Contributions to Development*, Perspectives No. 22. Gothenburg: University of Gothenburg, School of Global Studies.

Birdsall, Nancy and Homi Kharas. 2010. 'Quality of Official Development Assistance Assessment.' Washington, DC: 112.

Bjerninger, Jan. 2013. *Det Framgångsrika Biståndet : Om Svenskt Utvecklingssamarbete i Praktiken*. Stockholm: Vulkan.

Blomquist, Glenn C. 2004. 'Self-Protection and Averting Behavior, Values of Statistical Lives, and Benefit Cost Analysis of Environmental Policy.' *Review of Economics of the Household* 2(1): 89–110.

Blyth, Mark. 2002. *Great Transformations: Economic Ideas and Institutional Change in the Twentieth Century*. New York: Cambridge University Press.

2003. 'Structures Do Not Come with an Instruction Sheet: Interests, Ideas, and Progress in Political Science.' *Perspectives on Politics* 1(4): 695–706.

BMZ. 2008. 'Evaluation of the Implementation of the Paris Declaration: Case Study Germany, Bonn: BMZ (Evaluation Reports 032).'

Boussard, Valérie and Marc Loriol. 2008. "Les Cadres du Ministère des Affaires Etrangères et Européennes Face à la LOLF." Revue françaised'administrationpublique 128: 717–728.

Boutton, Andrew and David B. Carter. 2014. 'Fair-Weather Allies? Terrorism and the Allocation of US Foreign Aid.' *Journal of Conflict Resolution* 58(7): 1144–73.

Braithwaite, Jessica M. and Amanda A. Licht. 2020. 'The Effect of Civil Society Organizations and Democratization Aid on Civil War Onset.' *Journal of Conflict Resolution* 64(6): 1095–1120.

Brautigam, Deborah A. and Stephen F. Knack. 2004. 'Foreign Aid, Institutions, and Governance in Sub-Saharan Africa.' *Economic Development and Cultural Change* 52: 255–85.

Brech, Viktor and Niklas Potrafke. 2014. 'Donor Ideology and Types of Foreign Aid.' *Journal of Comparative Economics* 42(1): 61–75.

Broschek, Jörg. 2010. 'Federalism and Political Change: Canada and Germany in Historical-Institutionalist Perspective.' *Canadian Journal of Political Science/Revue canadienne de science politique* 43(1): 1–24.

Broz, J. Lawrence. 2005. 'Congressional Politics of International Financial Rescues.' *American Journal of Political Science* 49(3): 479–96.

Bueno de Mesquita, Bruce and Alastair Smith. 2009. 'A Political Economy of Aid.' *International Organization* 63: 309–40.

Buntaine, Mark T. (1986). *Giving Aid Effectively: The Politics of Environmental Performance and Selectivity at Multilateral Development Banks*. New York: Oxford University Press.

Buntaine, Mark T., Bradley C. Parks, and Benjamin P. Buch. 2017. 'Aiming at the Wrong Targets: The Domestic Consequences of International Efforts to Build Institutions.' *International Studies Quarterly* 61(2): 471–88.

Bush, Sarah S. 2015. *The Taming of Democracy Assistance: Why Democracy Promotion Does Not Confront Dictators*. Reprint edition. New York: Cambridge University Press.

2016. 'When and Why Is Civil Society Support 'Made-in-America'? Delegation to Non-State Actors in American Democracy Promotion.' *The Review of International Organizations* 11(3): 361–85.

Büthe, Tim, Solomon Major and André de Mello e Souza. 2012. 'The Politics of Private Foreign Aid: Humanitarian Principles, Economic Development Objectives, and Organizational Interests in NGO Private Aid Allocation.' *International Organization* 66(4): 571–607.

Campbell, Cole C. 2004. 'Journalism and Public Knowledge.' *National Civic Review* 93(3): 3–10.

Campbell, John L. 1998. 'Institutional Analysis and the Role of Ideas in Political Economy.' *Theory and Society* 27(3): 377–409.

Campbell, John L. and Ove K. Pedersen. 2001. *The Rise of Neoliberalism and Institutional Analysis*. Princeton, NJ: Princeton University Press.

Campbell, Susanna P. and Gabriele Spilker. 2020. Aiding War or Peace? The Insiders' View on Aid to Post-Conflict Transitions (December 21, 2020). SSRN: https://ssrn.com/abstract=3576116 or http://dx.doi.org/10.2139/ssrn.3576116.

Capoccia, Giovanni. 2015. Critical junctures and institutional change. In James Mahoney & Kathleen Thelen (Eds.), *Advances in Comparative-Historical Analysis* (Strategies for Social Inquiry, pp. 147–179). Cambridge: Cambridge University Press.

Capoccia, Giovanni and R. Daniel Kelemen. 2007. 'The Study of Critical Junctures: Theory, Narrative, and Counterfactuals in Historical Institutionalism.' *World Politics* 59(3): 341–69.

Carcelli, Shannon. 2019. *Bureaucracy at the Border: The Congressional Fragmentation of US Foreign Aid*. Unpublished Manuscript.

Carlsson, A. Gunilla. 2012. 'Speech by Ms Gunilla Carlsson at the Stockholm Internet Forum 2012.'

Chapman, Terrence L. 2011. *Securing Approval: Domestic Politics and Multilateral Authorization for War*. Chicago: University of Chicago Press.

Charness, Gary, Uri Gneezy, and Michael A. Kuhn. 2012. 'Experimental methods: Between-Subject and Within-Subject Design.' *Journal of Economic Behavior & Organization* 81(1): 1–8,

Chasukwa, Michael and Dan Banik. 2019. 'Bypassing Government: Aid Effectiveness and Malawi's Local Development Fund.' *Politics and Governance* 7(2): 103.

Chong, Alberto and Mark Gradstein. 2008. 'What Determines Foreign Aid? The Donors' Perspective.' *Journal of Development Economics* 87(1): 1–13.

Chorev, Nitsan. 2020. *Give and Take: Developmental Foreign Aid and The Pharmaceutical Industry in East Africa*. Princeton, NJ: Princeton University Press.

Christensen, Tom and Per Laegreid. 2002. 'New Public Management: Puzzles of Democracy and the Influence of Citizens.' *Journal of Political Philosophy* 10(3): 267–95.

Claessens, Stijn, Danny Cassimon, and Bjorn Van Campenhout. 2009. 'Evidence on Changes in Aid Allocation Criteria.' *The World Bank Economic Review* 23(2): 185–208.

Clarke, Harold D., David Hudson, Jennifer Hudson, Marianne C. Stewart, and Joe Twyman. 2017. Aid Attitudes Tracker – Wave 9 (Germany). Bill & Melinda Gates Foundation.

Cohen, Gary B., Ben W. Ansell, Robert H. Cox, and Jane Gingrich, eds. 2012. *Social Policy in the Smaller European Union States*. 1st edition. New York: Berghahn Books.

Collier, Paul and David Dollar. 2002. 'Aid Allocation and Poverty Reduction.' *European Economic Review* 46(8): 1475–1500.

Collier, Paul and Hoeffler, Anke. 2002. 'Aid, Policy and Peace: Reducing the Risks of Civil Conflict.' *Defence and Peace Economics* 13(6): 435–50.

Collier, Paul, Patrick Guillaumont, Sylviane Guillaumont, and Jan W. Gunning. 1997. 'Redesigning Conditionality.' *World Development* 25(9): 1399–1407.

Conceição-Heldt, Eugénia da. 2013. 'Do Agents 'Run Amok'? A Comparison of Agency Slack in the EU and US Trade Policy in the Doha Round.' *Journal of Comparative Policy Analysis: Research and Practice* 15(1): 21–36.

Cornell, Agnes. 2013. 'Does Regime Type Matter for the Impact of Democracy Aid on Democracy?' *Democratization* 20(4), 642–67.

Dahlström, Carl and Victor Lapuente. 2017. *Organizing Leviathan: Politicians, Bureaucrats, and the Making of Good Government*. Cambridge; New York: Cambridge University Press.

Dalton, Russell J. 2013. *Citizen Politics: Public Opinion and Political Parties in Advanced Industrial Democracies*. 1st edition. Los Angeles: CQ Press.

Dardot, Pierre and Christian Laval. 2009. *The New Way of the World: On Neoliberal Society*. Reprint edition. Brooklyn, NY: Verso.

De Hoogh, Annebel H. B., Lindred L. Greer and Deanne N. Den Hartog. 2015. 'Diabolical Dictators or Capable Commanders? An Investigation of the Differential Effects of Autocratic Leadership on Team Performance.' *The Leadership Quarterly* 26(5): 687–701.

de Renzio, Paolo, David Booth, Andrew Rogerson, and Zaza Curran. 2005. *Incentives for Harmonisation and Alignment in Aid Agencies*. Overseas Development Institute Working Paper 248, London.

Deaton, Angus S. 2015. *Great Escape: Health, Wealth, and the Origins of Inequality*. Reprint. Princeton, NJ: Princeton University Press.

Denly, Michael. 2021. Institutional Autonomy and Donor Strategic Interest in Multilateral Aid: Rules versus Influence. Paper Presented at the 2021 Conference for Political Economy of International Organizations

DEval. 2020. Home – Deutsches Evaluierungsinstitut Der Entwicklungszusammenarbeit GGmbH.

Diefenbach, Thomas. 2009. 'New Public Management in Public Sector Organizations: The Dark Sides of Managerialistic "Enlightenment".' *Public Administration* 87(4): 892–909.

Dietrich, Simone. 2013a. 'Bypass or Engage? Explaining Donor Delivery Tactics in Foreign Aid Allocation.' *International Studies Quarterly* 57(4): 698–712.

2016. 'Donor Political Economies and the Pursuit of Aid Effectiveness.' *International Organization* 70(1): 65–102.

Dietrich, Simone and Amanda Murdie. 2017. 'Human Rights Shaming through INGOs and Foreign Aid Delivery.' *The Review of International Organizations* 12(1): 95–120.

Dietrich, Simone, Bernhard Reinsberg, and Martin Steinwand. 2019b. *Networks in International Organizations: How Governance Principles Influence the Rise, Orientation, and Evolution of World Bank Trust Funds.* Rochester, NY: Social Science Research Network. SSRN Scholarly Paper.

Dietrich, Simone, Heidi Hardt, and Haley, J. Swedlund. 2021. 'How to Make Elite Experiments Work in International Relations.' *European Journal of International Relations.* February 2021.

Dietrich, Simone, Helen V. Milner, and Jonathan Slapin. 2020. 'From Text to Political Positions on Foreign Aid: Analysis of Aid Mentions in Party Manifestos from 1960 to 2015.' *International Studies Quarterly* 64(4): 980–90.

Dietrich, Simone and Joseph Wright. 2015. 'Foreign Aid Allocation Tactics and Democratic Change in Africa.' *The Journal of Politics* 77(1): 216–34.

Dietrich, Simone and Matthew S. Winters. 2015. 'Foreign Aid and Government Legitimacy.' *Journal of Experimental Political Science* 2: 164–71.

Dietrich, Simone, Minhaj Mahmud, and Matthew S. Winters. 2018. 'Foreign Aid, Foreign Policy, and Domestic Government Legitimacy: Experimental Evidence from Bangladesh.' *Journal of Politics* 80(1): 133–48.

Dietrich, Simone, Susan D. Hyde, and Matthew S. Winters. 2019a. 'Overseas Credit Claiming and Domestic Support for Foreign Aid.' *Journal of Experimental Political Science* 6(3): 159–70.

DiLorenzo, Matthew. 2018. 'Bypass Aid and Unrest in Autocracies.' *International Studies Quarterly* 62(1): 208–19.

Directorate-General of Global Affairs, Development and Partnership. 2011. Strategy 2011 – Development Cooperation: a French Vision. Framework Document published by MAEE.

Dixit, Avinash, K. 2002. "Incentives and Organizations in the Public Sector: An Interpretative Review." *The Journal of Human Resources* 37: 696–727.

Djankov, Simeon, Jose G. Montalvo, and Marta Reynal-Querol. 2008. 'The Curse of Aid.' *Journal of Economic Growth* 13(3): 169–94.

Dobbin, Frank. 1994. *Forging Industrial Policy: The United States, Britain, and France in the Railway Age.* New York: Cambridge University Press.

Doshi, Rush, Judith G. Kelley, and Beth A. Simmons. 2019. 'The Power of Ranking: The Ease of Doing Business Indicator and Global Regulatory Behavior.' *International Organization* 73(3): 611–43. doi: 10.1017/S0020818319000158.

Downs, Anthony. 1957. 'An Economic Theory of Political Action in a Democracy.' *Journal of Political Economy* 65(2): 135–50.

Dreher, Axel, Peter Nunnenkamp, and Maya Schmaljohann. 2015. *The Allocation of German Aid: Self-Interest and Government Ideology.* Rochester, NY: Social Science Research Network. SSRN Scholarly Paper.

Dreher, Axel, Peter Nunnenkamp, and Rainer Thiele. 2008. 'Does US Aid Buy UN General Assembly Votes? A Disaggregated Analysis.' *Public Choice* 136(1): 139–64.

Dreher, Axel, Valentin Lang, B. Peter Rosendorff, and James R. Vreeland. 2018. *Buying Votes and International Organizations: The Dirty Work-Hypothesis.* Rochester, NY: Social Science Research Network. SSRN Scholarly Paper.

Dunning, Casey and Ben Leo. 2016. Making USAID Fit for Purpose – A Proposal for a Top-to-Bottom Program Review. Washington, DC: Center for Global Development, p. 4.

Dunton, Caroline and Jack Hasler. 2021. 'Opening the Black Box of International Aid: Understanding Delivery Actors and Democratization.' *International Politics.* doi: 10.1057/s41311-020-00276-y.

Dupuy, Kendra, James Ron, and Aseem Prakash. 2015. 'Who Survived? Ethiopia's Regulatory Crackdown on Foreign-Funded NGOs.' *Review of International Political Economy* 22(2): 419–456.

2016. 'Hands Off My Regime! Governments' Restrictions on Foreign Aid to Non-Governmental Organizations in Poor and Middle-Income Countries.' *World Development* 84: 299–311.

Easterly, William R. (2002). 'The Cartel of Good Intentions: The Problem of Bureaucracy in Foreign Aid.' *Journal of Policy Reform* 5: 223–50. doi: 10.1080/1384128032000096823

2007. *The White Man's Burden: Why the West's Efforts to Aid the Rest Have Done So Much Ill and So Little Good.* Reprint edition. New York: Penguin Books.

2014. *The Tyranny of Experts: Economists, Dictators, and the Forgotten Rights of the Poor.* New York: Basic Books.

Easterly, William R. and Claudia R. Williamson. 2011. 'Rhetoric versus Reality: The Best and Worst of Aid Agency Practices.' *World Development* 39(11): 1930–49.

Economic Cooperation Administration. 1951. *Three Years of the Marshall Plan.*

The Economist. 2020. 'Building up the Pillars of State: Rich Countries Try Radical Economic Policies to Counter COVID-19.'

Ehn, Peter, Magnus Isberg, Claes Linde, and Gunnar Wallinn. 2003. 'Swedish Bureaucracy in an Era of Change.' *Governance: An International Journal of Policy, Administration, and Institutions* 16(3): 429–58.

Eichenauer, Vera Z. and Bernhard Reinsberg. 2017. 'What Determines Earmarked Funding to International Development Organizations? Evidence from the New Multi-Bi Aid Aata.' *The Review of International Organizations* 12(2): 171–97.

Eichenauer, Vera Z. and Simon Hug. 2018. 'The Politics of Special Purpose Trust Funds.' *Economics & Politics* 30(2): 211–55.

Eisinger, Robert W., Gregory K. Folkers, and Anthony S. Fauci. 2019. 'Ending the Human Immunodeficiency Virus Pandemic: Optimizing the Prevention and Treatment Toolkits.' *Clinical Infectious Diseases* 69(12): 2212–17.

Ekbladh, David. 2011. *The Great American Mission: Modernization and the Construction of an American World Order.* Princeton, NJ: Princeton University Press.

EM-DAT: The Emergency Events Database. Université catholique de Louvain (UCL) – CRED, D. Guha-Sapir – www.emdat.be, Brussels, Belgium.

England, Roger. 2007. 'Are We Spending Too Much on HIV?' *BMJ : British Medical Journal* 334(7589): 344.

Esping-Andersen, Gosta. 1999. *Social Foundations of Postindustrial Economies.* Oxford: Oxford University Press.

Essex, Jamey. 2013. *Development, Security, and Aid: Geopolitics and Geoeconomics at the U.S. Agency for International Development.* Athens: University of Georgia Press.

Estevez-Abe, Margarita, Torben Iversen, and David Soskice. 2001. *Social Protection and the Formation of Skills: A Reinterpretation of the Welfare State.* Oxford University Press.

Evans, Peter. 1995. *Embedded Autonomy: States and Industrial Transformation.* Princeton, NJ: Princeton University Press.

Ezrow, Lawrence and Timothy Hellwig. 2014. 'Responding to Voters or Responding to Markets? Political Parties and Public Opinion in an Era of Globalization.' *International Studies Quarterly* 58(4): 816–27.

Faust, Jörg, Svea Koch, Stefan Leiderer, and Nadia Molenaers. 2017. 'The Rise and Demise of European Budget Support: Political Economy of Collective European Union Donor Action.' *Development Policy Review* 35(4): 455–73.

Fearon, James D. 1994. 'Domestic Political Audiences and the Escalation of International Disputes.' *The American Political Science Review* 88(3): 577–92.

Fearon, James and Alexander Wendt. 2002. 'Rationalism v. Constructivism: A Skeptical View.' In *Handbook of International Relations*. London: SAGE, 52–72.

Ferlie, Ewan, Lynn Ashburner, Louise Fitzgerald, and Andrew Pettigrew. 1996. *The New Public Management in Action*. Oxford, UK: Oxford University Press.

Finkel, Steven E., Anibal Pérez-Liñán, and Mitchell, A. Seligson. 2007. 'The Effects of U.S. Foreign Assistance on Democracy Building, 1990–2003.' *World Politics*, 59(3), 404–38.

Fleck, Robert K. and Christopher Kilby. 2006a. 'How Do Political Changes Influence US Bilateral Aid Allocations? Evidence from Panel Data.' *Review of Development Economics* 10(2): 210–23.

2006b. 'World Bank Independence: A Model and Statistical Analysis of U.S. Influence.' *Review of Development Economics* 10(2): 224–40.

2010. 'Changing Aid Regimes? U.S. Foreign Aid from the Cold War to the War on Terror.' *Journal of Development Economics* 91(2): 185–97.

Flores, Thomas E. and Irfan Nooruddin. 2009. 'Democracy under the Gun: Understanding Postconflict Economic Recovery.' *Journal of Conflict Resolution* 53(1): 3–29.

2012. 'The Effect of Elections on Postconflict Peace and Reconstruction.' *The Journal of Politics* 74(2): 558–70.

Foucault, Paul-Michel. 2004. *S'ecurit'e, Territoire, Population Cours Au Colláege de France, 1977–1978*.

Fox, Justin and Kenneth W. Shotts. 2009. 'Delegates or Trustees? A Theory of Political Accountability.' *The Journal of Politics* 71(4): 1225–37.

Foyle, Douglas, C. 1999. *Counting the Public in: Presidents, Public Opinion, and Foreign Policy*. New York: Columbia University Press.

Franzese, Robert J. 2002. *Macroeconomic Policies of Developed Democracy*. Cambridge: Cambridge University Press.

Freedom House. 2018. *Freedom in the World.*, p. 19. https://freedomhouse .org/sites/default/files/FH_FITW_Report_2018_Final_SinglePage.pdf

Frot, Emmanuel. 2009a. *Aid and the Financial Crisis: Shall We Expect Development Aid to Fall?* Rochester, NY: Social Science Research Network. SSRN Scholarly Paper.

2009b. 'Aid and the Financial Crisis: Shall We Expect Development Aid to Fall?' *VoxEU.org*.

Frot, Emmanuel and Javier Santiso. 2011. 'Herding in Aid Allocation.' *Kyklos* 64(1): 54–74.

Fuchs, Andreas, Axel Dreher, and Peter Nunnenkamp. 2014. 'Determinants of Donor Generosity: A Survey of the Aid Budget Literature.' *World Development* 56(C): 172–99.

Fuchs, Andreas and Hannes Öhler. 2021. 'Does Private Aid Follow the Flag? An Empirical Analysis of Humanitarian Assistance.' *World Economies* 44: 671–705.

GAO. 1996. Foreign Assistance – Status of USAID's Reforms. Briefing Report to the Chairman, Committee on International Relations, GAO/ NSIAD-96-241BR. House of Representatives.

2003a. Foreign Assistance: Strategic Workforce Planning Can Help USAID Address Current and Future Challenges. GAO Report on Congressional Request, No. GAO-03-946. House of Representatives.

2003b. Foreign Assistance: USAID Needs to Improve Its Workforce Planning and Operating Expense Accounting, No. GAO-03-1171T. House of Representatives.

Gates, Robert M. 2008. Defense.gov Secretary of Defense Speech: U.S. Global Leadership Campaign (Washington, D.C.) [WWW Document]. URL https://archive.defense.gov/Speeches/Speech.aspx?SpeechID=1262 (accessed 25 August 2019).

Ganga, Paula D. and Desha Girod. 2019. 'Ties That Bind: The Impact of Tied Aid on Development.' Unpublished Manuscript: 34.

The George C. Marshall Foundation. 2019. 'The Marshall Plan – George C. Marshall.'

Giauque, David, Simon Anderfuhren-Biget, and Fréderic Varone. 2013. 'HRM Practices, Intrinsic Motivators and Organizational Performance in the Public Sector.' *Public Personnel Management* 42(2): 123–50.

Giauque, David, Adrian Ritz, Frédéric Varone, and Simon Anderfuhren-Biget. 2012. 'Resigned but Satisfied: The Negative Impact of Public Service Motivation and Red Tape on Work Satisfaction.' *Public Administration* 90(1): 175–93.

Gibson, Clark C., Krister Andersson, Elinor Ostrom, and Sujai Shivakumar. 2005. *The Samaritan's Dilemma: The Political Economy of Development Aid.* New York: Oxford University Press.

Gingrich, Jane R. 2011. *Making Markets in the Welfare State: The Politics of Varying Market Reforms.* 1st edition. Cambridge; New York: Cambridge University Press.

Girod, Desha M. 2008. 'Cut from the Same Cloth? Bilateral vs. Multilateral Aid.' Presented at the Annual Meeting of the International Political Economy Society, Philadelphia.

2018. 'The Political Economy of Aid Conditionality.' *Oxford Research Encyclopedia of Politics.* 26. Oxford University Press.

2019. 'How to Win Friends and Influence Development: Optimising US Foreign Assistance.' *Survival* 61(6): 99–114.

Girod, Desha M. and Jennifer L. Tobin. 2016. 'Take the Money and Run: The Determinants of Compliance with Aid Agreements.' *International Organization* 70(1): 209–39.

Girod, Desha M., Stephen D. Krasner, and Kathryn Stoner-Weiss. 2009. 'Governance and Foreign Assistance: The Imperfect Translation of Ideas into Outcomes.' In *Promoting Democracy and the Rule of Law: American and European Strategies*, Governance and Limited Statehood Series, eds. Amichai Magen, Thomas Risse, and Michael A. McFaul. London: Palgrave Macmillan, 61–92.

Gleditsch, Nils P. et al. 2002. 'Armed Conflict 1946–2001: A New Dataset.' *Journal of Peace Research* 39(5): 615–37.

Goldsmith, Arthur A. 2001. 'Risk, Rule and Reason: Leadership in Africa.' *Public Administration and Development* 21(2): 77–87.

Goldstein, Markus P. and Todd J. Moss. 2005. 'Compassionate Conservatives or Conservative Compassionates? US Political Parties and Bilateral Foreign Assistance to Africa.' *The Journal of Development Studies* 41(7): 1288–1302.

Goodsell, Charles T. 1981. 'Collegial State Administration: Design for Today?' *Western Political Quarterly* 34(3): 447–60.

Gould, Arthur. 1993. 'The End of the Middle Way. The Swedish Welfare State in Crisis.' In *New Perspectives on the Welfare State in Europe*, ed. Caherine Jones. London: Routledge, 157–76.

Gourevitch, Peter. 1986. *Politics in Hard Times: Comparative Responses to International Economic Crises.* 1st edition. Ithaca, NY: Cornell University Press.

Greene, Zachary D. and Amanda A. Licht. 2018. 'Domestic Politics and Changes in Foreign Aid Allocation: The Role of Party Preferences.' *Political Research Quarterly* 71(2): 284–301.

Guisinger, Alexandra. (2017). *American Opinion on Trade: Preferences without Politics*, 1st edition. New York: Oxford University Press.

Gulrajani, Nilima. 2011. 'Transcending the Great Foreign Aid Debate: Managerialism, Radicalism and the Search for Aid Effectiveness.' *Third World Quarterly* 32(2): 199–216.

The Guardian. 2011. 'Why Western Aid Workers Are Coming under Threat. Simon Reid-Henry. Global Development. Guardian.Co.Uk.' Poverty Matters Blog.

Hafner-Burton, Emilie M., D. Alex Hughes, and David G. Victor. 2013. 'The Cognitive Revolution and the Political Psychology of Elite Decision Making.' *Perspectives on Politics* 11(2): 368–86.

Hall, Peter A. and Daniel W. Gingerich. 2009. 'Varieties of Capitalism and Institutional Complementarities in the Political Economy: An Empirical Analysis.' *British Journal of Political Science* 39(3): 449–82.

Hall, Peter A. and David Soskice. 2001. *Varieties of Capitalism: The Institutional Foundations of Comparative Advantage*. Oxford University Press.

Hall, Peter A. and Rosemary C. R. Taylor. 1996. 'Political Science and the Three New Institutionalisms*.' *Political Studies* 44(5): 936–57.

Hammerschmid, Gerhard, Steven Van de Walle, Rhys Andrews, and Philippe Bezes. 2016. *Public Administration Reforms in Europe: The View from the Top*. Edward Elgar.

Hardt, Heidi. 2009. 'Rapid Response or Evasive Action? Regional Organization Responses to Peace Operation Demands.' *European Security* 18(4): 383–415.

Harvey, David. 2007. *A Brief History of Neoliberalism*. Oxford: Oxford University Press.

Hawkins, Darren G., David A. Lake, Daniel L. Nielson, and Michael J. Tierney, eds. 2006. *Delegation and Agency in International Organizations*. 1st edition. Cambridge; New York: Cambridge University Press.

Hawkins, Darren G. and Wade Jacoby. 2006. 'How Agents Matter.' In *Delegation and Agency in International Organizations*, eds. Darren Hawkins, David A. Lake, D. L. Nielson, and Michael J. Tierney. Cambridge: Cambridge University Press, 199–228.

Hays, Jude C. 2009. *Globalization and the New Politics of Embedded Liberalism*. New York: Oxford University Press.

Heinrich, Tobias, Carla Martinez Machain, and Jared Oestman. 2017. 'Does Counterterrorism Militarize Foreign Aid? Evidence from Sub-Saharan Africa.' *Journal of Peace Research* 54(4): 527–41.

Heinrich, Tobias, Yoshiharu Kobayashi, and Kristin A. Bryant. 2016. 'Public Opinion and Foreign Aid Cuts in Economic Crises.' *World Development* 77: 66–79.

Hermann, Christoph. 2014. 'Structural Adjustment and Neoliberal Convergence in Labour Markets and Welfare: The Impact of the Crisis and Austerity Measures on European Economic and Social Models.' *Competition & Change* 18(2): 111–30.

Herrera, Yoshiko M. 2005. *Imagined Economies: The Sources of Russian Regionalism*. Cambridge; New York: Cambridge University Press.

Hibou, B. 2015. *The Bureaucratization of the World in the Neoliberal Era: An International and Comparative Perspective*. New York: Palgrave Macmillan.

Hoadley, J. Stephen. 1980. 'Small States as Aid Donors.' *International Organization* 34(1): 121–37.

Hofmann, Stephanie C. 2009. 'Overlapping Institutions in the Realm of International Security: The Case of NATO and ESDP.' *Perspectives on Politics* 7(1): 45–52.

Holmgren, Wiveca and Arne Svensson. 2005. *Performance Management at Sida*. Stockholm: Department for Evaluation and Internal Audit, Sida.

Holzapfel, Sarah. 2016. 'Boosting or Hindering Aid Effectiveness? An Assessment of Systems for Measuring Donor Agency Results.' *Public Administration and Development* 36(1): 3–19.

Honig, Dan. 2018. *Navigation by Judgment: Why and When Top Down Management of Foreign Aid Doesn't Work*. New York; Oxford: Oxford University Press.

Honig, Dan and Catherine, Weaver. 2019. 'A Race to the Top? The Aid Transparency Index and the Social Power of Global Performance Indicators.' *International Organization* 73(3): 579–610.

Hood, Christopher. 1991. 'A Public Management for All Seasons?' *Public Administration* 69(1): 3–19.

Hood, Christopher and Ruth Dixon. 2015. *A Government That Worked Better and Cost Less?: Evaluating Three Decades of Reform and Change in UK Central Government*. Oxford; New York: Oxford University Press.

Hulme, David. 2007. 'The Making of the Millennium Development Goals: Human Development Meets Results-based Management in an Imperfect World.' Brooks World Poverty Institute Working Paper: 16.

Humphrey, Chris and Katharina Michaelowa. 2013. 'Shopping for Development: Multilateral Lending, Shareholder Composition and Borrower Preferences.' *World Development* 44(C): 142–55.

Iannantuoni, Alice, Charla Waeiss, and Matthew S. Winters. 2020. 'Project Design Decisions of Egalitarian and Non-Egalitarian International Organizations: Evidence from the Global Environment Facility and the World Bank.' *The Review of International Organizations*.

IMF (International Monetary Fund). 2018. 'Direction of Trade Statistics.' *IMF Data Access to Macroecomoic and Financial Data*.

Ireton, Barrie 2013a. *Britain's International Development Policies: A History of DFID and Overseas Aid*. London: Palgrave Macmillan.

2013b. *Britain's International Development Policies: A History of DFID and Overseas Aid*. London: Palgrave Macmillan.

Iversen, Torben, Jonas Pontusson, and David Soskice. 2000. *Unions, Employers and Central Banks: Macroeconomic Coordination and Institutional Change in Social Market Economies*. Cambridge; New York: Cambridge University Press.

Jabko, Nicolas. 2006. *Playing the Market: A Political Strategy for Uniting Europe, 1985–2005*. Ithaca, NY: Cornell University Press.

Jablonski, Ryan S. 2014. 'How Aid Targets Votes: The Impact of Electoral Incentives on Foreign Aid Distribution.' *World Politics* 66(2): 293–330.

Jann, Werner. 2003. 'State, Administration and Governance in Germany: Competing Traditions and Dominant Narratives.' *Public Administration* 81: 95–118.

Johnson, Tana. 2014. *Organizational Progeny: Why Governments Are Losing Control over the Proliferating Structures of Global Governance.* 1st edition. Oxford: Oxford University Press.

Judt Tony. 2001. Introduction. In: Schain, Martin (eds) The Marshall Plan: Fifty Years After. Europe in Transition: The NYU European Studies Series. Palgrave Macmillan, New York.

Kaboolian, Linda. 1998. 'The New Public Management: Challenging the Boundaries of the Management vs. Administration Debate.' *Public Administration Review* 58(3): 189–93.

Kaplan, Stephen B. 2021. Globalizing Patient Capital: The Political Economy of Chinese Finance in the Americas. New York: Cambridge University Press.

Katzenstein, Peter J., ed. 1978. *Between Power and Plenty: Foreign Economic Policies of Advanced Industrial States.* Madison: University of Wisconsin Press.

Katznelson, Ira, I. 1997. 'Liberal Maps for Technology's Powers: Six Question.' *Social Research: An International Quarterly* 64(3): 1333–37.

Kaufmann, Daniel, Aart Kraay, and Massimo Mastruzzi. 2011. 'The Worldwide Governance Indicators: Methodology and Analytical Issues.' *Hague Journal on the Rule of Law* 3(2): 220–46.

Kegley, Charles W. and Steven W. Hook. 1991. 'U.S. Foreign Aid and U.N. Voting: Did Reagan's Linkage Strategy Buy Deference or Defiance?' *International Studies Quarterly* 35(3): 295–312.

Kelley, Judith G. and Beth A. Simmons. 2019. 'Introduction: The Power of Global Performance Indicators.' *International Organization* 73(3): 491–510. doi: 10.1017/S0020818319000146.

Kertzer, Joshua D. 2020. 'Re-Assessing Elite-Public Gaps in Political Behavior.' *American Journal of Political Science* [Online version of Record before inclusion in an issue].

Kertzer, Joshua D. and Dustin H. Tingley. 2018. 'Political Psychology in International Relations: Beyond the Paradigms.' *Annual Review of Political Science* 21(1): 319–39.

Kertzer, Joshua D., Kathleen E. Powers, Brian C. Rathbun, and Ravi Iyer. 2014. 'Moral Support: How Moral Values Shape Foreign Policy Attitudes.' *The Journal of Politics* 76(3): 825–40.

Kertzer, Joshua D. and Thomas Zeitzoff. 2017. 'A Bottom-Up Theory of Public Opinion about Foreign Policy.' *American Journal of Political Science* 61(3): 543–58.

Kiewiet, D. Roderick and Mathew D. McCubbins. 1991. *The Logic of Delegation: Congressional Parties and the Appropriations Process.* 1st edition. Chicago: University of Chicago Press.

Kilby, Christopher. 2006. 'Donor Influence in Multilateral Development Banks: The Case of the Asian Development Bank.' *The Review of International Organizations* 1(2): 173–95.

Kilby, Christopher and Axel Dreher. 2010. 'The Impact of Aid on Growth Revisited: Do Donor Motives Matter?' *Economics Letters* 107(3): 338–40. doi: 10.1016/j.econlet.2010.02.015.

Killick, Tony, Ramani Gunatilaka, and Ana Marr. 1998. *Aid and the Political Economy of Policy Change*. New York: Routledge.

Kinder, Donald R. and Lynn M. Sanders. 1990. 'Mimicking Political Debate with Survey Questions: The Case of White Opinion on Affirmative Action for Blacks.' *Social Cognition* 8(1): 73–103.

Kinderman, Daniel. 2005. "Pressure from Without, Subversion from Within: The TwoPronged German Employer Offensive." Comparative European Politics 3(4): 432–63.

2008. 'The Political Economy of Sectoral Exchange Rate Preferences and Lobbying: Germany from 1960–2008, and Beyond.' *Review of International Political Economy* 15(5): 851–80.

Kinsey, Christopher. 2006. *Corporate Soldiers and International Security: The Rise of Private Military Companies*. New York: Routledge & CRC Press.

Knack, Stephen F. 2001. 'Aid Dependence and the Quality of Governance: Cross-Country Empirical Tests.' *Southern Economic Journal* 68(2): 310–29.

Knack, Stephen F. and Aminur Rahman. 2007. 'Donor Fragmentation and Bureaucratic Quality in Aid Recipients.' *Journal of Development Economics* 83(1): 176–97.

Kono, Daniel Y. and Gabriella R. Montinola. 2009. 'Does Foreign Aid Support Autocrats, Democrats, or Both?' *The Journal of Politics* 71: 704–18.

Krasner, Stephen D. and Jeremy M. Weinstein. 2014. 'Improving Governance from the Outside in.' *Annual Review of Political Science* 17: 123–45.

Kuhlmann, Sabine, Proeller, Isabella, Schimanke, Dieter & Ziekow, Jan (eds). 2021. Public Administration in Germany. Part of: Governance and Public Management. Cham: Springer Publishing. Palgrave Macmillan.

Kumlin, Staffan and Bo Rothstein. 2005. 'Making and Breaking Social Capital: The Impact of Welfare-State Institutions.' *Comparative Political Studies* 38(4): 339–65.

Kuziemko, Ilyana and Eric Werker. 2006. 'How Much Is a Seat on the Security Council Worth? Foreign Aid and Bribery at the United Nations.' *Journal of Political Economy* 114(5): 905–30.

Lake, David A. 2009a. 'Open Economy Politics: A Critical Review.' *The Review of International Organizations* 4(3): 219–44.

2009b. 'Relational Authority and Legitimacy in International Relations.' *American Behavioral Scientist* 53(3): 331–35.

Lancaster, Carol J. 2006. *Foreign Aid: Diplomacy, Development, Domestic Politics*. 11.1.2006 edition. Chicago: University of Chicago Press.

2007. *Foreign Aid: Diplomacy, Development, Domestic Politics*. Chicago: University of Chicago Press.

Latham, Michael E. 2000. *Modernization as Ideology: American Social Science and "Nation Building" in the Kennedy Era*. New edition. Chapel Hill: University of North Carolina Press.

Lawson, Marian L. 2011. 'Foreign Assistance: Public-Private Partnerships (PPPs).' CRS Report No. R41880. www.legistorm.com/reports/view/crs/124924/Foreign_Assistance_Public_Private_Partnerships_PPPs_.html.

Le Grand, Julian and Will Bartlett. 1993. *Quasi-Markets and Social Policy*. Basingstoke: Palgrave Macmillan.

Lebovic, James H. 2014. 'The Millennium Challenge Corporation: Organizational Constraints on US Foreign Aid, 2004–11.' *World Development* 58(C): 116–29.

Leepson, Marc. 2000. 'The Heart and Mind of USAID's Vietnam Mission.' *Foreign Service Journal*: 20–27.

Leiderer, Stefan. 2015. 'Donor Coordination for Effective Government Policies?' *Journal of International Development* 27(8): 1422–45. https://onlinelibrary.wiley.com/doi/abs/10.1002/jid.3184.

Levin, Victoria and David Dollar. 2006. 'The Increasing Selectivity of Foreign Aid, 1984–2003.' *World Development* 34(12): 2034–46.

Lewin, Leif. 1994. 'The Rise and Decline of Corporatism: The Case of Sweden.' *European Journal of Political Research* 26(1): 59–79.

Licht, Amanda A. 2010. 'Coming into Money: The Impact of Foreign Aid on Leader Survival.' *The Journal of Conflict Resolution* 54(1): 58–87.

Lieberman, Robert C. 2002. 'Ideas, Institutions, and Political Order: Explaining Political Change.' *The American Political Science Review* 96(4): 697–712.

Lim, Daniel Y. M. and James R. Vreeland. 2013. 'Regional Organizations and International Politics: Japanese Influence over the Asian Development Bank and the UN Security Council.' *World Politics* 65(01): 34–72.

Lippmann, Walter. 1937. *An Inquiry into the Principles of the Good Society*. Boston: Little, Brown and Company.

Loewen, Peter J. and Daniel Rubenson. 2011. 'For Want of a Nail: Negative Persuasion in a Party Leadership Campaign.' *Party Politics* 17(1): 45–65.

Luboga, Samuel A. et al. 2016. 'Did PEPFAR Investments Result in Health System Strengthening? A Retrospective Longitudinal Study Measuring Non-HIV Health Service Utilization at the District Level.' *Health Policy and Planning* 31(7): 897–909.

Lumsdaine, David H. 1993. *Moral Vision in International Politics: The Foreign Aid Regime, 1949–1989*. Princeton, NJ: Princeton University Press.

Lundsgaarde, Erik. 2012. *The Domestic Politics of Foreign Aid*, 1st edition. New York: Routledge.

Lupia, Arthur. 1994. 'Shortcuts Versus Encyclopedias: Information and Voting Behavior in California Insurance Reform Elections.' *The American Political Science Review* 88(1): 63–76.

Lynn Jr., Laurence E. 2006. *Public Management: Old and New*. 1st edition. New York: Routledge.

MacDonald, Peter. 2013. *Labour Substitution and the Scope for Military Outsourcing*.

McLean, Elena V. 2015. 'Multilateral Aid and Domestic Economic Interests.' *International Organization* 69: 97–130 doi: 10.1017/S0020818314000289.

Mahoney, James. 2002. *The Legacies of Liberalism: Path Dependence and Political Regimes in Central America*. Baltimore: The Johns Hopkins University Press.

Maizels, Alfred and Machiko K. Nissanke. 1984. 'Motivations for Aid to Developing Countries.' *World Development* 12(9): 879–900.

Mannheim, Karl and Edward Shils. 1940. *Man and Society in an Age of Reconstruction: Studies in Modern Social Structure*. 1st edition. New York: Harcourt, Brace and Co.

Manning, Richard. 2009. Using Indicators to Encourage Development Lessons from the Millennium Development Goals. Danish Institute for International Studies Report 09/01.

Mansfield, Edward D. and Jon C. Pevehouse. 2006. 'Democratization and International Organizations.' *International Organization* 60(1): 137–67.

Martens, Bertin et al. 2002. *The Institutional Economics of Foreign Aid*. New York: Cambridge University Press.

Mattli, Walter and Tim Bühte. 2013. *The New Global Rulers: The Privatization of Regulation in the World Economy*. Princeton, NJ: Princeton University Press.

Mawdsley, Emma. 2007. 'The Millennium Challenge Account: Neo-Liberalism, Poverty and Security1.' *Review of International Political Economy* 14(3): 487–509.

Mawdsley, Emma, Laura Savage, and Sung-Mi Kim. 2014. 'A "Post-Aid World"? Paradigm Shift in Foreign Aid and Development Cooperation at the 2011 Busan High Level Forum: A "Post-Aid World"?' *The Geographical Journal* 180(1): 27–38.

McDermott, Rose. 2002. 'Experimental Methods in Political Science.' *Annual Review of Political Science* 5: 31–61.

2011. 'Internal and External Validity.' In *Cambridge Handbook of Experimental Political Science*, eds. Arthur Lupia, Donald P. Greene,

James H. Kuklinski, and James N. Druckman. Cambridge: Cambridge University Press, 27–40.

McGillivray, Mark and Thi Kim Cuong Pham. 2017. 'Reforming Performance-Based Aid Allocation Practice.' *World Development* 90: 1–5.

McKinlay, Robert D. and R. Little. 1978. 'A Foreign-Policy Model of the Distribution of British Bilateral Aid, 1960–70.' *British Journal of Political Science* 8(3): 313–31.

1979. 'The US Aid Relationship: A Test of the Recipient Need and the Donor Interest Models*.' *Political Studies* 27(2): 236–50.

McLean, Elena V. 2015. 'Multilateral Aid and Domestic Economic Interests.' *International Organization* 69(1): 97–130.

Menz, Georg. 2011. 'Neo-Liberalism, Privatization and the Outsourcing of Migration Management: A Five-Country Comparison.' *Competition and Change* 15(2): 116–35.

Metzger, Laura, Peter Nunnenkamp, and Toman O. Mahmoud. 2010. 'Is Corporate Aid Targeted to Poor and Deserving Countries? A Case Study of Nestlé's Aid Allocation.' *World Development* 38(3): 228–43.

Micheletti, Michele. 1995. *Civil Society and State Relations in Sweden*. Aldershot: Avebury.

2000. 'End of Big Government: Is It Happening in the Nordic Countries?' *Governance* 13(2): 265–78.

Milner, Helen V. 1997. *Interests, Institutions, and Information: Domestic Politics and International Relations*. Princeton, NJ: Princeton University Press.

2006. 'Why Multilateralism? Foreign Aid and Domestic Principal-Agent Problems.' In *Delegation and Agency in International Organizations*, eds. Darren G. Hawkins, David A. Lake, Daniel L. Nielson, and Michael J. Tierney. New York: Cambridge University Press, 107–39.

Milner, Helen V., and Dustin H. Tingley. 2010. 'The Political Economy of U. s. Foreign Aid: American Legislators and the Domestic Politics of Aid.' *Economics & Politics* 22(2): 200–32.

2011a. *The Economic and Political Influences on Different Dimensions of United States Immigration Policy*. Rochester, NY: Social Science Research Network. SSRN Scholarly Paper.

2011b. 'Who Supports Global Economic Engagement? The Sources of Preferences in American Foreign Economic Policy.' *International Organization* 65(01): 37–68.

2012. 'The Choice for Multilateralism: Foreign Aid and American Foreign Policy.' *The Review of International Organizations* 8(3): 313–41.

2015. *Sailing the Water's Edge.: The Domestic Politics of American Foreign Policy*. Princeton, NJ; Oxford: Princeton University Press.

Molander, Per, Jan-Eric Nilsson, and Allen Schick. 2002. *Does Anyone Govern? The Relationship Between the Government Office and the Agencies in Sweden*. Center for Business and Policy Studies (SNS), Stockholm.

Molenaers, Nadia, Anna Gagiano, Lodewijk Smets, and Sebastian Dellepiane. 2015. 'What Determines the Suspension of Budget Support?' *World Development* 75: 62–73.

Morgenthau, Hans J. 1993. *Politics among Nations: The Struggle for Power and Peace*. New York: McGraw-Hill.

Morgenthau, Hans J., Kenneth A. Thompson, and David Clinton. 2005. *Politics Among Nations*. 7th edition. Boston: McGraw-Hill Education.

Morrison, Kevin M. 2009. 'Oil, Nontax Revenue, and the Redistributional Foundations of Regime Stability.' *International Organization* 63(1): 107–38.

Mosley, Paul. 1981. 'Models of the Aid Allocation Process: A Comment of McKinlay and Little.' *Political Studies*, 29(2): 245–53. doi: 10.1111/j.1467-9248.1981.tb00491.x.

Mosley, Paul, Jane Harrigan, and John F. J. Toye. 1991. *Aid and Power: The World Bank and Policy-Based Lending*. London: Routledge.

Muller, Jerry Z. 2018. *Tyranny of Metrics*. Princeton, NJ: Princeton University Press.

Natsios, Andrew. 2010. 'The Clash of Counter-Bureaucracy and Development.' Essay, Washington, DC: Center for Global Development.

Nelson, Stephen C. 2017. *The Currency of Confidence: How Economic Beliefs Shape the IMF's Relationship with Its Borrowers*. 1st edition. Ithaca, NY: Cornell University Press.

Nielson, Daniel L. and Michael J. Tierney. 2003. 'Delegation to International Organizations: Agency Theory and World Bank Environmental Reform.' *International Organization* 57(2): 241–76.

Noël, Alain and Jean-Philippe Therien. 1995. 'From Domestic to International Justice: The Welfare State and Foreign Aid.' *International Organization* 49(3): 523–53.

North, Douglass C. 1990. *Institutions, Institutional Change and Economic Performance*. 2nd edition. Cambridge; New York: Cambridge University Press.

1991. 'Institutions.' *The Journal of Economic Perspectives* 5(1): 97–112.

Nunnenkamp, Peter, Hannes Öhler, and Rainer Thiele. 2013. 'Donor Coordination and Specialization: Did the Paris Declaration Make a Difference?' *Review of World Economics* 149(3): 537–63.

OECD. 1996. *Integrating People Management into Public Service Reform*. Paris: OECD Publishing.

Adding People Management into Public Service Reform. Puma Report. Paris.

2003. *Development Co-Operation Report 2002 Efforts and Policies of the Members of the Development Assistance Committee: Efforts and Policies of the Members of the Development Assistance Committee.* Paris: OECD Publishing.

2006. Harmonising Donor Practices for Effective Aid Delivery. DAC Guidelines and References Series. Volume 2. Paris.

2008. *Accra Agenda for Action.* Paris: OECD Publishing, p. 1.

2017. *Government at a Glance 2017,* OECD Publishing, Paris.

OECD, D. A. C. 1996. *Shaping the 21st Century: The Role of Development Cooperation.* Paris.

OECD, N. A. Statistics. 2020. *Government at a Glance 2017 (Text).* Paris: OECD Publishing.

OECD, O. for E. C. and D., & DAC Task Force on Donor Practices, eds. 2003. *Harmonising Donor Practices for Effective Aid Delivery. DAC Guidelines and Reference Series.* Paris: Organisation for Economic Co-operation and Development.

OECD DAC. 2017. Results in Development Co-Operation – Provider Case Studies: Sweden – Ministry of Foreign Affairs and Swedish International Development Cooperation Agency. OECD Development Co- Operation Policy Paper – May 2017.

OECD Development Co-operation Peer Reviews: France. 2000.

OECD Development Co-operation Peer Reviews: France. 2004.

OECD Development Co-operation Peer Reviews: France. 2008.

OECD Development Co-operation Peer Reviews: France. 2013.

OECD Development Co-operation Peer Reviews: Germany. 1995.

OECD Development Co-operation Peer Reviews: Germany. 1998.

OECD Development Co-operation Peer Reviews: Germany. 2001.

OECD Development Co-operation Peer Reviews: Germany. 2005.

OECD Development Co-operation Peer Reviews: Germany. 2010.

OECD Development Co-operation Peer Reviews: Germany. 2015.

OECD Development Co-operation Peer Reviews: Sweden. 2000.

OECD Development Co-operation Peer Reviews: Sweden. 2005.

OECD Development Co-operation Peer Reviews: Sweden. 2009.

OECD Development Co-operation Peer Reviews: Sweden. 2013.

OECD Development Co-operation Peer Reviews: United Kingdom. 2001.

OECD Development Co-operation Peer Reviews: United Kingdom. 2006.

OECD Development Co-operation Peer Reviews: United Kingdom. 2010.

OECD Development Co-operation Peer Reviews: United Kingdom. 2014.

OECD Development Co-operation Peer Reviews: United States. 1989/1990.

OECD Development Co-operation Peer Reviews: United States. 1994/1995.
OECD Development Co-operation Peer Reviews: United States. 1998.
OECD Development Co-operation Peer Reviews: United States. 2002.
OECD Development Co-operation Peer Reviews: United States. 2006.
OECD Development Co-operation Peer Reviews: United States. 2011.
OECD Development Co-operation Peer Reviews: United States. 2016.
OECD. 2005. *Paris Declaration on Aid Effectiveness*. Paris: OECD
    Publishing Paris, https://doi.org/10.1787/9789264098084-en
Olken, Benjamin A. and Rohini Pande. 2012. 'Corruption in Developing
    Countries.' *Annual Review of Economics* 4(1): 479–509.
Olsen, Gregg M. 1996. 'Re-Modeling Sweden: The Rise and Demise of the
    Compromise in a Global Economy.' *Social Problems*, 43(1): 1–20.
Olsen, Johan P. 2008. 'The Ups and Downs of Bureaucratic Organization.'
    Annual Review of Political Science 11: 13–37.
Osborne, David and Ted Gaebler. 1992. *Reinventing Government: How the
    Entrepreneurial Spirit Is Transforming the Public Sector*. 1st edition.
    Reading, MA: Addison-Wesley.
O'Sullivan, Tim. 1991. 'Book Reviews.' *Media, Culture & Society* 13(3):
    426–28.
Parsons, Craig. 2003. *A Certain Idea of Europe*. Ithaca, NY: Cornell
    University Press.
Paxton, Pamela and Stephen F. Knack. 2012. 'Individual and Country-Level
    Factors Affecting Support for Foreign Aid.' *International Political
    Science Review* 33(2): 171–92.
Pepinsky, Thomas B, Jan H Pierskalla, and Audrey Sacks. 2017. 'Bureaucracy
    and Service Delivery.' *Annual Review of Political Science* 20(1): 249–68.
Peters, B. Guy. 1996. *The Future of Governing:Four Emerging Models*.
    Lawrence: University Press of Kansas.
Peters, B. Guy and John Pierre. 1998. 'Governance without Government?
    Rethinking Public Administration.' *Journal of Public Administration
    Research and Theory* 8(2): 223–43.
Peters, John. 2012. 'Neoliberal Convergence in North America and Western
    Europe: Fiscal Austerity, Privatization, and Public Sector Reform.'
    Review of International Political Economy 19(2): 208–35.
Peteson, Ulrich. 2008. *Outsourcing the Big Stick: The Consequences of
    Using Private Military Companies*. Cambridge, MA: Weatherhead
    Center for International Affairs.
Peterson, Robert A. 1994. 'A Meta-Analysis of Cronbach's Coefficient
    Alpha.' *Journal of Consumer Research* 21(2): 381–91.
Poate, Derek. 1997. *Measuring and Managing Results: Lessons for
    Development Cooperation*. Stockholm: Swedish International
    Development Cooperation Agency.

PIC, P. I. C. n.d. 'Performance Improvement Council – Who We Are'. www .pic.gov/

Piccio, Lorenzo. 2012. 'In Uganda, Donors Divided on Response to Aid Embezzlement Scandal.' *Devex*. www.devex.com/news/in-ugandadonors-divided-on-response-to-aid-embezzlement-scandal-79925.

Pierson, Paul 1995. *Dismantling the Welfare State?: Reagan, Thatcher and the Politics of Retrenchment*. Cambridge: Cambridge University Press.

2001. *The New Politics of the Welfare State*. Oxford: Oxford University Press.

Polanyi, Karl P. 2001. *The Great Transformation: The Political and Economic Origins of Our Time*. Boston: Beacon Press.

Pollitt, Christopher. 1990. *Managerialism and the Public Services: The Anglo-American Experience*. Oxford: Basil Blackwell.

Pollitt, Christopher and Geert Bouckaert. 2003. 'Evaluating Public Management Reforms: An International Perspective.' In *Evaluating Public Sector Reform: Concepts and Practice in International Perspective*, ed. Hellmut Wollmann. Cheltenham; Northampton, MA: Edward Elgar.

2011. *Public Management Reform: A Comparative Analysis: New Public Management, Governance, and the Neo-Weberian State*. Oxford: Oxford University Press.

Pontusson, Jonas. 1992. 'At the End of the Third Road: Swedish Social Democracy in Crisis.' *Politics & Society* 20(3): 305–32.

Pospieszna, Paulina. 2019. *Democracy Assistance Bypassing Governments in Recipient Countries*. New York: Routledge Press.

Powell, Walter W. and Paul J. DiMaggio, eds. 1991. *The New Institutionalism in Organizational Analysis*. 1st edition. Chicago: University of Chicago Press.

Prather, Lauren. 2014. 'Values at the Water's Edge: Social Welfare Values and Foreign Aid.' www.laurenprather.org/uploads/2/5/2/3/25239175/ prather-values_at_the_waters_edge.pdf: 42.

Pratt, Chris, William E. Tunmer, and Andrew R. Nesdale. 1989. 'Young Children's Evaluations of Experience- and Non–Experience-Based Oral Communications.' *British Journal of Developmental Psychology* 7(1): 83–91.

Premfors, Rune. 1991. 'The 'Swedish Model' and Public Sector Reform.' *West European Politics* 14(3): 83–95.

Presidential Directive on Global Development. 2010. Accessible at: https:// fas.org/irp/offdocs/ppd/ppd-6.pdf.

Pritchett, Lant, Michael Woolcock, and Matthew Andrews. 2010. 'Capability Traps? The Mechanisms of Persistent Implementation Failure.' *SSRN Electronic Journal*, Center for Global Development Working Paper No. 234, Washington DC.

Przeworski, Adam. 1975. 'Institutionalization of Voting Patterns, or Is Mobilization the Source of Decay?' *The American Political Science Review* 69(1): 49–67.

Przeworski, Adam, Susan Stokes, and Bernard Manin. 1999. *Democracy, Accountability, and Representation*. Cambridge: Cambridge University Press.

Quermonne, Jean-Louis and Luc Rouban. 1986. 'French Public Administration and Policy Evaluation: The Quest for Accountability.' *Public Administration Review* 46(5): 397–406.

Raadschelders, Jos C. N. and Theo A. J. Toonen. 1999. 'Public Sector Reform for Building and Recasting the Welfare State: Experiences in Western Europe.' *Research in Public Administration* 5: 39–62.

Radelet, Steven. 2004. 'Aid Effectiveness and the Millenium Development Goals.' Working Paper 39. Washington, DC: Center for Global Development.

2003. Challenging Foreign Aid: A Policymaker's Guide to the Millennium Challenge Account. New York: Columbia University Press.

Radin, Beryl A. 1998. 'Searching for Government Performance: The Government Performance and Results Act.' *PS: Political Science and Politics* 31(3): 553–55.

Randel, Judith and Tony German. 2015. Why the New UK Government Will Stick to Its Commitments on Aid. Brookings Future Development Blog.

Rathbun, Brian C. et al. 2016. 'Taking Foreign Policy Personally: Personal Values and Foreign Policy Attitudes.' *International Studies Quarterly* 60(1): 124–37.

Reinikka, Ritva and Jakob Svensson. 2004. 'Local Capture: Evidence from a Central Government Transfer Program in Uganda.' *The Quarterly Journal of Economics* 119(2): 679–705.

Reinsberg, Bernhard, Katharina Michaelowa, and Vera Z. Eichenauer. 2015. 'The Rise of Multi-Bi Aid and the Proliferation of Trust Funds.' In *Handbook on the Economics of Foreign Aid*, eds. Mak Arvin and Byron Lew. Cheltenham: Edward Elgar, 527–54.

Remmer, Karen L. 2004. 'Does Foreign Aid Promote the Expansion of Government?' *American Journal of Political Science* 48(1): 77–92.

Resnick, Danielle and Nicolas van de Walle (eds). 2013. Democratic Trajectories in Africa: Unravelling the Impact of Foreign Aid. Oxford: Oxford University Press.

Rhodes, R. A. W. 1997. *"Understanding Governance: Policy Networks, Governance, Reflexivity and Accountability."* Milton Keynes: Open University Press.

Riddell, Roger. 2007. *Does Foreign Aid Really Work?* Oxford: Oxford University Press.

Roberts, Susan M. 2014. 'Development Capital: USAID and the Rise of Development Contractors.' *Annals of the Association of American Geographers* 104(5): 1030–51.

Rodrik, Dani. 1995. 'Why Is There Multilateral Lending?' In *Annual World Bank Conference on Development Economics 1995*, eds. Michael Bruno and Boris Pleskovic. Washington, DC: World Bank, 167–205.

Rogerson, Andrew. 2005. 'Aid Harmonisation and Alignment: Bridging the Gaps between Reality and the Paris Reform Agenda.' *Development Policy Review* 23(5): 531–52.

Rose, Nikolas and Peter Miller. 2008. *Governing the Present: Administering Economic, Social and Personal Life*. 1st edition. Cambridge; Malden, MA: Polity.

Ross, David J. 1990. 'Aid Co-Ordination.' *Public Administration and Development* 10(3): 331–42.

Rothstein, Bo. 1998. *The Social Democratic State. The Swedish Model and the Bureaucratic Problem of Social Reforms*. Pittsburgh, PA: University of Pittsburgh Press.

Round, Jeffery I. and Matthew Odedokun. 2004. 'Aid Effort and Its Determinants.' *International Review of Economics & Finance, Aid Allocations and Development Financing* 13(3): 293–309. doi: 10.1016/j.iref.2003.11.0 06.

Ruggie, John G. 1982. 'International Regimes, Transactions, and Change: Embedded Liberalism in the Postwar Economic Order.' *International Organization* 36(2): 379–415.

Ryner, Magnus. 2004. 'Neo-liberalization of Social Democracy: The Swedish Case.' *Comparative European Politics* 2: 97–119.

Sachs, Jeffrey D. 2005. *The End of Poverty: Economic Possibilities for Our Time*. Reprint edition. New York: Penguin Books.

Sacks, Audrey. 2012. Can Donors and Non-State Actors Undermine Citizens' Legitimating Beliefs ?. Policy Research working paper no. WPS 6158. World Bank, Washington, DC. © World Bank. https://openknowledge.worldbank.org/handle/10986/11997 License: CC BY 3.0 IGO

Savun, Burcu and Daniel Tirone. 2018. 'Foreign Aid as a Counterterrorism Tool: More Liberty, Less Terror?' *Journal of Conflict Resolution* 62(8): 1607–35.

Scharpf, Fritz W. 1997a. 'Economic Integration, Democracy and the Welfare State.' *Journal of European Public Policy* 4(1): 18–36.

1997b. *Games Real Actors Play: Actor-Centered Institutionalism In Policy Research*. 1st edition. Boulder, CO: Westview Press.

1999. *Governing in Europe: Effective and Democratic?* Oxford: Oxford University Press.

Schneider, Christina J. and Jennifer L. Tobin. 2013. 'Interest Coalitions and Multilateral Aid Allocation in the European Union.' *International Studies Quarterly* 57(1): 103–14.

Schnyder, Gerhard. 2012. 'Like a Phoenix from the Ashes? Reassessing the Transformation of the Swedish Political Economy since the 1970s.' *Journal of European Public Policy* 19(8): 1126–45.

Schraeder, Peter J., Steven W. Hook, and Bruce Taylor. 1998. 'Clarifying the Foreign Aid Puzzle: A Comparison of American, Japanese, French and Swedish Aid Flows.' *World Politics* 50(2): 294–323.

Schröter, Eckhard and Helmut Wollmann. 1997. 'Public Sector Reforms in Germany: Whence and Where? A Case of Ambivalence.' *Administrative Studies/Hallinnon Tutkimus* 16(3): 184–200.

Schumpeter, Joseph A. 1950. *Capitalism, Socialism, and Democracy*. New York: Harper & Row. Sewell, William H., Jr. 1985.

Scott, James M. and Carie A. Steele. 2011. 'Sponsoring Democracy? The United States and Democracy Aid to the Developing World 1988–2001.' *International Studies Quarterly* 55(1): 47–69.

Scotto, Thomas, Jason Reifler, David Hudson, and Jennifer Hudson. 2017. 'We Spend How Much? Misperceptions, Innumeracy, and Support for the Foreign Aid in the United States and Great Britain.' *Journal of Experimental Political Science* 4(2): 119–28.

Simmons, David G. 1994. 'Tourism Alternatives: Potentials and Problems in the Development of Tourism.' *New Zealand Geographer* 50(2): 57–58.

Sjöstedt, Martin. 2013. 'Aid Effectiveness and the Paris Declaration: A Mismatch Between Ownership and Results-Based Management?' *Public Administration and Development* 33(2): 143–55.

Snyder, Susan and Barry Weingast. 2000. 'The American System of Shared Powers: The President, Congress, and the NLRB.' *Journal of Law, Economics and Organization* 16: 269–305.

Soifer, Hillel D. 2012. 'The Causal Logic of Critical Junctures.' *Comparative Political Studies* 45(12): 572–97.

Spero, Domani. 2010. 'Houston, We Have a Problem … at USAID.' *Diplopundit*. https://diplopundit.net/2010/04/15/houston-we-have-a-problem-at-usaid/

Steele, Abbey and Jacob N. Shapiro. 2017. 'Subcontracting State-Building: Small Wars & Insurgencies.' Taylor & Francis Journals, vol. 28(4–5): 887–905.

Steele, Carie A., Daniel Pemstein, and Stephen A. Meserve. 2020. 'Democracy promotion and electoral quality: A disaggregated analysis.' *Governance* 1–17.

Steinmo, Sven. 2010. 'The Evolution of Modern States: Sweden, Japan, and the United States.' *The Evolution of Modern States: Sweden, Japan, and the United States*: 1–269.

Steinmo, Sven, Kathleen Thelen, and Frank Longstreth, eds. 1992. *Structuring Politics: Historical Institutionalism in Comparative Analysis*. Cambridge; New York: Cambridge University Press.

Steinwand, Martin C. 2015. 'Compete or Coordinate? Aid Fragmentation and Lead Donorship.' *International Organization* 69(2): 443–72.

Stokke, Olav, ed. 1989. *Western Middle Powers and Global Poverty: The Determinants of the Aid Policies of Canada, Denmark, the Netherlands, Norway, and Sweden.* Uppsala; Stockholm: The Scandinavian Institute of African Studies, in cooperation with the Norwegian Institute of International Affairs; Distributed by Almqwist & Wiksell International.

Strand, Jonathan and Tina Zappile. 2015. 'Always Vote for Principle, Though You May Vote Alone: Explaining United States Political Support for Multilateral Development Loans.' *World Development* 72: 224–39.

Streeck, Wolfgang. 2010. *Re-Forming Capitalism Re-Forming Capitalism: Institutional Change in the German Political Economy.* Oxford: Oxford University Press.

Strøm, Kaare, Wolfgang C. Müller, and Torbjörn Bergman, eds. 2003. *Delegation and Accountability in Parliamentary Democracies.* Oxford; New York: Oxford University Press.

Suleiman, Ezra. 2003. *Dismantling Democratic States.* Princeton, NJ: Princeton University Press.

Svensson, Jakob. 2000. 'Foreign Aid and Rent-Seeking.' *Journal of International Economics* 51(2): 437–61.

Swank, Duane. 2002. *Global Capital, Political Institutions, and Policy Change in Developed Welfare States.* Cambridge: Cambridge University Press.

Swedlund, Haley J. 2017. The Development Dance: How Donors and Recipients Negotiate the Delivery of Foreign Aid. Ithaca, NY: Cornell University Press.

Tallberg, Jonas. 2002. 'Delegation to Supranational Institutions: Why, How, and with What Consequences?' *West European Politics*, 25(1): 23–46.

Tallberg, Jonas, Karin Bäckstrand, and Jan A. Scholte, eds. 2018. *Legitimacy in Global Governance: Sources, Processes, and Consequences.* Oxford; New York: Oxford University Press.

Tesler, Michael. 2015. 'Priming Predispositions and Changing Policy Positions: An Account of When Mass Opinion Is Primed or Changed.' *American Journal of Political Science* 59(4): 806–24.

Thelen, Kathleen. 1999. Historical Institutionalism in Comparative Politics. *Annual Review of Political Science* 2(1): 369–404.

2003. 'How Institutions Evolve. Insights from Comparative Historical Analysis.' In *Comparative Historical Analysis in the Social Sciences*, eds. James Mahoney and Dietrich Rueschemeyer. Cambridge: Cambridge University Press, 208–40.

2014. *Varieties of Liberalization and the New Politics of Social Solidarity.* Cambridge; New York: Cambridge University Press.

Therien, Jean-Philippe, and Alain Noël. 2000. 'Political Parties and Foreign Aid.' *American Political Science Review* 94(1): 151–62.

Tingley, Dustin H. 2010. 'Donors and Domestic Politics: Political Influences on Foreign Aid Effort.' *The Quarterly Review of Economics and Finance* 50(1): 40–49.

Tsebelis, George and Yataganas Xenophon. 2002. 'Veto Players and Decision-Making in the EU After Nice: Policy Stability and Bureaucratic/Judicial Discretion.' *Journal of Common Market Studies* 40(2): 283–307.

Tsopanakis, Georgios. 2016. 'What Is Development and Why Even Bother? Narratives, Experts and a Quest to End Poverty.' *Forum for Development Studies* 43(3): 521–30.

United States. Dept. of State. Office of Media Services, and United States. Dept. of State. Office of Public Communication. 1949. *The Department of State Bulletin.* Washington, DC : Office of Public Communication, Bureau of Public Affairs.

US Office of Management and Budget. 1993. Government Performance Results Act of 1993. Washington, DC. Available at http://www .whitehouse.gov/omb/mgmt-gpra/gplaw2m.

2011. Government Performance and Results Modernization Act of 2010. Washington, DC.Available at http://www.whitehouse.gov/omb/per formance/gprm-act.

USAID. 2019. 'USAID History | U.S. Agency for International Development.'

Valters, Craig and Brendan Whitty. 2017. *The Politics of the Results Agenda in DFID: 1997–2017.* London: Overseas Development Institute.

Van de Walle, Steven, Steven Van Roosbroek, and Geert Bouckaert. 2008. 'Trust in the Public Sector: Is There Any Evidence for a Long-Term Decline?' *International Review of Administrative Sciences* 74(1): 47–64.

Van der Veen, A. Maurits. 2011. *Ideas, Interests and Foreign Aid.* Cambridge: Cambridge University Press.

Van Dooren, Wouter, Gert Bouckaert, and John Halligan. 2010. Performance Management in the Public Sector (1st ed.). London: Routledge.

Veillette, Connie. 2007. *Restructuring U.S. Foreign Aid: The Role of the Director of Foreign Assistance in Transformational Development.* Washington, DC: Congressional Research Service.

Vestergaard, Jakob and Robert H. Wade. 2013. 'Protecting Power: How Western States Retain the Dominant Voice in the World Bank's Governance.' *World Development* 46(C): 153–64.

Vreeland, James R. 2008. 'Political Institutions and Human Rights: Why Dictatorships Enter into the United Nations Convention Against Torture.' *International Organization* 62(1): 65–101.

Vreeland, James R. and Axel Dreher. 2014. *The Political Economy of the United Nations Security Council: Money and Influence*. New York: Cambridge University Press.

Vähämäki, Janet 2017, *Matrixing Aid: The Rise and Fall of 'Results Initiatives' in Swedish Development Aid*. Dissertation. University of Stockholm.

Weaver, Catherine. 2008. *Hypocrisy Trap: The World Bank and the Poverty of Reform*. Princeton, NJ: Princeton University Press.

Weber, Max. 1978. *Economy and Society: An Outline of Interpretive Sociology*. Berkeley: University of California Press.

Weinstein, Jeremy M. 2005. 'Resources and the Information Problem in Rebel Recruitment.' *The Journal of Conflict Resolution* 49(4): 598–624.

Wendt, Alexander. 2001. 'Driving with the Rearview Mirror: On the Rational Science of Institutional Design.' *International Organization* 55(4): 1019–49.

Whitford, Andrew. 2005. 'The Pursuit of Political Control by Multiple Principals.' *The Journal of Politics* 67: 29–49.

Wildavsky, Aaron. 1966. 'The Two Presidencies.' *Trans-Action* 4 (2):7–14.

1998. 'The Two Presidencies.' *Society* 35 (2):23–31.

Williamson, Oliver E. 1985. 'The New Institutional Economics: Taking Stock, Looking Ahead.' *Journal of Economic Literature* 38(3): 595–613.

Wilson, James Q. 1991. *Bureaucracy: What Government Agencies Do and Why They Do It*. 1st Edition. New York: Basic Books.

Winters, Matthew S. 2010a. 'Accountability, Participation and Foreign Aid Effectiveness.' *International Studies Review* 12(2): 218–43.

2010b. 'Choosing to Target: What Types of Countries Get Different Types of World Bank Projects.' *World Politics* 62(3): 422–58.

2012. 'The Obstacles to Foreign Aid Harmonization: Lessons from Decentralization Support in Indonesia.' *Studies in Comparative International Development* 47(3): 316–41.

2014. 'Targeting, Accountability and Capture in Development Projects.' *International Studies Quarterly* 58(2): 393–404.

Winters, Matthew S., Simone Dietrich, and Minhaj Mahmud. 2017. 'Perceptions of Foreign Aid Project Quality in Bangladesh.' *Research & Politics* 4(4): 1–6.

Winters, Matthew S. and Jaclyn D. Streitfeld. 2018. 'Splitting the Check: Explaining Patterns of Counterpart Commitments in World Bank Projects.' *Review of International Political Economy*, 25(6): 884–908.

Wittkopf, Eugene R. 1973. 'Foreign Aid and United Nations Votes: A Comparative Study*.' *American Political Science Review* 67(3): 868–88.

Wohlgemuth, Lennart and Bertil Odén. 2013. 'Trend, Lessons Learned, and Directions for the Future.' Policy Report, Stockholm: Global Utmaning.

Wood, Stewart. 2001. 'Labour Market Regimes under Threat?: Sources of Continuity in Germany, Britain, and Sweden.' In *The New Politics of the Welfare State*, ed. Paul Pierson. Oxford: Oxford University Press.

Wood, Terence. 2018. Aid Policy and Australian Public Opinion. Asia & the Pacific Policy Studies 5(2): 235–248.

Wooldridge, Jeffrey M. 2002. *Econometric Analysis of Cross Section and Panel Data*. Cambridge, MA: MIT Press.

Yanguas, Pablo and David Hulme. 2015. 'Barriers to Political Analysis in Aid Bureaucracies: From Principle to Practice in DFID and the World Bank.' *World Development* 74: 209–19.

Yeung, Karen. 2010. 'The Regulatory State.' In *The Oxford Handbook of Regulation*, Oxford Handbooks, eds. Robert Baldwin, Martin Cave, and Martin Lodge. Oxford; New York: Oxford University Press.

Yoo, John. 2018. *Franklin Roosevelt and Presidential Power*. Rochester, NY: Social Science Research Network. SSRN Scholarly Paper.

Zaller, John R. 1992. *The Nature and Origins of Mass Opinion*. 1st Edition. Cambridge England; New York: Cambridge University Press.

Ziaja, Sebastian. 2020. 'More Donors, More Democracy.' *Journal of Politics* 82(2): 433–47.

Index

absorptive capacity, *see capacity of recipient country*
accountability
  bottom-up, 137
  ensuring of, 87, 92, 108
  in foreign aid, 18, 61, 116
  mutual, 94, 230
  organization of, 51, 83, 99
  -oriented, 119, 228
  voice and, 132
Accra conference, 230–32
aid agency, *see aid organisations*
aid delivery
  budget, 32
  challenges, 59
  decision-making, 3, 19, 21, 23, 31–33, 36, 39, 56, 58, 78, 80, 96, 123, 134, 154, 157–58, 160, 163, 190
  determinants of, 12, 19–21, 31, 224
  domestic political explanations of, 33, 55
  effectiveness or success of, 17, 28, 63, 155, 168, 173, 185
  ideological origins of, 29, 36, 56, 68, 149, 178, 186
  objectives of, 69, 231
  patterns of, 9, 28, 30, 33, 41, 63, 130, 191, 206, 212–13
  performance of, 105
  public opinion, 21, 33, 37, 186, 189–93, 200, 207, 212–13, 225
  recipient-based explanations of, 24–31
  tactics. *See aid delivery channel*
  trade-offs, 6–8, 35, 167, 175, 231
aid delivery channels, 12
aid officials
  as elites, 159, 162, 190, 193
  constrained, 5
  incentive-oriented, 4, 123

rational, 24, 178, 185
aid organisations
  AFD, *see Agence Française du Développement, under France*
  BMZ, *see BMZ under Germany*
  definition, 8
  mandate, mission, 8, 39–40, 55, 65, 68, 185, 191, 208, 214, 225
  national, 30, 60, 84, 96, 122–23, 153, 186, 236
  organisational, 28
  Sida, *see Swedish International Development Agency under Sweden*
  streamlining of (the bureaucracy), 72
  USAID, *see United States Development Agency under United States*
aid recipient countries
  characteristics, 161
  civil conflict, 135, 147
  clinics, 46, 62, 72
  democracy, 134, 136
  development, 52
  economic resources, 229
  health care systems, 175
  natural disaster, 135, 147
  quality of governance in, *see quality of governance*
  risk in, 161
  risk of aid capture, 131
Anglo-Saxon countries, 27, 51
Asian Development Bank, 64
Australia, 79, 129

beltway bandits, 27, 57
Bermeo, 2, 10, 12, 19, 42, 57, 245
Blair, 91, 111
Broz, 33

budget support, 10, 91, 109
building
  capacity (of recipient), 2
  bureaucratic organisation, 173, 184
  bureaucratic structures and
    administrative practices/processes
    formal rules, 39
  formal rules of the game, 22–23, 56,
    59, 123, 149
  independent variable, 32
Busan conference, 230, 256
Bush, George H, 104
Bush, George W. 61, 65, 82, 86
bypass aid
  actors, 2, 14, 127, 236
  definition, 2
  for-profit development actors,
    203
  international organisations, 30
  measure, 225, 236
  non-governmental organisations
    (NGOs), 11
  public–private partnerships, 11–12,
    60, 62, 236

capability traps, 7
capacity (of donors)
  bureaucratic, 45
  in-house expertise, 46
capacity (of recipient)
  absorptive capacity, 25, 58, 132,
    165
  building, 1
  local or indigenous, 45, 164, 166,
    194, 201
  strengthening of, 70, 230–31
Care International, 11
Carlsson, Gunilla, 94
Catholic Relief Services, 11, 125
Chemonics, 27, 57
civil conflict, see Aid recipient countries
civil society, 7, 45, 84, 96, 136, 182,
  236
Clinton, Bill, 85, 104
Clinton, Hillary, 87
Cold War, 41, 46–47, 87
colonies / former colonies, 19, 146
competition
  in aid delivery, 26, 71
  of ideas among donors, 93

contracting
  bypass actors, 2, 92
  monitoring of, 11, 102
  contractors/contracting, see contracting
    under foreign aid
coordinated market economies (CMEs),
  129
corporatization, 27
counterterrorism, 18
cost-effectiveness, see contracting under
  foreign aid
COVID-19, 231
critical juncture, see historical
  institutionalism
creditor reporting system (CRS), see
  foreign aid

DAI, 27, 57
DFID, see Department for International
  Development under United
  Kingdom
development, see objectives under aid
  delivery
democracy, see aid recipient countries
developing countries, 1–2, 11, 24, 30,
  57, 64, 68, 85, 100, 115, 124–25,
  164, 167, 170, 176–77, 182, 224,
  227, 229, 232
Development Assistant Committee
  (DAC)
  peer reviews, 78, 99, 105–6, 115–16,
    118–19
development policies, 6
distributive politics, 24
Doctors Without Borders, 11
domestic stability, aid for, 18
donor
  coordination, 9, 35, 156, 164, 177,
    232–33
  major versus minor, 146
  motives or motivation, 3, 5, 10, 12,
    19–20, 222
  politics, 19
  typology, 28, 36, 128
donor–recipient interactions, 5, 22–23,
  25, 32, 36, 40–41, 48, 54, 66, 70,
  78–79, 81, 113, 148, 154, 156,
  183, 192, 224, 226
donors
  major versus minor, 20

economic interests, 31
economic growth, *see objectives under aid delivery*
economic management, *see donor countries*
economic sector aid, 146
egalitarian values, 21
electorate, *see public opinion*
elites, *see aid officials*

financial liberalization, 49
foreign aid
  capture of, 13, 17
  contractors/contracting, 12, 27, 39, 45, 50, 57, 62, 83, 86–87, 92, 105, 109, 130, 235–36
  creditor reporting system (CRS), 17, 124, 126, 133
  curse, 18
  definition, 124
  delivery, *see aid delivery*
  domestic politics of, 20, 31, 55
  effectiveness metrics, 34, 40, 104, 112, 181, 226, 236
  effectiveness of, 7–8
  Official Development Assistance (ODA), 3, 126
  performance-based, 83
formal rules of the game, *see bureaucratic structures and administrative processes/practice*
former colony, *see aid recipient countries*
fragmentation
  of foreign aid literature, 232
France
  Agence Française du Développement (AFD), 100, 182
  aid structures, 80
  bureaucratic reform, 97
  government-to-government aid, 5
  grands corps, 73, 99
  Institutional Act on Finance Legislation, the so-called LOLF, 119
  Ministry of Finance, 99
  Ministry of Foreign Affairs, 99
  Ministry of Foreign Affairs (MAE), 120
  neoliberal governance, 119–20
  traditional public sector, 97
freedom house, 134

Germany
  aid structures, 80
  Bundesministerium für wirtschaftliche Zusammenarbeit (BMZ), 98, 116
  bureaucratic reform, 97
  Development Policy Framework for Contracts and Cooperation (AURA), 117
  German Institute for Development Evaluation (DEval), 117
  Gesellschaft für Internationale Zusammenarbeit (GIZ), 98, 100, 117, 182
  Kreditanstalt für Wiederaufbau (KfW), 98
  National Audit office, 117
  neoliberal governance, 116–22
  public opinion, 181–82
  Rechtsstaat, 74
  traditional public sector governance, 119
Global Alliance on Vaccines and Immunizations (GAVI), 2
The Global Fund to Fight AIDS, TB, and Malaria, 2
Global Fund to Fight AIDS, Tuberculosis, and Malaria, 62
globalization
  challenges of, 189
  national responses to, 53–54
  result of, 53
goods and service delivery, 28, 50, 62, 71, 79, 93–94, 102, 105, 129, 132, 167, 192
government effectiveness, 58, 132
governance quality, *see quality of governance*
government-to-government aid
  definition, 5
  measure, 14
great depression, 42, 44

health care system, *see aid recipient countries*
historical institutionalism
  critical juncture, 4, 52
  method of analysis, 4
  path-dependence, 7, 88

HIV/AIDS, 6, 61–62
Hulme, David, 229

ideas
    in foreign aid, 4–5, 8, 22, 228
ideational explanations, 40
ideological origin of aid delivery
    channels, see aid delivery channels
industrial development complex, 24
infection rates, 62
institutional
    autonomy, 23, 73
    constraints mechanism, 120, 124,
        161, 179, 185–86, 192, 225
    guidelines, 3
    legacy, 4, 77
    rulebooks, 5, 9, 41, 54–55, 63, 81, 120,
        153, 156, 160, 176, 178, 180, 185,
        191–92, 208, 212–13, 223, 227–28
interest group(s), 89
    explanations, 27, 57
    in development, 24
interests
    material, 32, 34, 161
international economic conditions, 1,
    54, 122, 222, 224–25
International Monetary Fund (IMF),
    23, 135, 228, 252, 258
international organisations, see aid
    delivery channels

Japan, vii, 10, 17, 31, 37, 40, 64–65,
    129–30, 132, 136, 143, 153, 155,
    157–58, 167–68, 170–72, 174,
    176, 181, 183, 187

KfW, see Kreditanstalt für
    Wiederaufbau under Germany

Lancaster, Carol, 87
legislators, 21, 24, 27, 57
liberal market economies (LMEs), 129
like-minded donors, 9, 233

Mahoney, 52
managerialism, 81, 115
    reform, see neoliberal reform
    and performance, see performance
market
    -based rationality, 26, 50, 59

liberalization, 48–49
    -oriented, orientation, 35, 158
    -type mechanisms, 53, 92
Marshall Plan, 42–46, 84
Millennium Challenge Account (MCA).
    See Millennium Challenge
    Corporation (MCC)
Millennium Challenge Corporation
    (MCC), 158
Millennium Development Goals
    (MDGs), 229
Milner, Helen, 12, 21, 24, 33, 56, 89,
    126, 190
Mitchell, Andrew, 111, 233
monitoring
    aid implementation, 3
Monterrey Consensus, 229
mortality, 62, 164–66, 229
multilateral aid
    literature, 12, 126
    multi-bi aid, bypass through IOs,
        125
    traditional multilateral aid, 125

national structures, see bureaucratic
    structures
Natsios, Andrew, 45, 106, 109
natural disaster, see aid recipient
    countries
needs-based, 19
neocorporatist structures, 26
neoliberal
    beliefs, 28, 63, 223
    beliefs, doctrine, 9
    donor, 8, 24, 75, 78, 133, 143–44,
        232
    ideas, 23, 30, 34, 41
    principles, 7, 31, 170, 176, 236
    reform, 27–28, 48, 52, 61, 63, 67,
        79, 82, 84, 92, 94, 97, 102, 114,
        158, 213
neoliberalism
    definition, 26
    history, 49–57
new public management, see
    managerialism
New Zealand, 79
non-governmental organisations
    (NGOs)
    as bypass actors, see bypass

from donor countries, *see Germany*; *France*; *United Kingdom, Unites States*; *Sweden*
Nordic countries, *see Scandinavian countries*

Obama, Barack, 82–83, 87, 104, 107
Offical development assistance (ODA), *see foreign aid*
Organization for Economic Cooperation and Development (OECD), 9
organisational
rules and practices, 5
outsourcing in aid, *see bypass*
ownership
for recipient country, 5, 230–31

Paris Conference/Declaration, 230
path-dependence, *see historical*
performance
frameworks, 103, 106, 112, 181, 228
monitoring, 51, 103, 105–7, 110–13, 116, 119–21
-orientation, 51
pay, 103
system, 112
Pevehouse, Jonathan, 33
Phnom Penh Water Supply Authority (PPWS), 64
point four program, 42, 44
policy concessions, 18
political economy types
neoliberal, *see neoliberal donor*
traditional public sector, *see traditional public also, see explanation of aid delivery*
political parties, 21, 93
politico-administrative, 74, 97
post-Cold War, 1, 19, 41
President's Emergency Program for Aids Relief (PEPFAR), 61
principal–agent theory, 50, 62, 80–81
private contractors, *see aid delivery*
prosperity, *see aid recipient countries*
public administration
literature of, 67
public opinion
in donor countries, *see aid delivery*

public sector governance, *see traditional public sector governance*

quality of governance
definition, 168
effects on risk assessment, 58, 63
effects on risk/assessment, 25
good versus bad/poor, 14
measure of, 66
World Bank Governance Indicators, 132, 179

rationalization, 41, 48, 50–51, 69, 72, 77, 122
Reagan, Ronald, 51, 85, 227, 253, 261
recipient capacity, *see capacity*
recipient countries, *see aid recipients*
recipient governance, 132
good, 132
poor, 5, 33, 37, 41, 61, 112, 122–23, 128, 145, 153, 155, 178, 183, 189, 191, 204, 206, 208–9, 212, 225
regulatory quality, 58, 132
right-leaning parties, *see political parties*
risk in recipient countries, *see aid recipient countries*
risk of aid capture, *see aid recipient countries*
rule of law, 58, 132

Scandinavian countries, 73, 78, 97, 130
Security Council Rotating Members
aid recipient countries, 136
short- versus long-term approaches, 35, 224
Sida, *see Swedish International Development Cooperation under Sweden*
social sector aid, 145–46
societal challenges, 4, 8, 29, 69, 73, 75, 85, 97, 227
solidarity
domestic, 21, 190
international, 21
Soviet Union, 46–47
Sri Lanka
aid to, 12, 14, 40, 132, 143, 222
standard-operating procedures, 3

states versus markets, *see ideological origins of aid delivery*
state-to-state aid, *see government-to-government* aid under aid delivery
statist structures, 48, 85, 89
Sudan
  aid to, 1, 12, 14, 132, 143, 222
survey experiment, 33, 37, 173, 191, 197
Sweden
  Agency for Public Management, 114
  budget bill, 113
  bureaucratic reform, 93, 115
  financial crisis, 71
  Ministry of Finance, 93
  Ministry of Foreign Affairs, 55
  Moderate Party, 94, 114
  National Audit Office, 94
  National Financial Management Authority, 114
  Quality Assurance Committee, 114
  Social Democratic Government, 114
  Swedish Directors-General Association, 114
  Swedish government, 28
  Swedish International Development Agency (Sida), 72
Swedlund, Hailey, 23, 228

Tanzania
  aid to, 14, 143
technical assistance, 44, 63–64, 125
Thatcher, Margaret, 51, 71, 89, 109, 227, 261
Tingley, Dustin, 12, 21, 24, 56, 89, 190, 193, 253, 257, 266
traditional public sector donor
  definition of, 145
traditional public sector governance
  ideas of, 116
  logic of, 119
trade-off(s), *see aid delivery*
Truman Doctrine, 42

Uganda, 14, 28, 62, 239–40, 259, 262
United Kingdom
  ARIES, 111
  bureacratic reform, 89
  Comprehensive Spending Reviews (CSRs), 110
  Department for International Development (DfID), 90, 110, 187
  Freedom of Information Act, 111
  labour government, 90
  National Audit Office, 111
  UK Citizen's Charter, 110
United Nations, 11, 229, 254, 267–68
  Security Council, 136, 255
  United Nations Office for Drugs and Crimes (UNODC), 60
United Nations Higher Commissioner for Refugees (UNHCR), 11
United States
  bureaucratic reform, 86
  Congress, 24
  Development Experience Clearinghouse (DEC), 107
  Economic Cooperation Agency (ECA), 43
  Federal Workforce Restructuring Act, 85
  Foreign Operations Administration, 44
  General Accounting Office (GAO), 108
  Government Performance and Results Act (GPRA), 79, 104
  great society, 45
  International Cooperation Administration, 44
  Mutual Security Agency, 44
  National Audit Office Act, 110
  National Performance Review, 104
  new deal, 45
  new frontier, 45
  The Office of Management and Budget (OMB), 108
  Performance Improvement Council (PIC), 108
  Performance of Routine Information System Management (PRISM), 105, 111
  Private Enterprise Initiative, 85
  public opinion, 188–214
  reinventing government, 85
  state department, 43–44, 55, 60, 158, 187
  Technical Cooperation Administration (TCA), 44

traditional public sector, 47, 109
US Agency for International
  Development (USAID), 45
USAID Forward, 82, 88
USAID's Office of the Inspector
  General (IG), 108

value for money, 67, 92, 102, 111
Varieties of Capitalism (VoC)
  literature, 79, 129
  measure, 129

Vietnam, 46, 64, 255
voting in elections, 22, 190

welfare state, 39–76
Weber, Max, 115
World Bank, 55, 179
  government matters project, 132
World Health Organization (WHO), 11
World War I, 42
World War II, 36, 42, 64, 73
  post-World War II, 1, 41, 46, 93

Made in the USA
Columbia, SC
06 June 2022